GREAT
AMERICAN
HUNTING
STORIES

LYONS PRESS CLASSICS

GREAT AMERICAN HUNTING STORIES

EDITED BY
LAMAR UNDERWOOD

LYONS
PRESS

GUILFORD
CONNECTICUT

An imprint of The Rowman & Littlefield Publishing Group, Inc.
4501 Forbes Blvd., Ste. 200
Lanham, MD 20706
www.rowman.com

Distributed by NATIONAL BOOK NETWORK

British Library Cataloguing in Publication Information available

Library of Congress Cataloging-in-Publication Data
Names: Underwood, Lamar, editor.
Title: Great American hunting stories / edited by Lamar Underwood.
Description: Guilford, Connecticut : Lyons Press Classics, [2019]
Identifiers: LCCN 2019005185 | ISBN 9781493040421 (paperback) | ISBN
9781493040438 (ebook)
Subjects: LCSH: Hunting—United States—Anecdotes.
Classification: LCC SK33 .G788 2019 | DDC 639/.1—dc23 LC record
available at https://lccn.loc.gov/2019005185

CONTENTS

INTRODUCTION by Lamar Underwood   vii

HUNTING THE GRISLY by Theodore Roosevelt   1

THE WHITE GOAT AND HIS COUNTRY by Owen Wister   35

DE SHOOTIN'EST GENT'MAN by Nash Buckingham   57

THAT TWENTY-FIVE-POUND GOBBLER by Archibald Rutledge   69

IN BUFFALO DAYS by George Bird Grinnell   81

TIGE'S LION by Zane Grey   115

RED LETTER DAYS IN BRITISH COLUMBIA
by Lieutenant Townsend Whelen   127

THE ALASKAN GRIZZLY by Harold McCracken   145

THE PLURAL OF MOOSE IS MISE by Irwin S. Cobb   161

BRANT SHOOTING ON GREAT SOUTH BAY by Edwin Main Post   181

BEAR HUNTING IN THE SMOKIES by Horace Kephart   189

AN ELK HUNT AT TWO-OCEAN PASS by Theodore Roosevelt   209

BOB WHITE, DOWN 'T ABERDEEN by Nash Buckingham   233

HUNTING ON THE OREGON TRAIL by Francis Parkman   247

THE MOUNTAIN GOAT AT HOME by William T. Hornaday   273

HUNTING THE BLACK BEAR by Theodore Roosevelt   303

THE QUEST OF THE PTARMIGAN by Rex Beach   313

BLACKTAILS IN THE BAD LANDS by Bronson Rumsey   325

SOURCES   334

INTRODUCTION

Back in the days when I was holding the reins and driving the wagon as editor-in-chief at *Sports Afield* and *Outdoor Life*, the most important word in any magazine was the word *New*.

New products, destinations, how-to ideas; even new ways of overcoming old problems. If budgets were fat with advertising dollars, you might have space to throw in some short essays, like *Field & Stream* with Robert Ruark, or my own *Sports Afield* with Gene Hill. But in the newsstand and subscription-renewal pit where magazines struggle to survive, there is no room for strolls down memory lane, or long-winded proclamations. Shower your readers with *New* or they will stay away. And you will be needing a *New* (there's that word again) résumé.

Books, thank God, are vastly different. You can dedicate an entire book to the word *New* attached to some subject if you want to. But within the stacks of book pages, stories can reside that excite the senses, fill the heart with longing or excitement. Unlike magazines, strolls down memory lane are welcome here—as long as they ignite reader reward. Gatekeepers—the editors—of the book domains seek good prose on any subject that will hold readers. Whether fiction for escape and inspiration, or nonfiction that illuminates topical interests, the editors seek the best prose they can find. The books where that prose ends up residing become treasured personal possessions, on shelves in homes, or available in libraries, or accessible in today's vast web resources.

Books, imperishable and enduring, feed the soul. And some of the best—the most enduring of all—are not the newest. Old writers, many of them under the earth for decades, and their stories have new life every time a reader picks up a book. That is exactly why the book you are holding right now—where these old stories are gaining new life—is the source of great pleasure for this editor.

In the outdoor field, stories about hunting, fishing, and outdoor adventures of all sorts are scarce in today's few surviving magazines. However, they survive in great numbers in the pages of books. It is my intention and hope that this volume of hunting stories can become a collector's classic, as enjoyable as a well-worn pair of boots or trusted shotgun. The writers represent the halcyon days of hunting, when game and space to hunt were more plentiful. Their names won't be found in today's magazines, but they will be old friends to veteran readers, like this editor who has sought to keep their works in print wherever I can.

Names like Nash Buckingham, Archibald Rutledge, Owen Wister, Theodore Roosevelt, and Rex Beach were once superstars in outdoor-related literature, and it is with great pride that I present them to you in this new collection. I am equally proud of the other contributors, knowing that their stories will make this book a permanent selection on the shelves of new and old readers who like hunting and hunters.

Today, artists like David Maass and Bob Kuhn preserve the action and emotions of hunting and wildlife encounters with precise and dramatic interpretation. Near these paintings in the hunter's home, probably within the light flickering from the glowing hearth, there will be books. Visit these and you will probably find useful and pragmatic treatises on whatever hunting skills you are interested in perfecting—from training a dog to training yourself to make the shot. And also present on the shelves, whether as a few scattered outriders or vast collections, there will be hunting stories.

Preserved in books, hunting stories transcend the ages for all to whom the call of the chase is irresistible and rewarding. To the brethren of the chase, the call is clear: Hunting, thinking about hunting, and talking about hunting. In this way of life, the best talk is always hunting talk, and some of the most engaging you'll ever find is gathered in books, both new and dusty.

To help make this book as authentic as possible, in preserving the voices of the authors, the stories here are presented without being copyedited. When Theodore Roosevelt spells grizzly as "grisly," we let it stand as written.

As any hunter knows, the hunting in print will never replace the real thing. But, whether you're hunting every chance you get, or simply enjoying your memories, you'll find great pleasure in the stories here. They're some of the best I've ever read.

—LAMAR UNDERWOOD

HUNTING THE GRISLY

BY THEODORE ROOSEVELT

If out in the late fall or early spring, it is often possible to follow a bear's trail in the snow; having come upon it either by chance or hard hunting, or else having found where it leads from some carcass on which the beast has been feeding. In the pursuit one must exercise great caution, as at such times the hunter is easily seen a long way off, and game is always especially watchful for any foe that may follow its trail.

Once I killed a grisly in this manner. It was early in the fall, but snow lay on the ground, while the gray weather boded a storm. My camp was in a bleak, wind-swept valley, high among the mountains which form the divide between the head-waters of the Salmon and Clarke's Fork of the Columbia. All night I had lain in my buffalo-bag, under the lea of a windbreak of branches, in the clump of fir-trees, where I had halted the preceding evening. At my feet ran a rapid mountain torrent, its bed choked with ice-covered rocks; I had been lulled to sleep by the stream's splashing murmur, and the loud moaning of the wind along the naked cliffs. At dawn I rose and shook myself free of the buffalo robe, coated with hoar-frost. The ashes of the fire were lifeless; in the dim morning the air was bitter cold. I did not linger a moment, but snatched up my rifle, pulled on my fur cap and gloves, and strode off up a side ravine; as I walked I ate some mouthfuls of venison, left over from supper.

Two hours of toil up the steep mountain brought me to the top of a spur. The sun had risen, but was hidden behind a bank of sullen clouds. On the divide I halted, and gazed out over a vast landscape, inconceivably wild and dismal. Around me towered the stupendous mountain masses which make up the backbone of the Rockies. From my feet, as far as I could see, stretched a rugged and barren chaos of ridges and detached rock masses. Behind me, far below, the stream wound like a silver ribbon, fringed with dark conifers and the changing, dying foliage of poplar and quaking aspen. In front the bottoms of the valleys were filled with the somber evergreen forest, dotted here and there with black, ice-skimmed tarns; and the dark spruces clustered also in the higher gorges, and were scattered thinly along the mountain sides. The snow which had fallen lay in drifts and streaks, while, where the wind had scope it was blown off, and the ground left bare.

For two hours I walked onwards across the ridges and valleys. Then among some scattered spruces, where the snow lay to the depth of half a foot, I suddenly came on the fresh, broad trail of a grisly. The brute was evidently roaming restlessly about in search of a winter den, but willing, in passing, to pick up any food that lay handy. At once I took the trail, travelling above and to one side, and keeping a sharp look-out ahead. The bear was going across wind, and this made my task easy. I walked rapidly, though cautiously; and it was only in crossing the large patches of bare ground that I had to fear making a noise. Elsewhere the snow muffled my footsteps, and made the trail so plain that I scarcely had to waste a glance upon it, bending my eyes always to the front.

At last, peering cautiously over a ridge crowned with broken rocks, I saw my quarry, a big, burly bear, with silvered fur. He had halted on an open hillside, and was busily digging up the caches of some rock gophers or squirrels. He seemed absorbed in his work, and the stalk was easy. Slipping quietly back, I ran towards the end of the spur, and in ten minutes struck a ravine, of which one branch ran past within seventy yards of where the bear was working. In this ravine was a rather close growth of stunted evergreens, affording good cover, although in one or two places I had to lie down and crawl through the snow. When I reached the point for which I was aiming, the bear had just finished rooting, and was starting off. A slight whistle brought him to a standstill, and I drew a bead behind his shoulder, and low down, resting the rifle across the crooked branch of a dwarf spruce. At the crack he ran off at speed, making no sound, but the thick spatter of blood splashes, showing clear on the white snow, betrayed the mortal nature of the wound. For some minutes I followed the trail; and then, topping a ridge, I saw the dark bulk lying motionless in a snow drift at the foot of a low rock-wall, from which he had tumbled.

The usual practice of the still-hunter who is after grisly is to toll it to baits. The hunter either lies in ambush near the carcass, or approaches it stealthily when he thinks the bear is at its meal.

One day while camped near the Bitter Root Mountains in Montana I found that a bear had been feeding on the carcass of a moose which lay some five miles from the little open glade in which my tent was pitched, and I made up my mind to try to get a shot at it that afternoon. I stayed in camp till about three o'clock, lying lazily back on the bed of sweet-smelling evergreen boughs, watching the pack ponies as they stood under the pines on the edge of the open, stamping now and then, and switching their tails. The air was still, the sky a glorious blue; at that hour in the afternoon even the September sun was hot. The smoke from the smouldering logs of the camp fire curled thinly upwards. Little chipmunks scuttled out from their holes to the packs, which lay in a heap on the ground, and then scuttled madly back again. A couple of drab-colored whisky-jacks, with bold mien and fearless bright eyes, hopped and fluttered round, picking up the scraps, and uttering an extraordinary variety of notes, mostly discordant; so tame were they that one of them lit on my outstretched arm as I half dozed, basking in the sunshine.

When the shadows began to lengthen, I shouldered my rifle and plunged into the woods. At first my route lay along a mountain side; then for half a mile over a windfall, the dead timber piled about in crazy confusion. After that I went up the bottom of a valley by a little brook, the ground being carpeted with a sponge of soaked moss. At the head of this brook was a pond covered with water-lilies; and a scramble through a rocky pass took me into a high, wet valley, where the thick growth of spruce was broken by occasional strips of meadow. In this valley the moose carcass lay, well at the upper end.

In moccasined feet I trod softly through the soundless woods. Under the dark branches it was already dusk, and the air had the cool chill of evening. As I neared the clump where the body lay, I walked with redoubled caution, watching and listening with strained alertness. Then I heard a twig snap; and my blood leaped, for I knew the bear was at his supper. In another moment I saw his shaggy, brown form. He was working with all his awkward giant strength, trying to bury the carcass, twisting it to one side and the other with wonderful ease. Once he got angry and suddenly gave it a tremendous cuff with his paw; in his bearing he had something half humorous, half devilish. I crept up within forty yards; but for several minutes he would not keep his head still. Then something attracted his attention in the forest, and he stood motionless looking towards it, broadside to me, with his fore-paws planted on the carcass. This gave me my chance. I drew a very fine bead between his eye and ear; and pulled trigger. He dropped like a steer when struck with a pole-axe.

If there is a good hiding-place handy it is better to lie in wait at the carcass. One day on the head-waters of the Madison, I found that a bear was coming to an elk I had shot some days before; and I at once determined to ambush the beast when he came back that evening. The carcass lay in the middle of a valley a quarter of a mile broad. The bottom of this valley was covered by an open forest of tall pines; a thick jungle of smaller evergreens marked where the mountains rose on either hand. There were a number of large rocks scattered here and there, one, of very convenient shape, being only some seventy or eighty yards from the carcass. Up this I clambered. It hid me perfectly, and on its top was a carpet of soft pine needles, on which I could lie at my ease.

Hour after hour passed by. A little black woodpecker with a yellow crest ran nimbly up and down the tree-trunks for some time and then flitted away with a party of chickadees and nut-hatches. Occasionally a Clarke's crow soared about overhead or clung in any position to the swaying end of a pine branch, chattering and screaming. Flocks of cross-bills, with wavy flight and plaintive calls, flew to a small mineral lick near by, where they scraped the clay with their queer little beaks.

As the westering sun sank out of sight beyond the mountains these sounds of bird-life gradually died away. Under the great pines the evening was still with the silence of primeval desolation. The sense of sadness and loneliness, the melancholy of the wilderness, came over me like a spell. Every slight noise made my pulses throb as I lay motionless on the rock gazing intently into the gathering gloom. I began to fear that it would grow too dark to shoot before the grisly came.

Suddenly and without warning, the great bear stepped out of the bushes and trod across the pine needles with such swift and silent footsteps that its bulk seemed unreal. It was very cautious, continually halting to peer around; and once it stood up on its hind legs and looked long down the valley towards the red west. As it reached the carcass I put a bullet between its shoulders. It rolled over, while the woods resounded with its savage roaring. Immediately it struggled to its feet and staggered off; and fell again to the next shot, squalling and yelling. Twice this was repeated; the brute being one of those bears which greet every wound with a great outcry, and sometimes seem to lose their feet when hit—although they will occasionally fight as savagely as their more silent brethren. In this case the wounds were mortal, and the bear died before reaching the edge of the thicket.

I spent much of the fall of 1889 hunting on the head-waters of the Salmon and Snake in Idaho, and along the Montana boundary line from the Big Hole Basin and the head of the Wisdom River to the neighborhood of Red Rock Pass and to the north and west of Henry's Lake. During the last fortnight my companion was the old mountain man, already mentioned, named Griffeth or Griffin—I cannot tell which, as he was always called either "Hank" or "Griff." He was a crabbedly honest old fellow, and a very skilful hunter; but he was worn out with age and rheumatism, and his temper had failed even faster than his bodily strength. He showed me a greater variety of game than I had ever seen before in so short a time; nor did I ever before or after make so successful a hunt. But he was an exceedingly disagreeable companion on account of his surly, moody ways. I generally had to get up first, to kindle the fire and make ready breakfast, and he was very quarrelsome. Finally, during my absence from camp one day, while not very far from Red Rock pass, he found my whisky-flask, which I kept purely for emergencies, and drank all the contents. When I came back he was quite drunk. This was unbearable, and after some high words I left him, and struck off homeward through the woods on my own account. We had with us four pack and saddle horses; and of these I took a very intelligent and gentle little bronco mare, which possessed the invaluable trait of always staying near camp, even when not hobbled. I was not hampered with much of an outfit, having only my buffalo sleeping-bag, a fur coat, and my washing kit, with a couple of spare pairs of socks and some handkerchiefs. A frying-pan, some salt pork, and a hatchet, made up a light pack, which, with the bedding, I fastened across the stock saddle by means of a rope and a spare packing cinch. My cartridges and knife were in my belt; my compass and matches, as always, in my pocket. I walked, while the little mare followed almost like a dog, often without my having to hold the lariat which served as halter.

The country was for the most part fairly open, as I kept near the foot-hills where glades and little prairies broke the pine forest. The trees were of small size. There was no regular trail, but the course was easy to keep, and I had no trouble of any kind save on the second day. That afternoon I was following a stream which at last "canyoned up," that is sank to the bottom of a canyon-like ravine impossible for a horse. I started up a side valley, intending to cross from its head coulies to those of another valley which would lead in below the canyon.

However, I got enmeshed in the tangle of winding valleys at the foot of the steep mountains, and as dusk was coming on I halted and camped in a little open spot by the side of a small, noisy brook, with crystal water. The place was carpeted with soft, wet, green moss, dotted red with the kinnikinnic berries, and at its edge, under the trees where the ground was dry, I threw down the buffalo bed on a mat of sweet-smelling pine needles. Making camp took but a moment. I opened the pack, tossed the bedding on a smooth spot, knee-haltered the little mare, dragged up a few dry logs, and then strolled off, rifle on shoulder, through the frosty gloaming, to see if I could pick up a grouse for supper.

For half a mile I walked quickly and silently over the pine needles, across a succession of slight ridges separated by narrow, shallow valleys. The forest here was composed of lodge-pole pines, which on the ridges grew close together, with tall slender trunks, while in the valleys the growth was more open. Though the sun was behind the mountains there was yet plenty of light by which to shoot, but it was fading rapidly.

At last, as I was thinking of turning towards camp, I stole up to the crest of one of the ridges, and looked over into the valley some sixty yards off. Immediately I caught the loom of some large, dark object; and another glance showed me a big grisly walking slowly off with his head down. He was quartering to me, and I fired into his flank, the bullet, as I afterwards found, ranging forward and piercing one lung. At the shot he uttered a loud, moaning grunt and plunged forward at a heavy gallop, while I raced obliquely down the hill to cut him off. After going a few hundred feet he reached a laurel thicket, some thirty yards broad, and two or three times as long which he did not leave. I ran up to the edge and there halted, not liking to venture into the mass of twisted, close-growing stems and glossy foliage. Moreover, as I halted, I heard him utter a peculiar, savage kind of whine from the heart of the brush. Accordingly, I began to skirt the edge, standing on tiptoe and gazing earnestly to see if I could not catch a glimpse of his hide. When I was at the narrowest part of the thicket, he suddenly left it directly opposite, and then wheeled and stood broadside to me on the hill-side, a little above. He turned his head stiffly towards me; scarlet strings of froth hung from his lips; his eyes burned like embers in the gloom.

I held true, aiming behind the shoulder, and my bullet shattered the point or lower end of his heart, taking out a big nick. Instantly the great bear turned with a harsh roar of fury and challenge, blowing the blood foam from his mouth, so that I saw the gleam of his white fangs; and then he charged straight at me, crashing and bounding through the laurel bushes, so that it was hard to aim. I waited until he came to a fallen tree, raking him as he topped it with a ball, which entered his chest and went through the cavity of his body, but he neither swerved nor flinched, and at the moment I did not know that I had struck him. He came steadily on, and in another second was almost upon me. I fired for his forehead, but my bullet went low, entering his open mouth, smashing his lower jaw and going into the neck. I leaped to one side almost as I pulled trigger; and through the hanging smoke the first thing I saw was his paw as he made a vicious side blow at me. The rush of his charge carried him past. As he struck he lurched forward, leaving a pool of bright blood where his muzzle hit the ground; but he recovered himself and made two or three jumps onwards, while I hurriedly jammed a couple of cartridges into the magazine, my rifle holding only four, all of which I had fired. Then he tried to pull up, but as he did so his muscles seemed suddenly to give way, his head drooped, and he rolled over and over like a shot rabbit. Each of my first three bullets had inflicted a mortal wound.

It was already twilight, and I merely opened the carcass, and then trotted back to camp. Next morning I returned and with much labor took off the skin. The fur was very fine, the animal being in excellent trim, and unusually bright-colored. Unfortunately, in packing it out I lost the skull, and had to supply its place with one of plaster. The beauty of the trophy, and the memory of the circumstances under which I procured it, make me value it perhaps more highly than any other in my house.

This is the only instance in which I have been regularly charged by a grisly. On the whole, the danger of hunting these great bears has been much exaggerated. At the beginning of the present century, when white hunters first encountered the grisly, he was doubtless an exceedingly savage beast, prone to attack without provocation, and a redoubtable foe to persons armed with the clumsy, small-bore muzzle-loading rifles of the day. But at present bitter experience has taught him caution. He has been hunted for the bounty, and hunted as a dangerous enemy to stock, until, save in the very wildest districts, he has learned to be more wary than a deer and to avoid man's presence almost as carefully as the most timid kind of game. Except in rare cases he will not attack of his own accord, and, as a rule, even when wounded his object is escape rather than battle.

Still, when fairly brought to bay, or when moved by a sudden fit of ungovernable anger, the grisly is beyond peradventure a very dangerous antagonist. The first shot, if taken at a bear a good distance off and previously unwounded and unharried, is not usually fraught with much danger, the startled animal being at the outset bent merely on flight. It is always hazardous, however, to track a wounded and worried grisly into thick cover, and the man who habitually follows and kills this chief of American game in dense timber, never abandoning the bloody trail whithersoever it leads, must show no small degree of skill and hardihood, and must not too closely count the risk to life or limb. Bears differ widely in temper, and occasionally one may be found who will not show fight, no matter how much he is bullied; but, as a rule, a hunter must be cautious in meddling with a wounded animal which has retreated into a dense thicket, and had been once or twice roused; and such a beast, when it does turn, will usually charge again and again, and fight to the last with unconquerable ferocity. The short distance at which the bear can be seen through the underbrush, the fury of his charge, and his tenacity of life make it necessary for the hunter on such occasions to have steady nerves and a fairly quick and accurate aim. It is always well to have two men in following a wounded bear under such conditions. This is not necessary, however, and a good hunter, rather than lose his quarry, will, under ordinary circumstances, follow and attack it, no matter how tangled the fastness in which it has sought refuge; but he must act warily and with the utmost caution and resolution, if he wishes to escape a terrible and probably fatal mauling. An experienced hunter is rarely rash, and never heedless; he will not, when alone, follow a wounded bear into a thicket, if by that exercise of patience, skill, and knowledge of the game's habits he can avoid the necessity; but it is idle to talk of the feat as something which ought in no case to be attempted. While danger ought never to be needlessly incurred, it is yet true that the keenest zest in sport comes from its presence, and from the consequent exercise of the qualities necessary to overcome it. The most thrilling moments of an American hunter's life are those in which, with every sense on the alert, and with nerves strung to the highest point, he is following alone into the heart of its forest fastness the fresh and bloody footprints of an angered grisly; and no other triumph of American hunting can compare with the victory to be thus gained.

These big bears will not ordinarily charge from a distance of over a hundred yards; but there are exceptions to this rule. In the fall of 1890 my friend Archibald Rogers was hunting in Wyoming, south of the Yellowstone Park, and killed seven bears. One, an old he, was out on a bare table-land, grubbing for roots, when he was spied. It was early in the afternoon, and the hunters, who were on a high mountain slope, examined him for some time through their powerful glasses before making him out to be a bear. They then stalked up to the edge of the wood which fringed on the table-land on one side, but could get no nearer than about three hundred yards, the plains being barren of all cover. After waiting for a couple of hours Rogers risked the shot, in despair of getting nearer, and wounded the bear, though not very seriously. The animal made off, almost broadside to, and Rogers ran forward to intercept it. As soon as it saw him it turned and rushed straight for him, not heeding his second shot, and evidently bent on charging home. Rogers then waited until it was within twenty yards, and brained it with his third bullet.

In fact bears differ individually in courage and ferocity precisely as men do, or as the Spanish bulls, of which it is said that not more than one in twenty is fit to stand the combat of the arena. One grisly can scarcely be bullied into resistance; the next may fight to the end, against any odds, without flinching, or even attack unprovoked. Hence men of limited experience in this sport, generalizing from the actions of the two or three bears each has happened to see or kill, often reach diametrically opposite conclusions as to the fighting temper and capacity of the quarry. Even old hunters—who indeed, as a class, are very narrow-minded and opinionated—often generalize just as rashly as beginners. One will portray all bears as very dangerous; another will speak and act as if he deemed them of no more consequence than so many rabbits. I knew one old hunter who had killed a score without ever seeing one show fight. On the other hand, Dr. James C. Merrill, U. S. A., who has had about as much experience with bears as I have had, informs me that he has been charged with the utmost determination three times. In each case the attack was delivered before the bear was wounded or even shot at, the animal being roused by the approach of the hunter from his day bed, and charging headlong at them from a distance of twenty or thirty paces. All three bears were killed before they could do any damage. There was a very remarkable incident connected with the killing of one of them. It occurred in the northern spurs of the Bighorn range. Dr. Merrill, in company with an old hunter, had climbed down into a deep, narrow canyon. The bottom was threaded with well-beaten elk trails. While following one of these the two men turned a corner of the canyon and were instantly charged by an old she-grisly, so close that it was only by good luck that one of the hurried shots disabled her and caused her to tumble over a cut bank where she was easily finished. They found that she had been lying directly across the game trail, on a smooth well beaten patch of bare earth, which looked as if it had been dug up, refilled, and trampled down. Looking curiously at this patch they saw a bit of hide only partially covered at one end; digging down they found the body of a well grown grisly cub. Its skull had been crushed, and the brains licked out, and there were signs of other injuries. The hunters pondered long over this strange discovery, and hazarded many guesses as to its meaning. At last they decided that probably the cub had been killed, and its brains eaten out, either by some old male-grisly or by a cougar, that the mother had returned and driven away the murderer, and that she had then buried the body and lain above it, waiting to wreak her vengeance on the first passer-by.

Old Tazewell Woody, during his thirty years' life as a hunter in the Rockies and on the great plains, killed very many grislies. He always exercised much caution in dealing with them; and, as it happened, he was by some suitable tree in almost every case when he was charged. He would accordingly climb the tree (a practice of which I do not approve however); and the bear would look up at him and pass on without stopping. Once, when he was hunting in the mountains with a companion, the latter, who was down in a valley, while Woody was on the hill-side, shot at a bear. The first thing Woody knew the wounded grisly, running up-hill, was almost on him from behind. As he turned it seized his rifle in its jaws. He wrenched the rifle round, while the bear still gripped it, and pulled trigger, sending a bullet into its shoulder; whereupon it struck him with its paw, and knocked him over the rocks. By good luck he fell in a snow bank and was not hurt in the least. Meanwhile the bear went on and they never got it.

Once he had an experience with a bear which showed a very curious mixture of rashness and cowardice. He and a companion were camped in a little tepee or wigwam, with a bright fire in front of it, lighting up the night. There was an inch of snow on the ground. Just after they went to bed a grisly came close to camp. Their dog rushed out and they could hear it bark round in the darkness for nearly an hour; then the bear drove it off and came right into camp. It went close to the fire, picking up the scraps of meat and bread, pulled a haunch of venison down from a tree, and passed and repassed in front of the tepee, paying no heed whatever to the two men, who crouched in the doorway talking to one another. Once it passed so close that Woody could almost have touched it. Finally his companion fired into it, and off it ran, badly wounded, without an attempt at retaliation. Next morning they followed its tracks in the snow, and found it a quarter or a mile away. It was near a pine and had buried itself under the loose earth, pine needles, and snow; Woody's companion almost walked over it, and putting his rifle to its ear blew out its brains.

In all his experience Woody had personally seen but four men who were badly mauled by bears. Three of these were merely wounded. One was bitten terribly in the back. Another had an arm partially chewed off. The third was a man named George Dow, and the accident happened to him on the Yellowstone about the year 1878. He was with a pack animal at the time, leading it on a trail through a wood. Seeing a big she-bear with cubs he yelled at her; whereat she ran away, but only to cache her cubs, and in a minute, having hidden them, came racing back at him. His pack animal being slow he started to climb a tree;

but before he could get far enough up she caught him, almost biting a piece out of the calf of his leg, pulled him down, bit and cuffed him two or three times, and then went on her way.

The only time Woody ever saw a man killed by a bear was once when he had given a touch of variety to his life by shipping on a New Bedford whaler which had touched at one of the Puget Sound ports. The whaler went up to a part of Alaska where bears were very plentiful and bold. One day a couple of boats' crews landed; and the men, who were armed only with an occasional harpoon or lance, scattered over the beach, one of them, a Frenchman, wading into the water after shell-fish. Suddenly a bear emerged from some bushes and charged among the astonished sailors, who scattered in every direction; but the bear, said Woody, "just had it in for that Frenchman," and went straight at him. Shrieking with terror he retreated up to his neck in the water; but the bear plunged in after him, caught him, and disembowelled him. One of the Yankee mates then fired a bomb lance into the bear's hips, and the savage beast hobbled off into the dense cover of the low scrub, where the enraged sailor folk were unable to get at it.

The truth is that while the grisly generally avoids a battle if possible, and often acts with great cowardice, it is never safe to take liberties with him; he usually fights desperately and dies hard when wounded and cornered, and exceptional individuals take the aggressive on small provocation.

During the years I lived on the frontier I came in contact with many persons who had been severely mauled or even crippled for life by grislies; and a number of cases where they killed men outright were also brought under my ken. Generally these accidents, as was natural, occurred to hunters who had roused or wounded the game.

A fighting bear sometimes uses his claws and sometimes his teeth. I have never known one to attempt to kill an antagonist by hugging, in spite of the popular belief to this effect; though he will sometimes draw an enemy towards him with his paws the better to reach him with his teeth, and to hold him so that he cannot escape from the biting. Nor does the bear often advance on his hind legs to the attack; though, if the man has come close to him in thick underbrush, or has stumbled on him in his lair unawares, he will often rise up in this fashion and strike a single blow. He will also rise in clinching with a man on horseback. In 1882 a mounted Indian was killed in this manner on one of the river bottoms some miles below where my ranch house now stands, not far from the junction of the Beaver and Little Missouri. The bear had been hunted into a thicket by a band of Indians, in whose company my informant, a white squaw-man, with whom I afterward did some trading, was travelling. One of them in the excitement of the pursuit rode across the end of the thicket; as he did so the great beast sprang at him with wonderful quickness, rising on its hind legs, and knocking over the horse and rider with a single sweep of its terrible fore-paws. It then turned on the fallen man and tore him open, and though the other Indians came promptly to his rescue and slew his assailant, they were not in time to save their comrade's life.

A bear is apt to rely mainly on his teeth or claws according to whether his efforts are directed primarily to killing his foe or to making good his own escape. In the latter event he trusts chiefly to his claws. If cornered, he of course makes a rush for freedom, and in that case he downs any man who is in his way with a sweep of his great paw, but passes on without stopping to bite him. If while sleeping or resting in thick brush some one suddenly stumbles on him close up he pursues the same course, less from anger than from fear, being surprised and startled. Moreover, if attacked at close quarters by men and dogs he strikes right and left in defence.

Sometimes what is called a charge is rather an effort to get away. In localities where he has been hunted, a bear, like every other kind of game, is always on the look-out for an attack, and is prepared at any moment for immediate flight. He seems ever to have in his mind, whether feeding, sunning himself, or merely roaming around, the direction—usually towards the thickest cover or most broken ground—in which he intends to run if molested. When shot at he instantly starts towards this place; or he may be so confused that he simply runs he knows not whither; and in either event he may take a line that leads almost directly to or by the hunter, although he had at first no thought of charging. In such a case he usually strikes a single knock-down blow and gallops on without halting, though that one blow may have taken life. If the claws are long and fairly sharp (as in early spring, or even in the fall, if the animal has been working over soft ground) they add immensely to the effect of the blow, for they cut like blunt axes. Often, however, late in the season, and if the ground has been dry and hard, or rocky, the claws are worn down nearly to the quick, and the blow is then given mainly with the under side of the paw; although even under this disadvantage a thump from a big bear will down a horse or smash in a man's breast. The hunter Hofer once lost a horse in this manner. He shot at and wounded a bear which rushed off, as ill luck would have it, past the place where his horse was picketed; probably more in fright than in anger it struck the poor beast a blow which, in the end, proved mortal.

If a bear means mischief and charges not to escape but to do damage, its aim is to grapple with or throw down its foe and bite him to death. The charge is made at a gallop, the animal sometimes coming on silently, with the mouth shut, and sometimes with the jaws open, the lips drawn back and teeth showing, uttering at the same time a succession of roars or of savage rasping snarls. Certain bears charge without any bluster and perfectly straight; while others first threaten and bully, and even when charging stop to growl, shake the head and bite at a bush or knock holes in the ground with their fore-paws. Again, some of them charge home with a ferocious resolution which their extreme tenacity of life renders especially dangerous; while others can be turned or driven back even by a shot which is not mortal. They show the same variability in their behavior when wounded. Often a big bear, especially if charging, will receive a bullet in perfect silence, without flinching or seeming to pay any heed to it; while another will cry out and tumble about, and if charging, even though it may not abandon the attack, will pause for a moment to whine or bite at the wound.

Sometimes a single bite causes death. One of the most successful bear hunters I ever knew, an old fellow whose real name I never heard as he was always called Old Ike, was killed in this way in the spring or early summer of 1886 on one of the head-waters of the Salmon. He was a very good shot, had killed nearly a hundred bears with the rifle, and, although often charged, had never met with any accident, so that he had grown somewhat careless. On the day in question he had met a couple of mining prospectors and was travelling with them, when a grisly crossed his path. The old hunter immediately ran after it, rapidly gaining, as the bear did not hurry when it saw itself pursued, but slouched slowly forwards, occasionally turning its head to grin and growl. It soon went into a dense grove of young spruce, and as the hunter reached the edge it charged fiercely out. He fired one hasty shot, evidently wounding the animal, but not seriously enough to stop or cripple it; and as his two companions ran forward they saw the bear seize him with its wide-spread jaws, forcing him to the ground. They shouted and fired, and the beast abandoned the fallen man on the instant and sullenly retreated into the spruce thicket, whither they dared not follow it. Their friend was at his last gasp; for the whole side of the chest had been crushed in by the one bite, the lungs showing between the rent ribs.

Very often, however, a bear does not kill a man by one bite, but after throwing him lies on him, biting him to death. Usually, if no assistance is at hand, such a man is doomed; although if he pretends to be dead, and has the nerve to lie quiet under very rough treatment, it is just possible that the bear may leave him alive, perhaps after half burying what it believes to be the body. In a very few exceptional instances men of extraordinary prowess with the knife have succeeded in beating off a bear, and even in mortally wounding it, but in most cases a single-handed struggle, at close quarters, with a grisly bent on mischief, means death.

Occasionally the bear, although vicious, is also frightened, and passes on after giving one or two bites; and frequently a man who is knocked down is rescued by his friends before he is killed, the big beast mayhap using his weapons with clumsiness. So a bear may kill a foe with a single blow of its mighty fore-arm, either crushing in the head or chest by sheer force of sinew, or else tearing open the body with its formidable claws; and so on the other hand he may, and often does, merely disfigure or maim the foe by a hurried stroke. Hence it is common to see men who have escaped the clutches of a grisly, but only at the cost of features marred beyond recognition, or a body rendered almost helpless for life. Almost every old resident of western Montana or northern Idaho has known two or three unfortunates who have suffered in this manner. I have myself met one such man in Helena, and another in Missoula; both were living at least as late as 1889, the date at which I last saw them. One had been partially scalped by a bear's teeth; the animal was very old and so the fangs did not enter the skull. The other had been bitten across the face, and the wounds never entirely healed, so that his disfigured visage was hideous to behold.

Most of these accidents occur in following a wounded or worried bear into thick cover; and under such circumstances an animal apparently hopelessly disabled, or in the death throes, may with a last effort kill one or more of its assailants. In 1874 my wife's uncle, Captain Alexander Moore, U. S. A., and my friend Captain Bates, with some men of the 2nd and 3rd Cavalry, were scouting in Wyoming, near the Freezeout Mountains. One morning they roused a bear in the open prairie and followed it at full speed as it ran towards a small creek. At one spot in the creek beavers had built a dam, and as usual in such places there was a thick growth of bushes and willow saplings. Just as the bear reached the edge of this little jungle it was struck by several balls, both of its forelegs being broken. Nevertheless, it managed to shove itself forward on its hind-legs, and partly rolled, partly pushed itself into the thicket, the bushes though low being so dense that its body was at once completely hidden. The thicket was a mere patch of brush, not twenty yards across in any direction. The leading troopers reached the edge almost as the bear tumbled in. One of them, a tall and powerful man named Miller, instantly dismounted and prepared to force his way in among the dwarfed willows, which were but breast-high. Among the men who had ridden up were Moore and Bates, and also the two famous scouts, Buffalo Bill—long a companion of Captain Moore,—and California Joe, Custer's faithful follower. California Joe had spent almost all his life on the plains and in the mountains, as a hunter and Indian fighter; and when he saw the trooper about to rush into the thicket he called out to him not to do so, warning him of the danger. But the man was a very reckless fellow and he answered by jeering at the old hunter for his over-caution in being afraid of a crippled bear. California Joe made no further effort to dissuade him, remarking quietly: "Very well, sonny, go in; it's your own affair." Miller then leaped off the bank on which they stood and strode into the thicket, holding his rifle at the port. Hardly had he taken three steps when the bear rose in front of him, roaring with rage and pain. It was so close that the man had no chance to fire. Its fore-arms hung useless and as it reared unsteadily on its hind-legs, lunging forward at him, he seized it by the ears and strove to hold it back. His strength was very great, and he actually kept the huge head from his face and braced himself so that he was not overthrown; but the bear twisted its muzzle from side to side, biting and tearing the man's arms and shoulders. Another soldier jumping down slew the beast with a single bullet, and rescued his comrade; but though alive he was too badly hurt to recover and died after reaching the hospital. Buffalo Bill was given the bear-skin, and I believe has it now.

The instances in which hunters who have rashly followed grislies into thick cover have been killed or severely mauled might be multiplied indefinitely. I have myself known of eight cases in which men have met their deaths in this manner.

It occasionally happens that a cunning old grisly will lie so close that the hunter almost steps on him; and he then rises suddenly with a loud, coughing growl and strikes down or seizes the man before the latter can fire off his rifle. More rarely a bear which is both vicious and crafty deliberately permits the hunter to approach fairly near to, or perhaps pass by, its hiding-place, and then suddenly charges him with such rapidity that he has barely time for the most hurried shot. The danger in such a case is of course great.

Ordinarily, however, even in the brush, the bear's object is to slink away, not to fight, and very many are killed even under the most unfavorable circumstances without accident. If an unwounded bear thinks itself unobserved it is not apt to attack; and in thick cover it is really astonishing to see how one of these large animals can hide, and how closely it will lie when there is danger. About twelve miles below my ranch there are some large river bottoms and creek bottoms covered with a matted mass of cottonwood, box-alders, bull-berry bushes, rosebushes, ash, wild plums, and other bushes. These bottoms have harbored bears ever since I first saw them; but, though often in company with a large party, I have repeatedly beaten through them, and though we must at times have been very near indeed to the game, we never so much as heard it run.

When bears are shot, as they usually must be, in open timber or on the bare mountain, the risk is very much less. Hundreds may thus be killed with comparatively little danger; yet even under these circumstances they will often charge, and sometimes make their charge good. The spice of danger, especially to a man armed with a good repeating rifle, is only enough to add zest to the chase, and the chief triumph is in outwitting the wary quarry and getting within range. Ordinarily the only excitement is in the stalk, the bear doing nothing more than keep a keen look-out and manifest the utmost anxiety to get away. As is but natural, accidents occasionally occur; yet they are usually due more to some failure in man or weapon than to the prowess of the bear. A good hunter whom I once knew, at a time when he was living in Butte, received fatal injuries from a bear he attacked in open woodland. The beast charged after the first shot, but slackened its pace on coming almost up to the man. The latter's gun jambed, and as he was endeavoring to work it he kept stepping slowly back, facing the bear which followed a few yards distant, snarling and threatening. Unfortunately, while thus walking backwards the man struck a dead log and fell over it, whereupon the beast instantly sprang on him and mortally wounded him before help arrived.

On rare occasions men who are not at the time hunting it fall victims to the grisly. This is usually because they stumble on it unawares and the animal attacks them more in fear than in anger. One such case, resulting fatally, occurred near my own ranch. The man walked almost over a bear while crossing a little point of brush, in a bend of the river, and was brained with a single blow of the paw. In another instance which came to my knowledge the man escaped with a shaking up, and without even a fight. His name was Perkins, and he was out gathering huckleberries in the woods on a mountain side near Pend'Oreille Lake. Suddenly he was sent flying head over heels, by a blow which completely knocked the breath out of his body; and so instantaneous was the whole affair that all he could ever recollect about it was getting a vague glimpse of the bear just as he was bowled over. When he came to he found himself lying some distance down the hill-side, much shaken, and without his berry pail, which had rolled a hundred yards below him, but not otherwise the worse for his misadventure; while the footprints showed that the bear, after delivering the single hurried stoke at the unwitting disturber of its day-dreams, had run off up-hill as fast as it was able.

A she-bear with cubs is a proverbially dangerous beast; yet even under such conditions different grislies act in directly opposite ways. Some she-grislies, when their cubs are young, but are able to follow them about, seem always worked up to the highest pitch of anxious and jealous rage, so that they are likely to attack unprovoked any intruder or even passer-by. Others when threatened by the hunter leave their cubs to their fate without a visible qualm of any kind, and seem to think only of their own safety.

In 1882 Mr. Casper W. Whitney, now of New York, met with a very singular adventure with a she-bear and cub. He was in Harvard when I was, but left it and, like a good many other Harvard men of that time, took to cow-punching in the West. He went on a ranch in Rio Arriba County, New Mexico, and was a keen hunter, especially fond of the chase of cougar, bear, and elk. One day while riding a stony mountain trail he saw a grisly cub watching him from the chaparral above, and he dismounted to try to capture it; his rifle was a 40-90 Sharp's. Just as he neared the cub, he heard a growl and caught a glimpse of the old she, and he at once turned up-hill, and stood under some tall, quaking aspens. From this spot he fired at and wounded the she, then seventy yards off; and she charged furiously. He hit her again, but as she kept coming like a thunderbolt he climbed hastily up the aspen, dragging his gun with him, as it had a strap. When the bear reached the foot of the aspen she reared, and bit and clawed the slender trunk, shaking it for a moment, and he shot her through the eye. Off she sprang for a few yards, and then spun round a dozen times, as if dazed or partially stunned; for the bullet had not touched the brain. Then the vindictive and resolute beast came back to the tree and again reared up against it; this time to receive a bullet that dropped her lifeless. Mr. Whitney then climbed down and walked to where the cub had been sitting as a looker-on. The little animal did not move until he reached out his hand; when it suddenly struck at him like an angry cat, dove into the bushes, and was seen no more.

In the summer of 1888 an old-time trapper, named Charley Norton, while on Loon Creek, of the middle fork of the Salmon, meddled with a she and her cubs. She ran at him and with one blow of her paw almost knocked off his lower jaw; yet he recovered, and was alive when I last heard of him.

Yet the very next spring the cowboys with my own wagon on the Little Missouri round-up killed a mother bear which made but little more fight than a coyote. She had two cubs, and was surprised in the early morning on the prairie far from cover. There were eight or ten cowboys together at the time, just starting off on a long circle, and of course they all got down their ropes in a second, and putting spurs to their fiery little horses started toward the bears at a run, shouting and swinging their loops round their heads. For a moment the old she tried to bluster and made a half-hearted threat of charging; but her courage failed before the rapid onslaught of her yelling, rope-swinging assailants; and she took to her heels and galloped off, leaving the cubs to shift for themselves. The cowboys were close behind, however, and after half a mile's run she bolted into a shallow cave or hole in the side of a butte, where she stayed cowering and growling, until one of the men leaped off his horse, ran up to the edge of the hole, and killed her with a single bullet from his revolver, fired so close that the powder burned her hair. The unfortunate cubs were roped, and then so dragged about that they were speedily killed instead of being brought alive to camp, as ought to have been done.

In the cases mentioned above the grisly attacked only after having been itself assailed, or because it feared an assault, for itself or for its young. In the old days, however, it may almost be said that a grisly was more apt to attack than to flee. Lewis and Clarke and the early explorers who immediately succeeded them, as well as the first hunters and trappers, the "Rocky Mountain men" of the early decades of the present century, were repeatedly assailed in this manner; and not a few of the bear hunters of that period found that it was unnecessary to take much trouble about approaching their quarry, as the grisly was usually prompt to accept the challenge and to advance of its own accord, as soon as it discovered the foe. All this is changed now. Yet even at the present day an occasional vicious old bear may be found, in some far-off and little-trod fastness, which still keeps up the former habit of its kind. All old hunters have tales of this sort to relate, the prowess, cunning, strength, and ferocity of the grisly being favorite topics for camp-fire talk throughout the Rockies; but in most cases it is not safe to accept these stories without careful sifting.

Still it is just as unsafe to reject them all. One of my own cowboys was once attacked by a grisly, seemingly in pure wantonness. He was riding up a creek bottom and had just passed a clump of rose and bull-berry bushes when his horse gave such a leap as almost to unseat him, and then darted madly forward. Turning round in the saddle to his utter astonishment he saw a large bear galloping after him, at the horse's heels. For a few jumps the race was close, then the horse drew away and the bear wheeled and went into a thicket of wild plums. The amazed and indignant cowboy, as soon as he could rein in his steed, drew his revolver and rode back to and around the thicket, endeavoring to provoke his late pursuer to come out and try conclusions on more equal terms; but prudent Ephraim had apparently repented of his freak of ferocious bravado, and declined to leave the secure shelter of the jungle.

Other attacks are of a much more explicable nature. Mr. Huffman, the photographer of Miles City, informed me once when butchering some slaughtered elk he was charged twice by a she-bear and two well-grown cubs. This was a piece of sheer bullying, undertaken solely with the purpose of driving away the man and feasting on the carcasses; for in each charge the three bears, after advancing with much blustering, roaring, and growling, halted just before coming to close quarters. In another instance a gentleman I once knew, a Mr. S. Carr was charged by a grisly from mere ill temper at being disturbed at mealtime. The man was riding up a valley; and the bear was at an elk carcass, near a clump of firs. As soon as it became aware of the approach of the horseman, while he was yet over a hundred yards distant, it jumped on the carcass, looked at him a moment, and then ran straight for him. There was no particular reason why it should have charged, for it was fat and in good trim, though when killed its head showed scars made by the teeth of rival grislies. Apparently it had been living so well, principally on flesh, that it had become quarrelsome; and perhaps its not over sweet disposition had been soured by combats with others of its own kind. In yet another case, a grisly charged with even less excuse. An old trapper, from whom I occasionally bought fur, was toiling up a mountain pass when he spied a big bear sitting on his haunches on the hill-side above. The trapper shouted and waved his cap; whereupon, to his amazement, the bear uttered a loud "wough" and charged straight down on him—only to fall a victim to misplaced boldness.

I am even inclined to think that there have been wholly exceptional occasions when a grisly has attacked a man with the deliberate purpose of making a meal of him; when, in other words, it has started on the career of a man-eater. At least, on any other theory I find it difficult to account for an attack which once came to my knowledge. I was at Sand point, on Pend'Oreille Lake, and met some French and Meti trappers, then in town with their bales of beaver, otter, and sable. One of them, who gave his name as Baptiste Lamoche, had his head twisted over to one side, the result of the bite of a bear. When the accident occurred he was out on a trapping trip with two companions. They had pitched camp right on the shore of a cove in a little lake, and his comrades were off fishing in a dugout or pirogue. He himself was sitting near the shore, by a little lean-to, watching some beaver meat which was sizzling over the dying embers. Suddenly, and without warning, a great bear, which had crept silently up beneath the shadows of the tall evergreens, rushed at him, with a guttural roar, and seized him before he could rise to his feet. It grasped him with its jaws at the junction of the neck and shoulder, making the teeth meet through bone, sinew, and muscle; and turning, tracked off towards the forest, dragging with it the helpless and paralyzed victim. Luckily the two men in the canoe had just paddled round the point, in sight of, and close to, camp. The man in the bow, seeing the plight of their comrade, seized his rifle and fired at the bear. The bullet went through the beast's lungs, and it forthwith dropped its prey, and running off some two hundred yards, lay down on its side and died. The rescued man recovered full health and strength, but never again carried his head straight.

Old hunters and mountain-men tell many stories, not only of malicious grislies thus attacking men in camp, but also of their even dogging the footsteps of some solitary hunter and killing him when the favorable opportunity occurs. Most of these tales are mere fables; but it is possible that in altogether exceptional instances they rest on a foundation of fact. One old hunter whom I knew told me such a story. He was a truthful old fellow and there was no doubt that he believed what he said, and that his companion was actually killed by a bear; but it is probable that he was mistaken in reading the signs of his comrade's fate, and that the latter was not dogged by the bear at all, but stumbled on him and was slain in the surprise of the moment.

At any rate, cases of wanton assaults by grislies are altogether out of the common. The ordinary hunter may live out his whole life in the wilderness and never know aught of a bear attacking a man unprovoked; and the great majority of bears are shot under circumstances of no special excitement, as they either make no fight at all, or, if they do fight, are killed before there is any risk of their doing damage. If surprised on the plains, at some distance from timber or from badly broken ground, it is no uncommon feat for a single horseman to kill them with a revolver. Twice of late years it has been performed in the neighborhood of my ranch. In both instances the men were not hunters out after game, but simply cowboys, riding over the range in early morning in pursuance of their ordinary duties among the cattle. I knew both men and have worked with them on the round-up. Like most cowboys, they carried 44-calibre Colt revolvers, and were accustomed to and fairly expert in their use, and they were mounted on ordinary cow-ponies—quick, wiry, plucky little beasts. In one case the bear was seen from quite a distance, lounging across a broad table-land. The cowboy, by taking advantage of a winding and rather shallow coulie, got quite close to him. He then scrambled out of the coulie, put spurs to his pony, and raced up to within fifty yards of the astonished bear ere the latter quite understood what it was that was running at him through the gray dawn. He made no attempt at fight, but ran at top speed towards a clump of brush not far off at the head of a creek. Before he could reach it, however, the galloping horseman was alongside, and fired three shots into his broad back. He did not turn, but ran on into the bushes and then fell over and died.

In the other case the cowboy, a Texan, was mounted on a good cutting pony, a spirited, handy, agile little animal, but excitable, and with a habit of dancing, which rendered it difficult to shoot from its back. The man was with the round-up wagon, and had been sent off by himself to make a circle through some low, barren buttes, where it was not thought more than a few head of stock would be found. On rounding the corner of a small washout he almost ran over a bear which was feeding on the carcass of a steer that had died in an alkali hole. After a moment of stunned surprise the bear hurled himself at the intruder with furious impetuosity; while the cowboy, wheeling his horse on its haunches and dashing in the spurs, carried it just clear of his assailant's headlong rush. After a few springs he reined in and once more wheeled half round, having drawn his revolver, only to find the bear again charging and almost on him. This time he fired into it, near the joining of the neck and shoulder, the bullet going downwards into the chest hollow; and again by a quick dash to one side he just avoided the rush of the beast and the sweep of its mighty forepaw. The bear then halted for a minute, and he rode close by it at a run, firing a couple of shots, which brought on another resolute charge. The ground was somewhat rugged and broken, but his pony was as quick on its feet as a cat, and never stumbled, even when going at full speed to avoid the bear's first mad rushes. It speedily became so excited, however, as to render it almost impossible for the rider to take aim. Sometimes he would come up close to the bear and wait for it to charge, which it would do, first at a trot, or rather rack, and then at a lumbering but swift gallop; and he would fire one or two shots before being forced to run. At other times, if the bear stood still in a good place, he would run by it, firing as he rode. He spent many cartridges, and though most of them were wasted occasionally a bullet went home. The bear fought with the most savage courage, champing its bloody jaws, roaring with rage, and looking the very incarnation of evil fury. For some minutes it made no effort to flee, either charging or standing at bay. Then it began to move slowly towards a patch of ash and wild plums in the head of a coulie, some distance off. Its pursuer rode after it, and when close enough would push by it and fire, while the bear would spin quickly round and charge as fiercely as ever, though evidently beginning to grow weak. At last, when still a couple of hundred yards from cover the man found he had used up all his cartridges, and then merely followed at a safe distance. The bear no longer paid heed to him, but walked slowly forwards, swaying its great head from side to side, while the blood streamed from between its half-opened jaws. On reaching the cover he could tell by the waving of the bushes that it walked to the middle and then halted. A few minutes afterwards some of the other cowboys rode up, having been attracted by the incessant firing. They surrounded the thicket, firing and throwing stones into the bushes. Finally, as nothing moved, they ventured in and found the indomitable grisly warrior lying dead.

Cowboys delight in nothing so much as the chance to show their skill as riders and ropers; and they always try to ride down and rope any wild animal they come across in favorable ground and close enough up. If a party of them meets a bear in the open they have great fun; and the struggle between the shouting, galloping, rough-riders and their shaggy quarry is full of wild excitement and not unaccompanied by danger. The bear often throws the noose from his head so rapidly that it is a difficult matter to catch him; and his frequent charges scatter his tormentors in every direction while the horses become wild with fright over the roaring, bristling beast—for horses seem to dread a bear more than any other animal. If the bear cannot reach cover, however, his fate is sealed. Sooner or later, the noose tightens over one leg, or perchance over the neck and fore-paw, and as the rope straightens with a "plunk," the horse braces itself desperately and the bear tumbles over. Whether he regains his feet or not the cowboy keeps the rope taut; soon another noose tightens over a leg, and the bear is speedily rendered helpless.

I have known of these feats being performed several times in northern Wyoming, although never in the immediate neighborhood of my ranch. Mr. Archibald Roger's cowhands have in this manner caught several bears, on or near his ranch on the Gray Bull, which flows into the Bighorn; and those of Mr. G. B. Grinnell have also occasionally done so. Any set of moderately good ropers and riders, who are accustomed to back one another up and act together, can accomplish the feat if they have smooth ground and plenty of room. It is, however, indeed a feat of skill and daring for a single man; and yet I have known of more than one instance in which it has been accomplished by some reckless knight of the rope and the saddle. One such occurred in 1887 on the Flathead Reservation, the hero being a half-breed; and another in 1890 at the mouth of the Bighorn, where a cowboy roped, bound, and killed a large bear single-handed.

My friend General "Red" Jackson, of Bellemeade, in the pleasant mid-county of Tennessee, once did a feat which casts into the shade even the feats of the men of the lariat. General Jackson, who afterwards became one of the ablest and most renowned of the Confederate cavalry leaders, was at the time a young officer in the Mounted Rifle Regiment, now known as the 3rd United States Cavalry. It was some years before the Civil War, and the regiment was on duty in the Southwest, then the debatable land of Comanche and Apache. While on a scout after hostile Indians, the troops in their march roused a large grisly which sped off across the plain in front of them. Strict orders had been issued against firing at game, because of the nearness of the Indians. Young Jackson was a man of great strength, a keen swordsman, who always kept the finest edge on his blade, and he was on a swift and mettled Kentucky horse, which luckily had but one eye. Riding at full speed he soon overtook the quarry. As the horse hoofs sounded nearer, the grim bear ceased its flight, and whirling round stood at bay, raising itself on its hind-legs and threatening its pursuer with bared fangs and spread claws. Carefully riding his horse so that its blind side should be towards the monster, the cavalryman swept by at a run, handling his steed with such daring skill that he just cleared the blow of the dreaded fore-paw, while with one mighty sabre stroke he cleft the bear's skull, slaying the grinning beast as it stood upright.

THE WHITE GOAT AND HIS COUNTRY

BY OWEN WISTER

(Editor's Note: The author of the first popular Western novel, *The Virginian*, shows his prose skills in this portrait of early mountain goat hunting. From *The Virginian*, Mr. Wister (1860–1938) is famous for the expression, "When you call me that, smile!" Also in *The Virginian*, he wrote, "When a man ain't got no ideas of his own, he'd ought to be kind o' careful who he borrows 'em from." He was a good friend of Theodore Roosevelt and shared hunting adventures with him.)

In a corner of what is occasionally termed "Our Empire of the Northwest," there lies a country of mountains and valleys where, until recently, citizens have been few. At the present time certain mines, and uncertain hopes, have gathered an eccentric population and evoked some sudden towns. The names which several of these bear are tolerably sumptuous: Golden, Oro, and Ruby, for instance; and in them dwell many colonels and judges, and people who own one suit of clothes and half a name (colored by adjuncts, such as Hurry Up Ed), and who sleep almost anywhere. These communities are brisk, sanguine, and nomadic, full of good will and crime; and in each of them you will be likely to find a weekly newspaper, and an editor who is busy writing things about the neighboring editors. The flume slants down the hill bearing water to the concentrator; buckets unexpectedly swing out from the steep pines into mid-air, sailing along their wire to the mill; little new staring shanties appear daily; somebody having trouble in a saloon upsets a lamp, and half the town goes to ashes, while the colonels and Hurry Up Eds carouse over the fireworks till morning. In a short while there are more little shanties than ever, and the burnt district is forgotten. All this is going on not far from the mountain goat, but it is a forlorn distance from the railroad; and except for the stage line which the recent mining towns have necessitated, my route to the goat country might have been too prolonged and uncertain to attempt.

I stepped down one evening from the stage, the last public conveyance I was to see, after a journey that certainly has one good side. It is completely odious; and the breed of sportsmen that takes into camp every luxury excepting, perhaps, cracked ice, will not be tempted to infest the region until civilization has smoothed its path. The path, to be sure, does not roughen until one has gone along it for twenty-eight hundred miles. You may leave New York in the afternoon, and arrive very early indeed on the fifth day at Spokane. Here the luxuries begin to lessen, and a mean once-a-day train trundles you away on a branch west of Spokane at six in the morning into a landscape that wastes into a galloping consumption. Before noon the last sick tree, the ultimate starved blade of wheat, has perished from sight, and you come to the end of all things, it would seem; a domain of wretchedness unspeakable. Not even a warm, brilliant sun can galvanize the corpse of the bare ungainly earth. The railroad goes no further,—it is not surprising,—and the stage arranges to leave before the train arrives. Thus you spend sunset and sunrise in the moribund terminal town, the inhabitants of which frankly confess that they are not staying from choice. They were floated here by a boom-wave, which left them stranded. Kindly they were, and anxious to provide the stranger with what comforts existed.

Geographically I was in the "Big Bend" country, a bulk of land looped in by the Columbia River, and highly advertised by railroads for the benefit of "those seeking homes." Fruit and grain no doubt grow somewhere in it. What I saw was a desert cracked in two by a chasm sixty-five miles long. It rained in the night, and at seven next morning, bound for Port Columbia, we wallowed northward out of town in the sweating canvas-covered stage through primeval mud. After some eighteen miles we drew out of the rain area, and from around the wheels there immediately arose and came among us a primeval dust, monstrous, shapeless, and blind. First your power of speech deserted you, then your eyesight went, and at length you became uncertain whether you were alive. Then hilarity at the sheer discomfort overtook me, and I was joined in it by a brother American; but two Jew drummers on the back seat could not understand, and seemed on the verge of tears. The landscape was entirely blotted out by the dust. Often you could not see the roadside,—if the road had any side. We may have been passing homes and fruit-trees, but I think not. I remember wondering if getting goat after all—But they proved well worth it.

Toward evening we descended into the sullen valley of the Columbia, which rushes along, sunk below the level of the desert we had crossed. High sterile hills flank its course, and with the sweeping, unfriendly speed of the stream, its bleak shores seemed a chilly place for home-seekers. Yet I blessed the change. A sight of running water once more, even of this overbearing flood, and of hills however dreary, was exhilaration after the degraded, stingy monotony of the Big Bend. The alkali trails in Wyoming do not seem paradises till you bring your memory of them here. Nor am I alone in my estimate of this impossible hole. There is a sign-post sticking up in the middle of it, that originally told the traveler it was thirty-five miles to Central Ferry. But now the traveler has retorted; and three different hand-writings on this sign-post reveal to you that you have had predecessors in your thought, comrades who shared your sorrows:

FORTY-FIVE MILES TO WATER.
SEVENTY-FIVE MILES TO WOOD.

AND THEN THE LAST WORD:

TWO AND ONE-HALF MILES TO HELL.

Perhaps they were home-seekers.

We halted a moment at the town of Bridgeport, identified by one wooden store and an inchoate hotel. The rest may be seen upon blue-print maps, where you would suppose Bridgeport was a teeming metropolis. At Port Columbia, which we reached by a land-slide sort of road that slanted the stage over and put the twin Jew drummers in mortal fear, we slept in one of the two buildings which indicate that town. It is another important center,—in blue print,—but invisible to the naked eye. In the morning, a rope ferry floated the new stage and us travelers across the river. The Okanagon flows south from lakes and waters above the British line, and joins the Columbia here. We entered its valley at once, crossed it soon by another rope ferry, and keeping northward, with the river to the east between us and the Colville Reservation, had one good meal at noon, and entering a smaller valley, reached Ruby that evening. Here the stage left me to continue its way to Conconally, six miles further on. With the friends who had come to meet me, I ascended out of Ruby the next day over the abrupt hill westward, and passing one night out in my blankets near a hospitable but limited cabin (its flowing-haired host fed us, played us the fiddle, and would have had us sleep inside), arrived bag and baggage the fourth day from the railroad at the forks of the Methow River—the next tributary of the Columbia below the Okanogan.

Here was a smiling country, winning the heart at sight. An ample beauty was over everything Nature had accomplished in this place; the pleasant trees and clear course of the stream, a fertile soil on the levels, the slopes of the foot-hills varied and gentle, unencumbered by woods, the purple cloak of forest above these on the mountains, and rising from the valley's head a crown of white, clean frozen peaks. These are known to some as the Isabella Range and Mount Gardner, though the maps do not name them. Moreover, I heard that now I was within twenty-five miles of goats; and definite ridges were pointed out as the promised land.

Many things were said to me, first and last. I remember a ragged old trapper, lately come over the mountains from the Skagit River. Goats, did I say? On top there the goats had tangled your feet walking in the trail. He had shot two in camp for staring at him. Another accurate observer had seen three hundred on a hill just above Early Winter as he was passing by. The cabined dwellers on the Methow tied their horses to the fence and talked to me—so I had come from the East after goats, had I?—and in the store of the Man at the Forks I became something of a curiosity. Day by day I sat on the kegs of nails, or lay along the counter devoted to his dry-goods, and heard what passed. Citizens and denizens—for the Siwash with his squaws and horses was having his autumn hunt in the valley—knocked at the door to get their mail, or buy tobacco, or sell horns and fur, or stare for an hour and depart with a grunt; and the grave Man at the Forks stood behind one counter while I lay on the other, acquiring a miscellaneous knowledge. One old medical gentleman had slain all wild animals without weapons, and had been the personal friend of so many distinguished historical characters that we computed he was nineteen about the time of Bunker Hill. They were hospitable with their information, and I followed my rule of believing everything that I hear. And they were also hospitable with whatever they possessed. The memory of those distant dwellers among the mountains, young and old, is a friendly one, like the others I carry, whether of Wind or Powder Rivers, or the Yellowstone, or wherever Western trails have led me.

Yet disappointment and failure were the first things. There was all the zeal you could wish. We had wedged painfully into a severe country—twelve miles in two days, and trail-cutting between—when sickness turned us back, goatless. By this time October was almost gone, and the last three days of it went in patching up our disintegrated outfit. We needed other men and other horses; and while these were being sought, nothing was more usual than to hear "if we'd only been along with So-and-So, he saw goats" here and there, and apparently everywhere. We had, it would seem, ingeniously selected the only place where there were none. But somehow the services of So-and-So could not be procured. He had gone to town; or was busy getting his winter's meat; or his married daughter had just come to visit him, or he had married somebody else's daughter. I cannot remember the number of obstacles always lying between ourselves and So-and-So.

At length we were once more in camp on a stream named the Twispt. In the morning—new stroke of misfortune—one of us was threatened with illness, and returned to the Forks. We three, the guide, the cook, and myself, went on, finally leaving the narrow valley, and climbing four hours up a mountain at the rate of about a mile an hour. The question was, had winter come in the park above, for which we were heading? On top, we skirted a bare ridge from which everything fell precipitously away, and curving round along a steep hollow of the hill, came to an edge and saw the snow lying plentifully among the pines through which we must go down into the bottom of the park. But on the other side, where the sun came, there was little or none, and it was a most beautiful place. At the head of it was a little frozen lake fringed with tamarack, and a stream flowed down from this through scattered birches and pines, with good pasture for the horses between. The park sank at its outlet into a tall impassable cañon through which the stream joined the Twispt, miles below. It was a little lap of land clear at the top of the mountains, the final peaks and ridges of which rose all around, walling it in completely. You must climb these to be able to see into it, and the only possible approach for pack-horses was the pine-tree slant, down which we came. Of course there was no trail.

We prospected before venturing, and T——, the guide, shook his head. It was only a question of days—possibly of hours—when snow must shut the place off from the world until spring. But T—— appreciated the three thousand miles I had come for goats; and if the worst came to the worst, said he, we could "make it in" to the Forks on foot, leading the horses, and leaving behind all baggage that weighed anything. So we went down. Our animals slipped a little, the snow balling their feet; but nothing happened, and we reached the bottom and chose a camp in a clump of tamarack and pine. The little stream, passing through shadows here, ran under a lid of frozen snow easily broken, and there was plenty of wood, and on the ground only such siftings of snow as could be swept clean for the tent. The saddles were piled handily under a tree, a good fireplace was dug, we had a comfortable supper; and nothing remained but that the goats should be where they ought to be—on the ridges above the park.

I have slept more soundly; doubt and hope kept my thoughts active. Yet even so, it was pleasant to wake in the quiet and hear the bell on our horse, Duster, occasionally tankle somewhere on the hill. My watch I had forgotten to place at T——'s disposal, so he was reduced to getting the time of day from the stars. He consulted the Great Bear, and seeing this constellation at an angle he judged to indicate five o'clock, he came back into the tent, and I heard him wake the cook, who crawled out of his blankets.

"Why, it's plumb night," the cook whined.

"Make the breakfast," said T——.

I opened my eyes, and shut them immediately in despair at the darkness that I saw. Presently I heard the fire and the pans, and knew that the inevitable had come. So I got my clothes on, and we looked at my watch. It was only 4.30 A.M. T—— and the Great Bear had made half an hour's miscalculation, and the face of the cook was so grievous that I secretly laughed myself entirely awake. "Plumb night" lasted some time longer. I had leisure to eat two plates of oatmeal and maple syrup, some potato-and-onion soup, bacon, and coffee, and digest these, before dawn showed.

T—— and I left camp at 6.40 A.M. The day was a dark one. On the high peaks behind camp great mounds of cloud moved and swung, and the sky was entirely overcast. We climbed one of the lower ridges, not a hard climb nor long, but very sliding, and often requiring hands and feet to work round a ledge. From the top we could see the open country lying comfortably below and out of reach of the howling wind that cut across the top of the mountain, straight from Puget Sound, bringing all that it could carry of the damp of the Pacific. The ridges and summits that surrounded our park continually came into sight and disappeared again among the dense vapors which bore down upon them.

We went cautiously along the narrow top of crumbling slate, where the pines were scarce and stunted, and had twisted themselves into corkscrews so they might grip the ground against the tearing force of storms. We came on a number of fresh goat-tracks in the snow or the soft shale. These are the reverse of those of the mountain sheep, the V which the hoofs make having its open end in the direction the animal is going. There seemed to be several, large and small; and the perverted animals invariably chose the sharpest slant they could find to walk on, often with a decent level just beside it that we were glad enough to have. If there were a precipice and a sound flat top, they took the precipice, and crossed its face on juts that did not look as if your hat would hang on them. In this I think they are worse than the mountain sheep, if that is possible. Certainly they do not seem to come down into the high pastures and feed on the grass levels as the sheep will.

T—— and I hoped we should find a bunch, but that was not to be, in spite of the indications. As we continued, I saw a singular-looking stone lying on a little ledge some way down the mountain ahead. I decided it must be a stone, and was going to speak of it, when the stone moved, and we crouched in the slanting gravel. T—— had been making up his mind it was a stone. The goat turned his head our way, but did not rise. He was two hundred yards across a split in the mountain, and the wind blowing hard. T—— wanted me to shoot, but I did not dare to run such a chance. I have done a deal of missing at two hundred yards, and much nearer, too. So I climbed, or crawled, out of sight, keeping any stone or little bush between me and the goat, till I got myself where a buttress of rock hid me, and then I ran along the ridge and down and up the scoop in it made by the split of the mountain, and so came cautiously to where I could peer over and see the goat lying turned away from me, with his head commanding the valley. He was on a tiny shelf of snow, beside him was one small pine, and below that the rock fell away steeply into the gorge. Ought I to have bellowed at him, and at least have got him on his legs? I know it would have been more honorable. He looked white, and huge, and strange; and somehow I had a sense of personality about him more vivid than any since I watched my first silver-tip lift a rotten log, and, sitting on his hind legs, make a breakfast on beetles, picking them off the log with one paw.

I fired, aiming behind the goat's head. He did not rise, but turned his head round. The white bead of my Lyman sight had not showed well against the white animal, and I thought I had missed him. Then I fired again, and he rolled very little—six inches—and lay quiet. He could not have been more than fifty yards away, and my first shot had cut through the back of his neck and buried itself in mortal places, and the second in his head merely made death instantaneous. Shooting him after he had become alarmed might have lost him over the edge; even if a first shot had been fatal, it could not have been fatal soon enough. Two struggles on that snow would have sent him sliding through space. As it was, we had a steep, unsafe scramble down through the snow to where he lay stretched out on the little shelf by the tree.

He was a fair-sized billy, and very heavy. The little lifting and shoving we had to do in skinning him was hard work. The horns were black, slender, slightly spreading, curved backward, pointed, and smooth. They measured six inches round the base, and the distance from one point to the other, measured down one horn, along the skull, and up the other, was twenty-one and a half inches. The hoofs were also black and broad and large, wholly unlike a tame goat's. The hair was extraordinarily thick, long, and of a weather-beaten white; the eye large and deep-brown.

I had my invariable attack of remorse on looking closely at the poor harmless old gentleman, and wondered what achievement, after all, could be discerned in this sort of surprise and murder. We did not think of securing any of his plentiful fat, but with head and hide alone climbed back up the ticklish slant, hung the trophies on a tree in a gap on the camp side of the ridge, and continued our hunt. It was not ten o'clock yet, and we had taken one hour to skin the goat. We now hunted the higher ridges behind camp until 1 P.M., finding tracks that made it seem as if a number of goats must be somewhere near by. But the fog came down and shut everything out of sight; moreover, the wind on top blew so that we could not have seen had it been clear.

We returned to camp, and found it greatly improved. The cook had carpentered an important annex to the tent. By slanting pine-logs against a ridge-pole and nailing them, he had built a room, proof against wind and rain, and in it a table. One end was against the opening of the tent, the other at the fire. The arrangement was excellent, and timely also. The storm revived during the night, and it rained fitfully. The roar of the wind coming down from the mountain into our park sounded like a Niagara, and its approach was tremendous. We had built up a barrier of pine-brush, and this, with a clump of trees, sheltered us well enough; but there were wild moments when the gust struck us, and the tent shuddered and strained, until that particular breeze passed on with a diminishing roar down the cañon.

The next morning the rain kept us from making an early start, and we did not leave camp until eight. Now and then a drizzle fell from the mist, and the banks of clouds were still driving across the higher peaks, but during the day the sun slowly got the better of them. Again we saw a solitary goat, this time far below down the ridge we had chosen. Like the sheep, these animals watch the valley. There is no use in attempting to hunt them from there. Their eyes are watchful and keen, and the chances are that if you are working up from below and see a goat on the hill, he will have been looking at you for some time. Once he is alarmed, ten minutes will be enough for him to put a good many hours of climbing between himself and you. His favorite trick is to remain stock-still, watching you till you pass out of his sight behind something, and then he makes off so energetically that when you see him next he will be on some totally new mountain. But his intelligence does not seem to grasp more than the danger from below. While he is steadfastly on the alert against this, it apparently does not occur to him that anything can come down upon him. Consequently from above you may get very near before you are noticed. The chief difficulty is the noise of falling stones your descent is almost sure to make. The character of these mountain-sides is such that even with the greatest care in stepping we sent a shower rattling down from time to time. We had a viciously bad climb. We went down through tilted funnels of crag, avoiding jumping off places by crossing slides of brittle slate and shale, hailing a dead tree as an oasis. And then we lost count, and T—— came unexpectedly on the goat, which was up and away and was shot by T—— before I could get a sight of him. I had been behind some twenty yards, both of us supposing we had to go considerably further. T—— was highly disgusted. "To think of me managing such a botch as that," he said, "when you've come so far"; and he wanted me to tell the people that I had shot the goat myself. He really cared more than I did.

This goat was also a billy, and larger than the first. We sat skinning him where he had fallen at the edge of a grove of tamarack, and T—— conversed about the royal family of England. He remarked that he had always rather liked "that chap Lorne."

I explained to him that "that chap Lorne" had made himself ridiculous forever at the Queen's Jubilee. Then, as T—— did not know, I told him how the marquis had insisted on riding in the procession upon a horse, against which the Prince of Wales, aware of the tame extent of his horsemanship, had warned him. In the middle of the pageant, the Queen in her carriage, the crowned heads of Europe escorting her on horseback, and the whole world looking on—at this picturesque moment, Lorne fell off. I was not sure that T—— felt fully how inappropriate a time this was for a marquis to tumble from his steed.

"I believe the Queen sent somebody," I continued.

"Where?" said T——.

"To him. She probably called the nearest king and said: 'Frederick, Lorne's off. Go and see if he's hurt.'"

"'And if he ain't hurt, *hurt him*,'" said T——, completing her Majesty's thought.

This second billy seemed to me twice the size of a domestic goat. He was certainly twice the weight. His hide alone weighed thirty pounds, as far as one could determine by balancing it against weights that we knew, such as a sack of flour or sugar. But I distrust the measurements of wild animals made by guesswork on a mountain-top during the enthusiastic state of the hunter's mind which follows at once upon a lucky shot. Therefore, I can positively vouch for this only, that all the goats which I have seen struck me as being larger and heavier animals than the goat of civilization. After all, the comparison is one into which we are misled by the name. This is an antelope; and though, through certain details of his costume, he is able to masquerade as a goat, it must be remembered that he is of a species wholly distinct.

We took the web tallow, and the tallow of one kidney. The web was three quarters of an inch thick.

Neither elk, nor any animal I have seen, except bear, has such quantities of fat, and I do not think even a bear has a thicker hide. On the rump it was as thick as the sole of my boot, and the masses of hair are impenetrable to anything but modern firearms. An arrow might easily stick harmless; and I am told that carnivorous animals who prey upon the deer in these mountains respectfully let the goat alone. Besides his defensive armor, he is an ugly customer in attack. He understands the use of his thin, smooth horns, and, driving them securely into the belly of his enemy, jumps back and leaves him a useless, ripped-open sack. Male and female have horns of much the same size; and in taking a bite out of one of either sex, as T—— said, a mountain lion would get only a mouthful of hair.

But modern firearms have come to be appreciated by the wild animals; and those which were once unquestionably dangerous to pioneers, now retreat before the Winchester rifle. Only a bear with cubs to defend remains formidable.

I said this to T——, who told me a personal experience that tends to destroy even this last chance for the sportsman to be doughty. T—— came on a bear and cubs in the spring, and of course they made off, but his dog caught and held one little cub which cried out like a child—and its contemptible mama hurried straight on and away.

Not so a goat mama of which T—— also told me. Some prospectors came on a bunch of goats when the kids were young enough to be caught. One of the men captured a kid, and was walking off with it, when the mother took notice and charged furiously down on him. He flew by in ignominious sight of the whole camp with the goat after him, till he was obliged to drop the kid, which was then escorted back to its relatives by its most competent parent.

Yet no room for generalizing is here. We cannot conclude that the *Ursus* family fails to think blood as thick as other people do. These two incidents merely show that the race of bears is capable of producing unmaternal females, while, on the other hand, we may expect occasionally to find in a nanny-goat a Mother of the Gracchi.

I wished to help carry the heavy hide of the second billy; but T——— inflicted this upon himself, "every step to camp," he insisted, "for punishment at disappointing you." The descent this day had been bad enough, taking forty minutes for some four hundred yards. But now we were two hours getting up, a large part of the way on hands and knees. I carried the two rifles and the glass, going in front to stamp some sort of a trail in the sliding rocks, while T——— panted behind me, bearing the goat-hide on his back.

Our next hunt was from seven till four, up and down, in the presence of noble and lonely mountains. The straight peaks which marshal round the lake of Chelan were in our view near by, beyond the valley of the Twispt, and the whole Cascade range rose endlessly, and seemed to fill the world. Except in Switzerland, I have never seen such an unbroken area of mountains. And all this beauty going begging, while each year our American citizens of the East, more ignorant of their own country and less identified with its soil than any race upon earth, herd across the sea to the tables d'hôte they know by heart! But this is wandering a long way from goats, of which this day we saw none.

A gale set in after sunset. This particular afternoon had been so mellow, the sun had shone so clear from a stable sky, that I had begun to believe the recent threats of winter were only threats, and that we had some open time before us still. Next morning we waked in midwinter, the flakes flying thick and furious over a park that was no longer a pasture, but a blind drift of snow. We lived in camp, perfectly comfortable. Down at the Forks I had had made a rough imitation of a Sibley stove. All that its forger had to go on was my unprofessional and inexpert description, and a lame sketch in pencil; but he succeeded so well that the hollow iron cone and joints of pipe he fitted together turned out most efficient. The sight of the apparatus packed on a horse with the

panniers was whimsical, and until he saw it work I know that T——
despised it. After that, it commanded his respect. All this stormy day
it roared and blazed, and sent a lusty heat throughout the tent. T——
cleaned the two goat-heads, and talked Shakspere and Thackeray to
me. He quoted Henry the Fourth, and regretted that Thackeray had
not more developed the character of George Warrington. Warrington
was the *man* in the book. When night came the storm was gone.

By eight the next morning we had sighted another large solitary
billy. But he had seen us down in the park from his ridge. He had
come to the edge, and was evidently watching the horses. If not quick-
witted, the goat is certainly wary; and the next time we saw him he
had taken himself away down the other side of the mountain, along a
spine of rocks where approach was almost impossible. We watched his
slow movements through the glass, and were both reminded of a bear.
He felt safe, and was stepping deliberately along, often stopping, often
walking up some small point and surveying the scenery. He moved
in an easy, rolling fashion, and turned his head importantly. Then he
lay down in the sun, but saw us on our way to him, and bounced off.
We came to the place where he had jumped down sheer twenty feet
at least. His hoof-tracks were on the edge, and in the gravel below the
heavy scatter he made in landing; and then,—hasty tracks round a corner of rock, and no more goat that day.

I had become uneasy about the weather. It was all sunshine again,
and though our first goat was irretrievably gone, we had the afternoon
before us. Nevertheless, when I suggested we should spend it in taking
the shoes off the horses, so they might be able to walk homeward
without falling in the snow, T—— thought it our best plan. We wanted
to find a bunch of goats now, nannies and kids, as well as billies. It
had been plain that these ridges here contained very few, and those
all hermits; males who from age, or temperament, or disappointment

in love, had retired from society, and were spending the remainder of their days in a quiet isolation and whatever is the goat equivalent for reading Horace. It was well enough to have begun with these philosophers, but I wanted new specimens.

We were not too soon. A new storm had set in by next morning, and the unshod horses made their journey down the mountain, a most odious descent for man and beast, in the sliding snow. But down on the Twispt it was yet only autumn, with no snow at all. This was a Monday, the 7th of November, and we made haste to the Forks, where I stopped a night to read a large, accumulated mail, and going on at once, overtook my outfit, which had preceded me on the day before.

Our new camp—and our last one—was up the Methow, twenty-three miles above the Forks, in a straight line. Here the valley split at right angles against a tall face of mountain, and each way the stream was reduced to a brook one could cross afoot. The new valley became steep and narrow almost at once, and so continued to the divide between Columbia water and tributaries of the Skagit. We lived comfortably in an old cabin built by prospectors. The rain filtered through the growing weeds and sand on the roof and dropped on my head in bed; but not much, and I was able to steer it off by a rubber blanket. And of course there was no glass in the windows; but to keep out wind and wet we hung gunny sacks across those small holes, and the big stone fireplace was magnificent.

By ten next morning T—— and I saw "three hundred" goats on the mountain opposite where we had climbed. Just here I will risk a generalization. When a trapper tells you he has seen so many hundred head of game, he has not counted them, but he believes what he says. The goats T—— and I now looked at were a mile away in an air-line, and they seemed numberless. The picture which the white, slightly moving dots made, like mites on a cheese, inclined one to a large estimate of them, since they covered the whole side of a hill. The more we looked the more we found; besides the main army there were groups, caucuses, families sitting apart over some discourse too intimate for the general public; and beyond these single animals could be discerned, moving, gazing, browsing, lying down.

"Megod and Begod," said T—— (he occasionally imitated a brogue for no hereditary reason), "there's a hundred thousand goats!"

"Let's count 'em," I suggested, and we took the glasses. There were thirty-five.

We found we had climbed the wrong hill, and the day was too short to repair this error. Our next excursion, however, was successful. The hill where the goats were was not two miles above camp,— you could have seen the animals from camp but for the curve in the cañon,—yet we were four hours and a half climbing the ridge, in order to put ourselves above them. It was a hard climb, entirely through snow after the first. On top the snow came at times considerably above the knees. But the judicious T—— (I have never hunted with a more careful and thorough man) was right in the route he had chosen, and after we had descended again to the edge of the snow, we looked over a rock, and saw, thirty yards below us, the nanny and kid for which we had been aiming. I should have said earlier that the gathering of yesterday had dispersed during the night, and now little bunches of three and four goats could be seen up and down the cañon. We were on the exact ground they had occupied, and their many tracks were plain. My first shot missed—thirty yards!—and as nanny and kid went bounding by on the hill below, I knocked her over with a more careful bullet, and T—— shot the kid. The little thing was not dead when we came up, and at the sight of us it gave a poor little thin bleat that turns me remorseful whenever I think of it. We had all the justification that any code exacts. We had no fresh meat, and among goats the kid alone is eatable; and I justly desired specimens of the entire family.

We carried the whole kid to camp, and later its flesh was excellent. The horns of the nanny, as has been said before, are but slightly different from those of the male. They are, perhaps, more slender, as is also the total makeup of the animal. In camp I said to T—— that I desired only one more of those thirty-five goats, a billy; and that if I secured him the next day, that should be the last. Fortune was for us. We surprised a bunch of several. They had seen me also, and I was obliged to be quick. This resulted in some shots missing, and in two, perhaps three, animals going over ledges with bullets in them, leaving safe behind the billy I wanted. His conduct is an interesting example of the goat's capacity to escape you and die uselessly, out of your reach.

I had seen him reel at my first shot, but he hurried around a corner, and my attention was given to others. As I went down, I heard a shot, and came round the corner on T——, who stood some hundred yards further along the ledge beside a goat. T—— had come on him lying down. He had jumped up and run apparently unhurt, and T—— had shot him just as he reached the end of the ledge. Beyond was a fall into inaccessible depths. Besides T——'s shot we found two of mine—one clean through from the shoulder—the goat had faced me when I fired first—to the ham, where the lead was flat against the bone. This goat was the handsomest we had, smaller than the other males, but with horns of a better shape, and with hair and beard very rich and white. Curiously enough, his lower jaw between the two front teeth had been broken a long time ago, probably from some fall. Yet this accident did not seem to have interfered with his feeding, for he was in excellent plump condition.

This completely satisfied me, and I willingly decided to molest no more goats. I set neither value nor respect on numerical slaughter.

One cannot expect Englishmen to care whether American big game is exterminated or not; that Americans should not care is a disgrace. The pervading spirit of the far West as to game, as to timber, as to everything that a true American should feel it his right to use and his duty to preserve for those coming after, is— "What do I care, so long as it lasts my time?"

There remain a few observations to make, and then I have said the little that I know about goats. Their horns are not deciduous, so far at least as I could learn, and the books say this also. But I read a somewhat inaccurate account of the goat's habits in winter-time. It was stated that at that season, like mountain sheep, he descends and comes into the valleys. This does not seem to be the case. He does not depend upon grass, if indeed he eats grass at all. His food seems to be chiefly the short, almost lichen-like moss that grows on the faces and at the base of the rocks and between them in the crevices. The community of goats I watched was feeding; afterward, when on the spot where they had been, I found there was no grass growing anywhere near, and signs pointed to its having been the moss and rock plants that they had been eating. None of the people in the Methow country spoke of seeing goats come out of the mountains during winter. I have not sufficient data to make the assertion, but I am inclined to believe that the goat keeps consistently to the hills, whatever the season may be, and in this differs from the mountain sheep as he differs in appearance, temperament, and in all characteristics excepting the predilection for the inclined plane; and in this habit he is more vertical than the sheep.

Lest the region I hunted in may have remained vague to Eastern readers, it is as well to add that in an air-line I was probably some thirty miles below the British border, and some hundred and twenty east of Puget Sound.

DE SHOOTIN'EST GENT'MAN

BY NASH BUCKINGHAM

Supper was a delicious memory. In the matter of a certain goose stew, Aunt Molly had fairly outdone herself. And we, in turn, had jolly well done her out of practically all the goose. It may not come amiss to explain frankly and aboveboard the entire transaction with reference to said goose. Its breast had been deftly detached, lightly grilled and sliced into ordinary "mouth-size" portions. The remainder of the dismembered bird, back, limbs and all parts of the first part thereunto pertaining were put into an iron pot. Keeping company with the martyred fowl, in due proportion of culinary wizardry, were sundry bell peppers, two cans of mock turtle soup, diced roast pork, scrambled ham rinds, peas, potatoes, some corn and dried garden okra, shredded onions and pretty much anything and everything that wasn't tied down or that Molly had lying loose around her kitchen. This stew, served right royally, and attended by outriders of "cracklin' bread," was flanked by a man-at-arms in the form of a saucily flavored brown gravy. I recall a dish of broiled teal and some country puddin' with ginger pour-over, but merely mention these in passing.

So the Judge and I, in rare good humor (I forgot to add that there had been a dusty bottle of the Judge's famous port), as becomes sportsmen blessed with a perfect day's imperfect duck shooting, had discussed each individual bird brought to bag, with reasons, pro and con, why an undeniably large quota had escaped uninjured. We bordered upon that indecisive moment when bedtime should be imminent, were it not for the delightful trouble of getting started in that direction. As I recollect it, ruminating upon our sumptuous repast, the Judge had just countered upon my remark that I had never gotten enough hot turkey hash and beaten biscuits, by stating decisively that his craving for smothered quail remained inviolate, when the door opened softly and in slid "Ho'ace!" He had come, following a custom of many years, to tale final breakfast instructions before packing the embers in "Steamboat Bill," the stove, and dousing our glim.

Seeing upon the center table, t'wixt the Judge and me, a bottle and the unmistakable ingredients and tools of the former's ironclad rule for a hunter's nightcap, Ho'ace paused in embarrassed hesitation and seated himself quickly upon an empty shell case. His attitude was a cross between that of a timid gazelle's scenting danger and a wary hunter's sighting game and effacing himself gently from the landscape.

Long experience in the imperative issue of securing an invitation to "get his'n" had taught Ho'ace that it were ever best to appear humbly disinterested and thoroughly foreign to the subject until negotiations, if need be even much later, were opened with him directly or indirectly. With old-time members he steered along the above lines. But with newer ones or their uninitiated guests, he believed in quicker campaigning, or, conditions warranting, higher pressure sales methods. The Judge, reaching for the sugar bowl, mixed his sweetening water with adroit twirl and careful scrutiny as to texture; fastening upon Ho'ace meanwhile a melting look of liquid mercy. In a twinkling, however, his humor changed and he found himself in the glare of a forbidding menace, creditable in his palmiest days to the late Mister Chief Justice Jeffries himself.

"Ho'ace," demanded the Judge, tilting into his now ready receptacle a gurgling, man-size libation, "who is the best shot—the best duck-shot—you have ever paddled on this lake—barring—of course—a-h-e-m-m—myself?" Surveying himself with the coyness of a juvenile, the Judge stirred his now beading toddy dreamily and awaited the encore. Ho'ace squirmed a bit as the closing words of the Judge's query struck home with appalling menace upon his ears. He plucked nervously at his battered headpiece. His eyes, exhibiting a vast expanse of white, roamed pictured walls and smoke-dimmed ceiling in furtive, reflective, helpless quandry. Then speaking slowly and gradually warming to his subject, he fashioned the following alibi.

"Jedge, y' know, suh, us all has ouh good an' ouh bad days wid de ducks. Yes, my Lawdy, us sho' do. Dey's times whin de ducks flies all ovah ev'ything an' ev'ybody, an' still us kain't none o' us hit nuthin'—lak me an' you wuz dis mawnin'." At this juncture the Judge interrupted, reminding Ho'ace that he meant when the Judge—and not the Judge and Ho'ace—was shooting.

"An' den deys times whin h'it look lak dey ain't no shot too hard nur nary a duck too far not t'be kilt. But Mister Buckin'ham yonder—Mister Nash—he brung down de shootin'est gent'man what took all de cake. H'it's lots o' d' members here whut's darin' shooters, but dat fren' o' Mister Nash's—uummppphhh—don't never talk t' me 'bout him whur de ducks kin hear. 'Cause dey'll leave de laik ef dey hears he's even comin' dis way.

"Dat gent'man rode me jes' lak I wuz' er saddle, an' he done had on rooster spurs. Mister Nash he brung him on down here an' say, 'Ho'ace,' he say, 'here's a gent'man frum Englan', 'he say,

'Mister Money—Mister Harol' Money—an' say I wants you t' paddle him tomorrow an' see dat he gits er gran' shoot—unnerstan'?' I say, 'Yaas, suh, Mister Nash,' I say, 'dat I'll sho'ly do, suh. Mister Money gwi' hav' er fine picnic ef I has t' see dat he do my sef—but kin he shoot, suh?'

"Mister Nash, he say, 'Uh—why—uh—yaas, Ho'ace, Mister Money he's—uh—ve'y fair shot—'bout lak Mister Immitt Joyner or Mister Hal Howard.' I say t' mysef, I say, 'Uuummmpphhh—huuummmpppphhh—well—he'ah now—ef dats d' case, me an' Mister Money gwi' do some shootin' in d' mawnin.'

"Mister Money he talk so kin'er queer an' brief like, dat I hadda pay clos't inspection t' whut he all de time asayin'. But nex' mawnin', whin me an' him goes out in de bote, I seen he had a gre't big ol' happy bottle o' Brooklyn Handicap in dat shell box so I say t' m'sef, I say, 'W-e-l-l-l—me an' Mister Money gwi' got erlong someway, us is.'

"I paddles him on up de laik an' he say t' me, say, 'Hawrice—uh— hav yo'—er—got anny wager,' he say, 'or proposition t' mek t' me, as regards," he say, 't' shootin' dem dar eloosive wil'fowls?' he say.

"I kinder studies a minit, 'cause, lak I done say, he talk so brief. Den I says, 'I guess you is right 'bout dat, suh.'

"He say, 'Does you follow me, Hawrice, or is I alone?' he say.

"I says, 'Naw, suh, Mister, I'm right wid you in dis bote.'

"'You has no proposition t' mek wid me den?' he say.

"S' I, 'Naw, suh, Boss, I leaves all dat wid you, suh, trustin' t' yo' gin'rosity, suh.'

"'Ve'y good, Hawrice,' he say, 'I sees you doan grasp de principul. Now I will mek you de proposition,' he say. I jes' kep' on paddlin'. He say, 'Ev'y time I miss er duck you gits er dram frum dis hu'ah bottle—ev'y time I kills er duck—I gits de drink—which is h'it—come— come—speak up, my man.'

"I didn' b'lieve I done heard Mister Money rightly, an' I say, 'Uh—Mister Money,' I say, 'suh, does you mean dat I kin d' chice whedder you misses or kills ev'y time an' gits er drink?'

"He say, 'Dat's my defi',' he say.

"I says, 'Well, den—w-e-l-l—den—ef dat's de case, I gwi' choose ev'y time yo' misses, suh.' Den I say t'm'sef, I say, 'Ho'ace, right hu'ah whar you gotta be keerful, 'ginst you fall outa d' bote an' git fired frum d' lodge; 'cause ef'n you gits er drink ev'y time dis gent'man misses an' he shoot lak Mister Hal Howard, you an' him sho' gwi' drink er worl' o' liquah—er worl' o' liquah.'

"I pushes on up nurly to de Han'werker stan', an' I peeks in back by da li'l pocket whut shallers off'n de laik, an' sees some sev'ul blackjacks—four on 'em—settin' in dar. Dey done seen us, too. An' up come dey haids. I spy 'em twis'in', an' turnin'—gittin' raidy t' pull dey freight frum dar. I says, 'Mister Money,' I says, 'yawnder sets some ducks—look out now, suh, 'cause dey gwi' try t' rush on out pas' us whin dey come outa dat pocket.' Den I think, 'W-e-l-l-l, hu'ah whar I knocks d' gol' fillin' outa d' mouf' o' Mister Money's bottle o' Brooklyn Handicap!'

"I raised de lid o' d' shell box an' dar laid dat ol' bottle—still dar. I say, 'Uuummmppphhh—hummmph.' Jus' 'bout dat time up goes dem black-haids an' outa dar dey come—dey did—flyin' low t' d' watah—an' sorta raisin' lak—y' knows how dey does h'it, Jedge?'

"Mister Money he jus' pick up dat fas' feedin' gun—t'war er pump—not one o' dese hu'ah new afromatics—an' whin he did, I done reach f' d' bottle, 'cause I jes' natcherly know'd dat my time had done come. Mister Money he swings down on dem bullies. Ker-py—ker-py-powie-powie—splamp-splamp-splamp—ker-splash—Lawdy mussy—gent'mans—fo' times, right in d' same place, h'it sounded lak—an' d' las' duck fell ker-flop almos' in ouh bote.

"I done let go d' bottle, an' Mister Money say—mighty cool lak—say, 'Hawrice, say, kin'ly to examine dat las' chap clos'ly,' he say, 'an' obsurve,' he say, 'ef'n he ain' shot thru de eye.'

"I rakes in dat blackjack, an' sho' nuff—bofe eyes done shot plum out—yaas, suh, bofe on 'em right on out. Mister Money say, 'I wuz—er—slightly afraid,' he say, 'dat I had unknowin'ly struck dat fella er trifle too far t' win'ward,' he say. 'A ve'y fair start, Hawrice,' he say. 'You'd bettah place me in my station, so we may continue on wid'out interruption,' he say.

"Yaas, suh," I say. 'I'm on my way right dar now, suh, 'an I say t' m'sef, I say, 'Mek haste, Man, an' put dis gent'man in his bline an' giv' him er proper chanc't to miss er duck. I didn' hones'ly b'lieve but whut killin' all four o' dem other ducks so peart lak wuz er sorter accident. So I put him on de Han' werker bline. He seen I kep' de main shell bucket an' d' liquah, but he never said nuthin'. I put out d' m 'coys an' den creep back wid d' bote into d' willows t' watch.

"Pretty soon, hu'ah come er big ole drake flyin' mighty high. Ouh ole hen bird she holler t' him, an' d' drake he sorter twis' his haid an' look down. 'Warn't figurin' nuthin' but whut Mister Money gwi' let dat drake circle an' come 'mongst d' m 'coys—but—aw—aw! All uv er sudden he jus' raise up sharp lak an'—kerzowie! Dat ole drake jus' throw his haid on his back an' ride on down—looked t' me lak he fell er mile—an' whin he hit he thow'd watah fo' feet. Mister Money he nuvver said er word—jus' sot dar!

"Hu'ah come another drake—way off t' d' lef'—up over back o' me. He turn eroun'—quick lak—he did an'—kerzowie—he cut him on down, too. Dat drake fall way back in d' willows an' cose I hadda wade after 'im.

"Whilst I wuz gone, Mister Money shoot twice. An' whin I come stumblin' back, dar laid two mo' ducks wid dey feets in de air. Befo' I hav' time t' git in de bote again he done knock down er hen away off in d' elbow brush.

"I say, 'Mister Money, suh, I hav' behin' some far-knockin' guns in my time an' I'se er willin' worker, shoe—but ef you doan, please suh, kill dem ducks closer lak, you gwi' kill yo' willin' supporter Ho'ace in de mud.' He say, 'Da's all right 'bout dat,' he say. 'Go git d' bird—he kain't git er-way 'cause h'its dead ez er wedge.'

"Whin I crawls back t' d' bote dat las' time—it done got mighty col'. Dar us set—me in one en' ashiverin' an' dat ole big bottle wid de gol' haid in de far en'. Might jus' ez well bin ten miles so far ez my chances had done gone.

"Five mo' ducks come in—three singles an' er pair o' sprigs. An' Mister Money he chewed 'em all up lak good eatin'. One time, tho' he had t' shoot one o' them high-flyin' sprigs twice, an' I done got halfway in de bote reachin' fer dat bottle—but de las' shot got 'im. Aftah while, Mister Money say—'Hawrice,' he say, 'how is you hittin' off—my man?'

"'Mister Money,' I say, 'I'se pow'ful col', suh, an' ef you wants er 'umble, no 'count paddler t' tell you d' truth, suh, I b'lieves I done made er pow'ful po' bet.' He say 'Poss'bly so, Hawrice, poss'bly so.' But dat 'poss'bly' didn' git me nuthin'.

"Jedge, y' Honor, you know dat gent'man sot dar an' kill ev'ry duck come in, an' had his limit long befo' de eight-o'clock train runned. I done gone t' watchin' an' de las' duck whut come by wuz one o' dem lightnin'-express teals. Hu'ah he come—er greenwing drake—look lak' somebody done blowed er buckshot pas' us. I riz' up an' hollered, 'Fly fas', ole teal, do yo' bes'—caus' Ho'ace needs er drink.' But Mister Money jus' jumped up an' thow'd him forty feet—skippin' 'long d' watah. I say, 'Hol' on, Mister Money, hol' on—you done kilt d' limit.'

"'Oh,' he say, 'I hav'—hav' I?'

"I say, 'Yaas, suh, an' you ain't bin long 'bout h'it—neither.

"He say, 'What are you doin' gittin' so col' then?'

"I say, 'I spec' findin' out dat I hav' done made er bad bet had er lot t' do wid d' air.'

"An' dar laid dat Brooklyn Handicap all dat time—he nuvver touched none—an' me neither. I paddles him on back to de house, an' he comes er stalkin' on in hu'ah, he did—lookin' kinda mad lak—never said nuthin' 'bout no drink. Finally he say, 'Hawrice,' he say, 'git me a bucket o' col' watah.' I say t' m'sef, I say, 'W-e-l-l-l, das mo' lak h'it—ef he wants er bucket o' watah. Boy—you gwi' see some real drinkin' now.'

"Whin I come in wid d' pail, Mister Money took offin all his clothes an' step out onto d' side po'ch an' say, 'Th'ow dat watah ovah me, Hawrice. I am lit'rully compel,' he say, 't' have my col' tub ev'y mawnin'.' M-a-n-n-n-n! I sho' tow'd dat ice col' watah onto him wid all my heart an' soul. But he jus' gasp an' hollah, an' jump up an' down an' slap hisse'f. Den he had me rub him red wid er big rough towel. I sho' rubbed him, too. Come on in d' clubroom hu'ah, he did, an' mek hisse'f comfort'ble in dat big ol' rockin' chair yonder—an' went t' rea-din'. I brought in his shell bucket an' begin cleanin' his gun. But I seen him kinder smilin' t' hisse'f. Atta while, he says 'Hawrice,' he say, 'you hav' done los' yo' bet?'

"I kinder hang my haid lak, an' 'low, 'Yaas, suh, Mister Money, I don' said farewell t' d' liquah!'

"He say, 'Yo' admits den dat you hav' done los' fair an' square—an' dat yo' realizes h'it?'

"Yaas, suh!'

"He say, 'Yo' judgmint,' he say, 'wuz ve'y fair, considerin',' he say, 'de great law uv' av'ridge—but circumstance,' he say, 'has done render de ult'mate outcome subjec' t' d' mighty whims o' chance?'

"I say, 'Yaas, suh,' ve'y mournful lak.

"He say, 'In so far as realizin' on anything 'ceptin' de mercy o' d' Cote—say—you is absolutely non-est—eh, my man?'

"I say, 'Yaas, suh, barrin' yo' mercy, suh.'

"Den he think er moment, an' say, 'Verrree—verree—good!'

"Den he 'low, 'Sence you acknowledges d' cawn, an' admits dat you hav' done got grabbed,' he say, 'step up,' he say, 'an' git you a tumbler—po' yo'sef er drink—po' er big one, too.'

"I never stopped f' nuthin' den—jes' runned an' got me a glass outa de kitchen. Ole Molly, she say, 'Whur you goin' so fas'?' I say, 'Doan stop me now ole 'ooman—I got business—p'ticler business— an' I sho' poh'd me er big bait o' liquah—er whole sloo' o' liquah. Mister Money say, 'Hawrice—de size o' yo' po'tion,' he say, 'is primus facious ev'dence,' he say, 'dat you gwi' spout er toast in honor,' he say, 'o' d' occasion.'

"I say, 'Mister Money, suh,' I say, 'all I got t' say, suh, is dat you is de kingpin, champeen duck shotter so far as I hav' done bin' in dis life—an' ve'y prob'ly as far as I'se likely t' keep on goin', too.' He sorter smile t' hisse'f!

"Now, suh, please, suh, tell me dis—is you ever missed er duck— anywhar'—anytime—anyhow—suh?'

"He say 'Really, Hawrice,' he say, 'you embarrasses me,' he say, 'so hav' another snifter—there is mo', considerably mo',' he say, 'in yo' system what demands utt'rance,' he say.

"I done poh'd me another slug o' Brooklyn Handicap an' say, 'Mister Money,' I say, 'does you expec' t' ever miss another duck ez long ez you lives, suh?'

"He say, 'Hawrice,' he say, 'you embarrasses me,' he say, 'beyon' words—you overwhelms me,' he say. 'Git t' hell outa hu'ah befo' you gits us bofe drunk.'"

THAT TWENTY-FIVE-POUND GOBBLER

ARCHIBALD RUTLEDGE

I suppose that there are other things which make a hunter uneasy, but of one thing I am very sure: that is to locate and to begin to stalk a deer or a turkey, only to find that another hunter is doing precisely the same thing at the same time. The feeling I had was worse than uneasy. It is, in fact, as inaccurate as if a man should say, after listening to a comrade swearing roundly, "Bill is expressing himself uneasily."

To be frank, I was jealous; and all the more so because I knew that Dade Saunders was just as good a turkey-hunter as I am—and maybe a good deal better. At any rate, both of us got after the same whopping gobbler. We knew this turkey and we knew each other; and I am positive that the wise old bird knew both of us far better than we knew him.

But we hunters have ways of improving our acquaintance with creatures that are over-wild and shy. Both Dade and I saw him, I suppose, a dozen times; and twice Dade shot at him. I had never fired at him, for I did not want to cripple, but to kill; and he never came within a hundred yards of me. Yet I felt that the gobbler ought to be mine; and for the simple reason that Dade Saunders was a shameless poacher and a hunter-out-of-season.

I have in mind the day when I came upon him in the pine-lands in mid-July, when he had in his wagon five bucks in the velvet, all killed that morning. Now, this isn't a fiction story; this is fact. And after I have told you of those bucks, I think you'll want me to beat Dade to the great American bird.

This wild turkey had the oddest range that you could imagine. You hear of turkeys ranging "original forests," "timbered wilds," and the like. Make up your mind that if wild turkeys have a chance they are going to come near civilization. The closer they are to man, the farther they are away from their other enemies. Near civilization they at least have (but for the likes of Dade Saunders) the protection of the law. But in the wilds what protection do they have from wildcats, from eagles, from weasels (I am thinking of young turkeys as well as old), and from all their other predatory persecutors?

Well, as I say, time and again I have known wild turkeys to come, and to seem to enjoy coming, close to houses. I have stood on the porch of my plantation home and have watched a wild flock feeding under the great live-oaks there. I have repeatedly flushed wild turkeys in an autumn cornfield. I have shot them in rice stubble.

Of course they do not come for sentiment. They are after grain. And if there is any better wild game than a rice-field wild turkey, stuffed with peanuts, circled with browned sweet potatoes, and fragrant with a rich gravy that plantation cooks know how to make, I'll follow you to it.

The gobbler I was after was a haunter of the edges of civilization. He didn't seem to like the wild woods. I think he got hungry there. But on the margins of fields that had been planted he could get all he wanted to eat of the things he most enjoyed. He particularly liked the edges of cultivated fields that bordered either on the pinewoods or else on the marshy rice-lands.

One day I spent three hours in the gaunt chimney of a burned rice-mill, watching this gobbler feeding on such edges. Although I was sure that sooner or later he would pass the mouth of the chimney, giving me a chance for a shot, he kept just that distance between us that makes a gun a vain thing in a man's hands. But though he did not give me my chance, he let me watch him all I pleased. This I did through certain dusty crevices between the bricks of the old chimney.

If I had been taking a post-graduate course in caution, this wise old bird would have been my teacher. Whatever he happened to be doing, his eyes and his ears were wide with vigilance. I saw him first standing beside a fallen pine log on the brow of a little hill where peanuts had been planted. I made the shelter of the chimney before he recognized me. But he must have seen the move I made.

I have hunted turkeys long enough to be thoroughly rid of the idea that a human being can make a motion that a wild turkey cannot see. One of my woodsman friends said to me, "Why, a gobbler can see anything. He can see a jaybird turn a somersault on the verge of the horizon." He was right.

Watching from my cover I saw this gobbler scratching for peanuts. He was very deliberate about this. Often he would draw back one huge handful (or footful) of viney soil, only to leave it there while he looked and listened. I have seen a turkey do the same thing while scratching in leaves. Now, a buck while feeding will alternately keep his head up and down; but a turkey gobbler keeps his down very little. That bright black eye of his, set in that sharp bluish head, is keeping its vision on every object on the landscape.

My gobbler (I called him mine from the first time I saw him) found many peanuts, and he relished them. From that feast he walked over into a patch of autumn-dried crabgrass. The long pendulous heads of this grass, full of seeds, he stripped skilfully. When satisfied with this food, he dusted himself beside an old stump. It was interesting to watch this; and while he was doing it I wondered if it was not my chance to leave the chimney, make a detour, and come up behind the stump. But of course just as I decided to do this, he got up, shook a small cloud of dust from his feathers, stepped off into the open, and there began to preen himself.

A short while thereafter he went down to a marshy edge, there finding a warm sandy hole on the sunny side of a briar patch, where he continued his dusting and loafing. I believe that he knew the stump, which shut off his view of what was behind it, was no place to choose for a midday rest.

All this time I waited patiently; interested, to be sure, but I would have been vastly more so if the lordly old fellow had turned my way. This I expected him to do when he got tired of loafing. Instead, he deliberately walked into the tall ranks of the marsh, which extended riverward for half a mile. At that I hurried forward, hoping to flush him on the margin; but he had vanished for that day. But though he had escaped me, the sight of him had made me keen to follow him until he expressed a willingness to accompany me home.

Just as I was turning away from the marsh I heard a turkey call from the shelter of a big live-oak beside the old chimney. I knew that it was Dade Saunders, and that he was after my gobbler. I walked over to where he was making his box-call plead. He expressed no surprise on seeing me. We greeted each other as two hunters, who are not over-friendly, greet when they find themselves after the same game.

"I seen his tracks," said Dade. "I believe he limps in the one foot since I shot him last Sunday will be a week."

"He must be a big bird," I said; "you were lucky to have a shot."

Dade's eyes grew hungrily bright.

"He's the biggest in these woods, and I'll git him yet. You jest watch me."

"I suppose you will, Dade. You are the best turkey-hunter of these parts."

I hoped to make him overconfident; and praise is a great corrupter of mankind. It is not unlikely to make a hunter miss a shot. I remember that a friend of mine once said laughingly: "If a man tells me I am a good shot, I will miss my next chance, as sure as guns; but if he cusses me and tells me I'm not worth a darn, then watch me shoot!"

Dade and I parted for the time. I went off toward the marsh, whistling an old song. I wanted to have the gobbler put a little more distance between himself and the poacher. Besides, I felt that it was right of me to do this: for while I was on my own land, my visitor was trespassing. I hung around in the scrub–oak thickets for awhile; but no gun spoke out, I knew that the old gobbler's intelligence plus my whistling game had "foiled the relentless" Dade. It was a week later that the three of us met again.

Not far from the peanut field there is a plantation corner. Now, most plantation corners are graveyards; that is, cemeteries of the old days, where slaves were buried. Occasionally now Negroes are buried there, but pathways have to be cut through the jungle-like growths to enable the cortege to enter.

Such a place is a wilderness for sure. Here grow towering pines, mournful and moss-draped. Here are hollies, canopied with jasmine-vines; here are thickets of myrtle, sweet gum, and young pines. If a covey of quail goes into such a place, you might as well whistle your dog off and go after another lot of birds.

Here deer love to come in the summer, where they can hide from the heat and the gauze-winged flies. Here in the winter is a haunt for woodcock, a good range (for great live-oaks drop their sweet acorns) for wild turkeys, and a harbor for foxes. In those great pines and oaks turkeys love to roost. It was on the borders of just such a corner that I roosted the splendid gobbler.

It was a glowing December sunset. I had left the house an hour before to stroll the plantation roads, counting (as I always do) the number of deer and turkey tracks that had recently been made in the soft damp sand. Coming near the dense corner, I sat against the bole of a monster pine. I love to be a mere watcher in woodlands as well as a hunter.

About two hundred yards away there was a little sunny hill, grown to scrub-oaks. They stood sparsely; that enabled me to see well what I now saw. Into my vision, with the rays of the sinking sun gleaming softly on the bronze of his neck and shoulders, the great gobbler stepped with superb beauty. Though he deigned to scratch once or twice in the leaves, and peck indifferently at what he thus uncovered, I knew he was bent on roosting; for not only was it nearly his bedtime, but he seemed to be examining with critical judgment every tall tree in his neighborhood.

He remained in my sight ten minutes; then he stepped into a patch of gallberries. I sat where I was. I tried my best to be as silent and as motionless as the bodies lying in the ancient graves behind me. The big fellow kept me on the anxious bench for five minutes. Then he shot his great bulk into the air, beating his ponderous way into the huge pine that seemed to sentry that whole wild tract of woodland.

I marked him when he came to his limb. He sailed up to it and alighted with much scraping of bark with his No. 10 shoes. There was my gobbler poised against the warm red sky of that winter twilight. It was hard to take my sight from him; but I did so in order to get my bearings in relation to his position. His flight had brought him nearer to me than he had been on the ground. But he was still far out of gun-range.

There was no use for me to look into the graveyard, for a man cannot see a foot into such a place. I glanced down the dim pine-wood road. A moving object along its edge attracted my attention. It skulked. It seemed to flit like a ghostly thing from pine to pine. But, though I was near a cemetery, I knew I was looking at no "haunt." It was Dade Saunders.

He had roosted the gobbler, and he was trying to get up to him. Moreover, he was at least fifty yards closer to him than I was. I felt like shouting to him to get off my land; but then a better thought came. I pulled out my turkey call.

The first note was good, as was intended. But after that there came some heart-stilling squeaks and shrills. In the dusk I noted two things; I saw Dade make a furious gesture, and at almost the same instant the old gobbler launched out from the pine, winging a lordly way far across the graveyard thicket. I walked down slowly and peeringly to meet Dade.

"Your call's broke," he announced.

"What makes you think so?" I asked.

"Sounds awful funny to me," he said; "more than likely it might scare a turkey. Seen him lately?" he asked.

"You are better at seeing that old bird than I am, Dade."

Thus I put him off; and shortly thereafter we parted. He was sure that I had not seen the gobbler; and that suited me all right.

Then came the day of days. I was up at dawn, and when certain red lights between the stems of the pines announced daybreak, I was at the far southern end of the plantation, on a road on either side of which were good turkey woods. I just had a notion that my gobbler might be found there, as he had of late taken to roosting in a tupelo swamp near the river, and adjacent to these woodlands.

Where some lumbermen had cut away the big timber, sawing the huge short-leaf pines close to the ground, I took my stand (or my seat) on one of these big stumps. Before me was a tangle of undergrowth; but it was not very thick or high. It gave me the screen I wanted; but if my turkey came out through it, I could see to shoot.

It was just before sunrise that I began to call. It was a little early in the year (then the end of February) to lure a solitary gobbler by a call; but otherwise the chance looked good. And I am vain enough to say that my willow box was not broken that morning. Yet it was not I but two Cooper's hawks that got the old wily rascal excited.

They were circling high and crying shrilly over a certain stretch of deep woodland; and the gobbler, undoubtedly irritated by the sounds, or at least not to be outdone by two mere marauders on a domain which he felt to be his own, would gobble fiercly every time one of the hawks would cry. The hawks had their eye on a building site; wherefore their excited maneuvering and shrilling continued; and as long as they kept up their screaming, so long did the wild gobbler answer in rivalry or provoked superiority, until his wattles must have been fiery red and near to bursting.

I had an idea that the hawks were directing some of their crying at the turkey, in which case the performance was a genuine scolding match of the wilderness. And before it was over, several gray squirrels had added to the already raucous debate their impatient coughing barks. This business lasted nearly an hour, until the sun had begun to make the thickets "smoke off" their shining burden of morning dew.

I had let up on my calling for awhile; but when the hawks had at last been silenced by the distance, I began once more to plead. Had I had a gobbler-call, the now enraged turkey would have come to me as straight as a surveyor runs a line. But I did my best with the one I had. I had answered by one short gobble, then by silence.

I laid down my call on the stump and took up my gun. It was in such a position that I could shoot quickly without much further motion. It is a genuine feat to shoot a turkey on the ground after he has made you out. I felt that a great moment was coming.

But you know how hunter's luck sometimes turns. Just as I thought it was about time for him to be in the pine thicket ahead of me, when, indeed, I thought I had heard his heavy but cautious step, from across the road, where lay the companion tract of turkey-woods to the one I was in, came a delicately pleading call from a hen turkey. The thing was irresistible to the gobbler; but I knew it to be Dade Saunders. What should I do?

At such a time a man has to use all the headwork he has. And in hunting I had long since learned that that often means not to do a darn thing but to sit tight. All I did was to put my gun to my face. If the gobbler was going to Dade, he might pass me. I had started him coming; if Dade kept him going, he might run within hailing distance. Dade was farther back in the woods than I was. I waited.

No step was heard. No twig was snapped. But suddenly, fifty yards ahead of me, the great bird emerged from the thicket of pines. For an instant the sun gleamed on his royal plumage. My gun was on him, but the glint of the sun along the barrel dazzled me. I stayed my finger on the trigger. At that instant he made me out. What he did was smart. He made himself so small that I believed it to be a second turkey. Then he ran crouching through the vines and huckleberry bushes.

Four times I thought I had my gun on him, but his dodging was that of an expert. He was getting away; moreover, he was making straight for Dade. There was a small gap in the bushes sixty yards from me, off to my left. He had not yet crossed that. I threw my gun in the opening. In a moment he flashed into it, running like a racehorse. I let him have it. And I saw him go down.

Five minutes later, when I had hung him on a scrub-oak, and was admiring the entire beauty of him, a knowing, cat-like step sounded behind me.

"Well, sir," said Dade, a generous admiration for the beauty of the great bird overcoming other less kindly emotions, "so you beat me to him."

There was nothing for me to do but to agree. I then asked Dade to walk home with me so that we might weigh him. He carried the scales well down at the 25-pound mark. An extraordinary feature of his manly equipment was the presence of three separate beards, one beneath the other, no two connected. And his spurs were respectable rapiers.

"Dade," I said, "what am I going to do with this gobbler? I am alone here on the plantation."

The pineland poacher did not solve my problem for me.

"I tell you," said I, trying to forget the matter of the five velveted bucks, "some of the boys from down the river are going to come up on Sunday to see how he tastes. Will you join us?"

You know Dade Saunders' answer; for when a hunter refuses an invitation to help eat a wild turkey, he can be sold to a circus.

IN BUFFALO DAYS

BY GEORGE BIRD GRINNELL

On the floor, on either side of my fireplace, lie two buffalo skulls. They are white and weathered, the horns cracked and bleached by the snows and frosts and the rains and heats of many winters and summers. Often, late at night, when the house is quiet, I sit before the fire, and muse and dream of the old days; and as I gaze at these relics of the past, they take life before my eyes. The matted brown hair again clothes the dry bone, and in the empty orbits the wild eyes gleam. Above me curves the blue arch; away on every hand stretches the yellow prairie, and scattered near and far are the dark forms of buffalo. They dot the rolling hills, quietly feeding like tame cattle, or lie at ease on the slopes, chewing the cud and half asleep. The yellow calves are close by their mothers; on little eminences the great bulls paw the dust, and mutter and moan, while those whose horns have grown one, two, and three winters are mingled with their elders.

Not less peaceful is the scene near some river-bank, when the herds come down to water. From the high prairie on every side they stream into the valley, stringing along in single file, each band following the deep trail worn in the parched soil by the tireless feet of generations of their kind. At a quick walk they swing along, their heads held low.

The long beards of the bulls sweep the ground; the shuffling tread of many hoofs marks their passing, and above each long line rises a cloud of dust that sometimes obscures the westering sun.

Life, activity, excitement, mark another memory as vivid as these. From behind a near hill mounted men ride out and charge down toward the herd. For an instant the buffalo pause to stare, and then crowd together in a close throng, jostling and pushing one another, a confused mass of horns, hair, and hoofs. Heads down and tails in air, they rush away from their pursuers, and as they race along herd joins herd, till the black mass sweeping over the prairie numbers thousands. On its skirts hover the active, nimble horsemen, with twanging bow-strings and sharp arrows piercing many fat cows. The naked Indians cling to their naked horses as if the two were parts of one incompara-ble animal, and swing and yield to every motion of their steeds with the grace of perfect horsemanship. The ponies, as quick and skillful as the men, race up beside the fattest of the herd, swing off to avoid the charge of a maddened cow, and, returning, dart close to the victim, whirling hither and yon, like swallows on the wing. And their riders, with the unconscious skill, grace, and power of matchless archery, are drawing their bows to the arrow's head, and driving the feathered shaft deep through the bodies of the buffalo. Returning on their tracks, they skin the dead, then load the meat and robes on their horses, and with laughter and jest ride away.

After them, on the deserted prairie, come the wolves to tear at the carcasses. The rain and the snow wash the blood from the bones, and fade and bleach the hair. For a few months the skeleton holds together; then it falls apart, and the fox and the badger pull about the whitening bones and scatter them over the plain. So this cow and this bull of mine may have left their bones on the prairie, where I found them and picked them up to keep as mementos of the past, to dream over, and in such reverie to see again the swelling hosts which yesterday covered the plains, and to-day are but a dream.

So the buffalo passed into history. Once an inhabitant of this continent from the Arctic slope to Mexico, and from Virginia to Oregon, and, within the memory of men yet young, roaming the plains in such numbers that it seemed as if it could never be exterminated, it has now disappeared as utterly as has the bison from Europe. For it is probable that the existing herds of that practically extinct species, now carefully guarded in the forests of Grodno, about equal in numbers the buffalo in the Yellowstone Park; while the wild bison in the Caucasus may be compared with the "wood" buffalo which survive in the Peace River district. In view of the former abundance of our buffalo, this parallel is curious and interesting.

The early explorers were constantly astonished by the multitudinous herds which they met with, the regularity of their movements, and the deep roads which they made in traveling from place to place. Many of the earlier references are to territory east of the Mississippi, but even within the last fifteen years buffalo were to be seen on the Western plains in numbers so great that an entirely sober and truthful account seems like fable. Describing the abundance of buffalo in a certain region, an Indian once said to me, in the expressive sign-language of which all old frontiersmen have some knowledge: "The country was one robe."

Much has been written about their enormous abundance in the old days, but I have never read anything that I thought an exaggeration of their numbers as I have seen them. Only one who has actually spent months in traveling among them in those old days can credit the stories told about them. The trains of the Kansas Pacific Railroad used frequently to be detained by herds which were crossing the tracks in front of the engines; and in 1870, trains on which I was traveling were twice so held, in one case for three hours. When railroad travel first began on this road, the engineers tried the experiment of running through these passing herds; but after their engines had been thrown from the tracks they learned wisdom, and gave the buffalo the right of way. Two or three years later, in the country between the Platte and Republican rivers, I saw a closely massed herd of buffalo so vast that I dared not hazard a guess as to its numbers; and in later years I have traveled, for weeks at a time, in northern Montana without ever being out of sight of buffalo. These were not in close herds, except now and then when alarmed and running, but were usually scattered about, feeding or lying down on the prairie at a little distance from one another, much as domestic cattle distribute themselves in a pasture or on the range. As far as we could see on every side of the line of march, and ahead, the hillsides were dotted with dark forms, and the field-glass revealed yet others stretched out on every side, in one continuous host, to the most distant hills. Thus was gained a more just notion of their numbers than could be had in any other way, for the sight of this limitless territory occupied by these continuous herds was far more impressive than the spectacle of a surging, terrified mass of fleeing buffalo, even though the numbers which passed rapidly before the observer's gaze in a short time were very great.

The former range of the buffalo has been worked out with painstaking care by Dr. Allen, to whom we owe an admirable monograph on this species. He concludes that the northern limit of this range was north of the Great Slave Lake, in latitude about 63° N.; while to the south it extended into Mexico as far as latitude 25° N. To the west it ranged at least as far as the Blue Mountains of Oregon, while on the east it was abundant in the western portions of New York, Pennsylvania, Virginia, North and South Carolinas, and Georgia. In the interior the buffalo were very abundant, and occupied Ohio, Kentucky, West

Virginia, Tennessee, West Georgia, Illinois, Indiana, and Iowa, parts of Michigan, Wisconsin, and Minnesota, the whole of the great plains, from southern Texas north to their northern limit, and much of the Rocky Mountains. In Montana, Idaho, Wyoming, and most of New Mexico they were abundant, and probably common over a large part of Utah, and perhaps in northern Nevada. So far as now known, their western limit was the Blue Mountains of Oregon and the eastern foothills of the Sierra Nevada.

Thus it will be seen that the buffalo once ranged over a large part of the American continent,—Dr. Allen says one third of it,—but it must not be imagined that they were always present at the same time in every part of their range. They were a wandering race, sometimes leaving a district and being long absent, and again returning and occupying it for a considerable period. What laws or what impulses governed these movements we cannot know. Their wandering habits were well understood by the Indians of the Western plains, who depended upon the buffalo for food. It was their custom to follow the herds about, and when, as sometimes occurred, these moved away and could not be found, the Indians were reduced to great straits for food, and sometimes even starved to death.

Under natural conditions the buffalo was an animal of rather sluggish habits, mild, inoffensive, and dull. In its ways of life and intelligence it closely resembled our domestic cattle. It was slow to learn by experience, and this lack of intelligence greatly hastened the destruction of the race. Until the very last years of its existence as a species, it did not appear to connect the report of firearms with any idea of danger to itself, and though constantly pursued, did not become wild. If he used skill and judgment in shooting, a hunter who had "got a stand" on a small bunch could kill them all before they had moved out of rifle-shot. It was my fortune, one summer, to hunt for a camp of soldiers, and more than once I have lain on a hill above a little herd of buffalo, shot down what young bulls I needed to supply the camp, and then walked down to the bunch and, by waving my hat and shouting, driven off the survivors, so that I could prepare the meat for transportation to camp. This slowness to take the alarm, or indeed to realize the presence of danger, was characteristic of the buffalo almost up to the very last. A time did come when they were alarmed readily enough, but this was not until all the large herds had been broken up and scattered, and the miserable survivors had been so chased and harried that at last they learned to start and run even at their own shadows.

Another peculiarity of the buffalo was its habit, when stampeded, of dashing blindly forward against, over, or through anything that might be in the way. When running, a herd of buffalo followed its leaders, and yet these leaders lost the power of stopping, or even of turning aside, because they were constantly crowded upon and pushed forward by those behind. This explains why herds would dash into mire or quicksands, as they often did, and thus perish by the thousand. Those in front could not stop, while those behind could not see the danger toward which they were rushing. So, too, they ran into rivers, or into traps made for them by the Indians, or against railroad cars, or even dashed into the rivers and swam blindly against the sides of steamboats. If an obstacle lay squarely across their path, they tried to go through it, but if it lay at an angle to their course, they would turn a little to follow it, as will be shown further on.

The buffalo calf is born from April to June, and at first is an awkward little creature, looking much like a domestic calf, but with a shorter neck. The hump at first is scarcely noticeable, but develops rapidly. They are odd-looking and very playful little animals. They are easily caught and tamed when quite young, but when a few months old they become as shy as the old buffalo, and are much more swift of foot.

Although apparently very sluggish, buffalo are really extremely active, and are able to go at headlong speed over a country where no man would dare to ride a horse. When alarmed they will throw themselves down the almost vertical side of a cañon and climb the opposite wall with cat-like agility. Sometimes they will descend cut banks by jumping from shelf to shelf of rock like the mountain sheep. To get at water when thirsty, they will climb down bluffs that seem altogether impracticable for such great animals. Many years ago, while descending the Missouri River in a flatboat with two companions, I landed in a wide bottom to kill a mountain sheep. As we were bringing the meat to the boat, we saw on the opposite side of the river, about half-way down the bluffs, which were here about fifteen hundred feet high, a large buffalo bull. The bluffs were almost vertical, and this old fellow was having some difficulty in making his way down to the water. He went slowly and carefully, at times having pretty good going, and at others slipping and sliding for thirty or forty feet, sending the clay and stones rolling ahead of him in great quantities. We watched him for a little while, and then it occurred to some malicious spirit among us that it would be fun to see whether the bull could go up where he had come down. A shot was fired so as to strike near him,—for no one wanted to hurt the old fellow,—and as soon as the report reached his ears, he turned about and began to scramble up the bluffs. His first rush carried him, perhaps, a hundred feet vertically, and then he stopped and looked around. He seemed not to have the slightest difficulty in climbing up, nor did he use any caution, or appear to pick his way at all. A second shot caused another rush up the steep ascent, but this time he went only half as far as before, and again stopped. Three or four other shots drove him by shorter and shorter rushes up the bluffs, until at length he would go no further, and subsequent shots only caused him to shake his head angrily. Plainly he had climbed until his wind had given out, and now he would stand and fight. Our fun was over, and looking back as we floated down the river, our last glimpse was of the old bull, still standing on his shelf, waiting with lowered head for the unknown enemy that he supposed was about to attack him.

It is not only under the stress of circumstances that the bison climbs. The mountain buffalo is almost as active as the mountain sheep, and was often found in places that tested the nerve and activity of a man to reach; and even the buffalo of the plains had a fondness for high places, and used to climb up on to broken buttes or high rocky points. In recent years I have often noticed the same habit among range cattle and horses.

The buffalo were fond of rolling in the dirt, and to this habit, practised when the ground was wet, are due the buffalo wallows which so frequently occur in the old ranges, and which often contain water after all other moisture, except that of the streams, is dried up. These wallows were formed by the rolling of a succession of buffalo in the same moist place, and were frequently quite deep. They have often been described. Less well known was the habit of scratching themselves against trees and rocks. Sometimes a solitary erratic boulder, five or six feet high, may be seen on the bare prairie, the ground immediately around it being worn down two or three feet below the level of the surrounding earth. This is where the buffalo have walked about the stone, rubbing against it, and, where they trod, loosening the soil, which has been blown away by the wind, so that in course of time a deep trench was worn about the rock. Often single trees along streams were worn quite smooth by the shoulders and sides of the buffalo.

When the first telegraph line was built across the continent, the poles used were light and small, for transportation over the plains was slow and expensive, and it was not thought necessary to raise the wires high above the ground. These poles were much resorted to by the buffalo to scratch against, and before long a great many of them were pushed over. A story, now of considerable antiquity, is told of an ingenious employee of the telegraph company, who devised a plan for preventing the buffalo from disturbing the poles. This he expected to accomplish by driving into them spikes which should prick the animals when they rubbed against them. The result somewhat astonished the inventor, for it was discovered that where formerly one buffalo rubbed against the smooth telegraph poles, ten now struggled and fought for the chance to scratch themselves against the spiked poles, the iron furnishing just the irritation which their tough hides needed.

It was in spring, when its coat was being shed, that the buffalo, odd-looking enough at any time, presented its most grotesque appearance. The matted hair and wool of the shoulders and sides began to peel off in great sheets, and these sheets, clinging to the skin and flapping in the wind, gave it the appearance of being clad in rags.

The buffalo was a timid creature, but brought to bay would fight with ferocity. There were few sights more terrifying to the novice than the spectacle of an old bull at bay: his mighty bulk, a quivering mass of active, enraged muscle; the shining horns; the little, spiky tail; and the eyes half hidden beneath the shaggy frontlet, yet gleaming with rage, combined to render him an awe-inspiring object. Nevertheless, owing to their greater speed and activity, the cows were much more to be feared than the bulls.

It was once thought that the buffalo performed annually extensive migrations, and it was even said that those which spent the summer on the banks of the Saskatchewan wintered in Texas. There is no reason for believing this to have been true. Undoubtedly there were slight general movements north and south, and east and west, at

certain seasons of the year; but many of the accounts of these movements are entirely misleading, because greatly exaggerated. In one
portion of the northern country I know that there was a decided east
and west seasonal migration, the herds tending in spring away from
the mountains, while in the autumn they worked back again, seeking
shelter in the rough, broken country of the foot-hills from the cold
west winds of the winter.

The buffalo is easily tamed when caught as a calf, and in all its ways
of life resembles the domestic cattle. It at once learns to respect a
fence, and, even if at large, manifests no disposition to wander.

Three years ago there were in this country about two hundred and
fifty domesticated buffalo, in the possession of about a dozen individuals. Of these the most important herd was that of Hon. C. J. Jones, of
Garden City, Kansas, which, besides about fifty animals captured and
reared by himself, included also the Bedson herd of over eighty, purchased in Manitoba. The Jones herd at one time consisted of about one
hundred and fifty head. Next came that of Charles Allard and Michel
Pablo, of the Flathead Agency in Montana, which in 1888 numbered
thirty-five, and has now increased to about ninety. Mr. Jones's herd
has been broken up, and he now retains only about forty-five head, of
which fifteen are breeding cows. He tells me that within the past year
or two he has sold over sixty pure buffalo, and that nearly as many
more have died through injuries received in transporting them by rail.

Mr. Jones is the only individual who, of recent years, has made any
systematic effort to cross the buffalo with our own domestic cattle.
As far back as the beginning of the present century, this was successfully done in the West and Northwest; and in Audubon and Bachman's
"Quadrupeds of America" may be found an extremely interesting
account, written by Robert Wickliffe, of Lexington, Kentucky, giving the results of a series of careful and successful experiments which

he carried on for more than thirty years. These experiments showed that the cross for certain purposes was a very valuable one, but no systematic efforts to establish and perpetuate a breed of buffalo cattle were afterward made until within the past ten years. Mr. Jones has bred buffalo bulls to Galloway, Polled Angus, and ordinary range cows, and has succeeded in obtaining calves from all. Such half-breeds are of very large size, extremely hardy, and, as a farmer would say, "easy keepers." They are fertile among themselves or with either parent. A half-breed cow of Mr. Jones's that I examined was fully as large as an ordinary work-ox, and in spring, while nursing a calf, was fat on grass. She lacked the buffalo hump, but her hide would have made a good robe. The great size and tremendous frame of these crossbred cattle should make them very valuable for beef, while their hardiness would exempt them from the dangers of winter,—so often fatal to domestic range cattle,—and they produce a robe which is quite as valuable as that of the buffalo, and more beautiful because more even all over. If continued, these attempts at cross-breeding may do much to improve our Western range cattle.

Mr. Jones has sold a number of buffalo to persons in Europe, where there is a considerable demand for them. It is to be hoped that no more of these domesticated buffalo will be allowed to leave the country where they were born. Indeed, it would seem quite within the lines of the work now being carried on by the Agricultural Department, for the government to purchase all the domesticated American buffalo that can be had, and to start, in some one of the Western States, an experimental farm for buffalo breeding and buffalo crossing. With a herd of fifty pure-bred buffalo cows and a sufficient number of bulls, a series of experiments could be carried on which might be of great value to the cattle-growers of our western country. The stock of pure buffalo could be kept up and increased; surplus bulls, pure and half bred, could be sold to farmers; and, in time, the new race of buffalo cattle might become so firmly established that it would endure.

To undertake this with any prospect of success, such a farm would have to be managed by a man of intelligence and of wide experience in this particular field; otherwise all the money invested would be wasted. Mr. Jones is perhaps the only man living who knows enough of this subject to carry on an experimental farm with success.

Although only one species of buffalo is known to science, old mountaineers and Indians tell of four kinds. These are, besides the ordinary animal of the plains, the "mountain buffalo," sometimes called "bison," which is found in the timbered Rocky Mountains; the "wood buffalo" of the Northwest, which inhabits the timbered country to the west and north of Athabasca Lake; and the "beaver buffalo." The last named has been vaguely described to me by northern Indians as small and having a very curly coat. I know of only one printed account of it, and this says that it had "short, sharp horns which were small at the root and curiously turned up and bent backward, not unlike a ram's, but quite unlike the bend of the horn in the common buffalo." It is possible that this description may refer to the musk-ox, and not to a buffalo. The "mountain" and "wood" buffalo seem to be very much alike in habit and appearance. They are larger, darker, and heavier than the animal of the plains, but there is no reason for thinking them specifically distinct from it. Such differences as exist are due to conditions of environment.

The color of the buffalo in its new coat is a dark liver-brown. This soon changes, however, and the hides, which are at their best in November and early December, begin to grow paler toward spring; and when the coat is shed, the hair and wool from young animals is almost a dark smoky-gray. The calf when just born is of a bright yellow color, almost a pale red on the line of the back. As it grows older it becomes darker, and by late autumn is almost as dark as the adults. Variations from the normal color are very rare, but pied, spotted, and roan animals are sometimes killed. Blue or mouse-colored buffalo were occasionally seen, and a bull of this color was observed in the National Park last January. White buffalo—though often referred to as mythical—sometimes occurred. These varied from gray to cream-white. The rare and valuable "silk" or "beaver" robe owes its name to its dark color and its peculiar sheen or gloss. White or spotted robes were highly valued by the Indians. Among the Blackfeet they were presented to the Sun as votive offerings. Other tribes kept them in their sacred bundles.

Apart from man, the buffalo had but few natural enemies. Of these the most destructive were the wolves, which killed a great many of them. These, however, were principally old, straggling bulls, for the calves were protected by their mothers, and the females and young stock were so vigorous and so gregarious that they had but little to fear from this danger. It is probable that, notwithstanding the destruction which they wrought, the wolves performed an important service for the buffalo race, keeping it vigorous and healthy by killing weak, disabled, and superannuated animals, which could no longer serve any useful purpose in the herd, and yet consumed the grass which would support a healthy breeding animal. It is certainly true that sick buffalo, or those out of condition, were rarely seen.

The grizzly bear fed to some extent on the carcasses of buffalo drowned in the rivers or caught in the quicksands, and occasionally they caught living buffalo and killed them. A Blackfoot Indian told me of an attempt of this kind which he witnessed. He was lying hidden by a buffalo trail in the Bad Lands, near a little creek, waiting for a small bunch to come down to water, so that he might kill one. The buffalo came on in single file as usual, the leading animal being a young heifer. When they had nearly reached the water, and were passing under a vertical clay wall, a grizzly bear, lying hid on a shelf of this wall, reached down, and with both paws caught the heifer about the neck and threw himself upon her. The others at once ran off, and a short struggle ensued, the bear trying to kill the heifer, and she to escape. Almost at once, however, the Indian saw a splendid young bull come rushing down the trail toward the scene of conflict, and charge the bear, knocking him down. A fierce combat ensued. The bull would charge the bear, and when he struck him fairly would knock him off his feet, often inflicting severe wounds with his sharp horns. The bear struck at the bull, and tried to catch him by the head or shoulders, and to hold him, but this he could not do. After fifteen or twenty minutes of fierce and active fighting, the bear had received all the punishment he cared for, and tried to escape, but the bull would not let him go, and kept up the attack until he had killed his adversary. Even after the bear was dead the bull would gore the carcass and sometimes lift it clear of the ground on his horns. He seemed insane with rage, and, notwithstanding the fact that most of the skin was torn from his head and shoulders, appeared to be looking about for something else to fight. The Indian was very much afraid lest the bull should discover and kill him, and was greatly relieved when he finally left the bear and went off to join his band. This Blackfoot had never heard of Uncle Remus's tales, but he imitated Brer Rabbit—laid low and said nothing.

To the Indians the buffalo was the staff of life. It was their food, clothing, dwellings, tools. The needs of a savage people are not many, perhaps, but whatever the Indians of the plains had, that the buffalo gave them. It is not strange, then, that this animal was reverenced by most plains tribes, nor that it entered largely into their sacred ceremonies, and was in a sense worshiped by them. The Pawnees, in explaining their religious customs, say, "Through the corn and the buffalo we worship the Father." The Blackfeet ask, "What one of all the animals is most sacred?" and the reply given is, "The buffalo."

The robe was the Indian's winter covering and his bed, while the skin, freed from the hair and dressed, constituted his summer sheet or blanket. The dressed hide was used for moccasins, leggings, shirts, and women's dresses. Dressed cow-skins formed the lodges, the warmest and most comfortable portable shelters ever devised. Braided strands of rawhide furnished them with ropes and lines, and these were made also from the twisted hair. The green hide was sometimes used as a kettle, in which to boil meat, or, stretched over a frame of boughs, gave them coracles, or boats, for crossing rivers. The tough, thick hide of the bull's neck, allowed to shrink smooth, made a shield which would turn a lance-thrust, an arrow, or even the ball from an old-fashioned smooth-bore gun. From the rawhide, the hair having been shaved off, were made parfleches—envelop-like cases which served for trunks or boxes—useful to contain small articles. The cannon-bones and ribs were used to make implements for dressing hides; the shoulder-blades lashed to sticks made hoes and axes, and the ribs runners for small sledges drawn by dogs. The hoofs were boiled to make a glue for fastening the feathers and heads on their arrows, the hair used to stuff cushions, and later saddles, strands of the long black beard to ornament articles of wearing-apparel and implements of war, such as shields and quivers. The sinews lying along the back gave them thread and bowstrings, and backed their bows. The horns furnished spoons and ladles, and ornamented their war-bonnets. Water-buckets were made from the lining of the paunch. The skin of the hind leg cut off above the pastern, and again a short distance above the hock, was once used for a moccasin or boot. Fly-brushes were made from the skin of the tail dried on sticks. Knife-sheaths, quivers, bow-cases, gun-covers, saddle-cloths, and a hundred other useful and necessary articles, all were furnished by the buffalo.

The Indians killed some smaller game, as elk, deer, and antelope, but for food their dependence was on the buffalo. But before the coming of the whites their knives and arrowheads were merely sharpened stones, weapons which would be inefficient against such great, thick-skinned beasts. Even under the most favorable circumstances, with these primitive implements, they could not kill food in quantities sufficient to supply their needs. There must be some means of taking the buffalo in considerable numbers. Such wholesale capture was accomplished by means of traps or surrounds, which all depended for success on one characteristic of the animal, its curiosity.

The Blackfeet, Plains Crees, Gros Ventres of the Prairie, Sarcees, some bands of the Dakotas, Snakes, Crows, and some others, drove the herds of buffalo into pens from above, or over high cliffs, where the fall killed or crippled a large majority of the herd. The Cheyennes and Arapahoes drove them into pens on level ground; the Blackfeet, Aricaras, Mandans, Gros Ventres of the Village, Pawnees, Omahas, Otoes, and others, surrounded the herds in great circles on the prairie, and then, frightening them so that they started running, kept them from breaking through the line of men, and made them race round and round in a circle, until they were so exhausted that they could not run away, and were easily killed.

These primitive modes of slaughter have been described by earlier writers, and frequently quoted in recent years; yet, in all that has been written on this subject, I fail to find a single account which gives at all a true notion of the methods employed, or the means by which the buffalo were brought into the inclosures. Eye-witnesses have been careless observers, and have taken many things for granted. My understanding of this matter is derived from men who from childhood have been familiar with these things, and from them, during years of close association, I have again and again heard the story of these old hunting methods.

The Blackfoot trap was called the *piskun*. It was an inclosure, one side of which was formed by the vertical wall of a cut bank, the others being built of rocks, logs, poles, and brush six or eight feet high. It was not necessary that these walls should be very strong, but they had to be tight, so that the buffalo could not see through them. From a point on the cut bank above this inclosure, in two diverging lines stretching far out into the prairie, piles of rock were heaped up at short intervals, or bushes were stuck in the ground, forming the wings of a V-shaped chute, which would guide any animals running down the chute to its angle above the piskun. When a herd of buffalo were feeding near at hand, the people prepared for the hunt, in which almost the whole camp took part. It is commonly stated that the buffalo were driven into the piskun by mounted men, but this was not the case. They were not driven, but led, and they were led by an appeal to their curiosity. The man who brought them was usually the possessor of a "buffalo rock," a talisman which was believed to give him greater power to call the buffalo than was had by others. The previous night was spent by this man in praying for success in the enterprise of the morrow. The help of the Sun, *Napi*, and all Above People was asked for, and sweet-grass was burned to them. Early in the morning, without eating or drinking, the man started away from the camp and went up on the prairie. Before he left the lodge, he told his wives that they must not go out, or even look out, of the lodge during his absence. They should stay there, and pray to the Sun for his success, and burn sweet-grass until he returned. When he left the camp and went up on to the prairie toward the buffalo, all the people followed him, and distributed themselves along the wings of the chute, hiding behind the piles of rock or brush. The caller sometimes wore a robe and a bull's-head bonnet, or at times was naked. When he had approached close to the buffalo, he endeavored to attract their attention by moving about, wheeling round and round, and alternately appearing and disappearing. The feeding buffalo soon began to raise their heads and stare at him, and presently the nearest ones would walk toward him to discover what this strange creature might be, and the others would follow. As they began to approach, the man withdrew toward the entrance of the chute. If the buffalo began to trot, he increased his speed, and before very long he had the herd well within the wings. As soon as they had passed the first piles of rock, behind which some of the people were concealed, the Indians sprang into view, and by yelling and waving robes frightened the hind-most of the buffalo, which then began to run down the chute. As they passed along, more and more people showed themselves and added to their terror, and in a very short time the herd was in a headlong stampede, guided toward the angle above the piskun by the piles of rock on either side.

About the walls of the piskun, now full of buffalo, were distributed the women and children of the camp, who, leaning over the inclosure, waving their arms and calling out, did all they could to frighten the penned-in animals, and to keep them from pushing against the walls or trying to jump or climb over them. As a rule the buffalo raced round within the inclosure, and the men shot them down as they passed, until all were killed. After this the people all entered the piskun and cut up the dead, transporting the meat to camp. The skulls, bones, and less perishable offal were removed from the inclosure, and the wolves, coyotes, foxes, and badgers devoured what was left.

It occasionally happened that something occurred to turn the buffalo, so that they passed through the guiding arms and escaped. Usually they went on straight to the angle and jumped over the cliff into the inclosure below. In winter, when snow was on the ground, their straight course was made additionally certain by placing on, or just above, the snow a line of buffalo-chips leading from the angle of the V, midway between its arms, out on to the prairie. These dark objects, only twenty or thirty feet apart, were easily seen against the white snow, and the buffalo always followed them, no doubt thinking this a trail where another herd had passed.

By the *Siksikau* tribe of the Blackfoot nation and the Plains Crees, the piskun was built in a somewhat different way, but the methods employed were similar. With these people, who inhabited a flat country, the inclosure was built of logs and near a timbered stream. Its circular wall was complete; that is, there was no opening or gateway in it, but at one point this wall, elsewhere eight feet high, was cut away so that its height was only four feet. From this point a bridge or causeway of logs, covered with dirt, sloped by a gradual descent down to the level of the prairie. This bridge was fenced on either side with logs, and the arms of the V came together at the point where the bridge reached the ground. The buffalo were driven down the chute as before, ran up on this bridge, and were forced to leap into the pen. As soon as all had entered, Indians who had been concealed near by ran up and put poles across the opening through which the buffalo had passed, and over these poles hung robes so as entirely to conceal the outer world. Then the butchering of the animals took place.

Further to the south, out on the prairie, where timber and rocks and brush were not obtainable for making traps like these, simpler but less effective methods were adopted. The people would go out on the prairie and conceal themselves in a great circle, open on one side. Then some man would approach the buffalo, and decoy them into the circle. Men would now show themselves at different points and start the buffalo running in a circle, yelling and waving robes to keep them from approaching or trying to break through the ring of men. This had to be done with great judgment, however; for often if the herd got started in one direction it was impossible to turn it, and it would rush through the ring and none would be secured. Sometimes, if a herd was found in a favorable position, and there was no wind, a large camp of people would set up their lodges all about the buffalo, in which case the chances of success in the surround were greatly increased.

The tribes which used the piskun also practised driving the buffalo over high, rough cliffs, where the fall crippled or killed most of the animals which went over. In such situations, no inclosure was built at the foot of the precipice.

In the later days of the piskun in the north, the man who brought the buffalo often went to them on horseback, riding a white horse. He would ride backward and forward before them, zigzagging this way and that, and after a little they would follow him. He never attempted to drive, but always led them. The driving began only after the herd had passed the outer rock piles, and the people had begun to rise up and frighten them.

This method of securing meat has been practised in Montana within thirty years, and even more recently among the Plains Crees of the north. I have seen the remains of old piskuns, and the guiding wings of the chute, and have talked with many men who have taken part in such killings.

All this had to do, of course, with the primitive methods of buffalo killing. As soon as horses became abundant, and sheet-iron arrow-heads and, later, guns were secured by the Indians, these old practices began to give way to the more exciting pursuit of running buffalo and of surrounding them on horseback. Of this modern method, as practised twenty years ago, and exclusively with the bow and arrow, I have already written at some length in another place.

To the white travelers on the plains in early days the buffalo furnished support and sustenance. Their abundance made fresh meat easily obtainable, and the early travelers usually carried with them bundles of dried meat, or sacks of pemmican, food made from the flesh of the buffalo, that contained a great deal of nutriment in very small bulk. Robes were used for bedding, and in winter buffalo moccasins were worn for warmth, the hair side within. Coats of buffalo-skin are the warmest covering known, the only garment which will present an effective barrier to the bitter blasts that sweep over the plains of the Northwest.

Perhaps as useful to early travelers as any product of the buffalo, was the "buffalo chip," or dried dung. This, being composed of comminuted woody fiber of the grass, made an excellent fuel, and in many parts of the treeless plains was the only substance which could be used to cook with.

The dismal story of the extermination of the buffalo for its hides has been so often told, that I may be spared the sickening details of the butchery which was carried on from the Mexican to the British boundary line in the struggle to obtain a few dollars by a most ignoble means. As soon as railroads penetrated the buffalo country, a market was opened for the hides. Men too lazy to work were not too lazy to hunt, and a good hunter could kill in the early days from thirty to seventy-five buffalo a day, the hides of which were worth from $1.50 to $4 each. This seemed an easy way to make money, and the market for hides was unlimited. Up to this time the trade in robes had been mainly confined to those dressed by the Indians, and these were for the most part taken from cows. The coming of the railroad made hides of all sorts marketable, and even those taken from naked old bulls found a sale at some price. The butchery of buffalo was now something stupendous. Thousands of hunters followed millions of buffalo and destroyed them wherever found and at all seasons of the year. They pursued them during the day, and at night camped at the watering-places, and built lines of fires along the streams, to drive the buffalo back so that they could not drink. It took less than six years to destroy all the buffalo in Kansas, Nebraska, Indian Territory, and northern Texas. The few that were left of the southern herd retreated to the waterless plains of Texas, and there for a while had a brief respite. Even here the hunters followed them, but as the animals were few and the territory in which they ranged vast, they held out here for some years. It was in this country, and against the last survivors of this southern herd, that "Buffalo Jones" made his successful trips to capture calves.

The extirpation of the northern herd was longer delayed. No very terrible slaughter occurred until the completion of the Northern Pacific Railroad; then, however, the same scenes of butchery were enacted. Buffalo were shot down by tens of thousands, their hides stripped off, and the meat left to the wolves. The result of the crusade was soon seen, and the last buffalo were killed in the Northwest near the boundary line in 1883, and that year may be said to have finished up the species, though some few were killed in 1884 to 1885.

After the slaughter had been begun, but years before it had been accomplished, the subject was brought to the attention of Congress, and legislation looking to the preservation of the species was urged upon that body. Little general interest was taken in the subject, but in 1874, after much discussion, Congress did pass an act providing for the protection of the buffalo. The bill, however, was never signed by the President.

During the last days of the buffalo, a remarkable change took place in its form, and this change is worthy of consideration by naturalists, for it is an example of specialization—of development in one particular direction—which was due to a change in the environment of the species, and is interesting because it was brought about in a very few years, and indicates how rapidly, under favoring conditions, such specialization may sometimes take place.

This change was noticed and commented on by hunters who followed the northern buffalo, as well as by those who assisted in the extermination of the southern herd. The southern hunters, however, averred that the "regular" buffalo had disappeared—gone off somewhere—and that their place had been taken by what they called the southern buffalo, a race said to have come up from Mexico, and characterized by longer legs and a longer, lighter body than the buffalo of earlier years, and which was also peculiar in that the animals never became fat. Intelligent hunters of the northern herd, however, recognized the true state of the case, which was that the buffalo, during the last years of their existence, were so constantly pursued and driven from place to place that they never had time to lay on fat as in earlier years, and that, as a consequence of this continual running, the animal's form changed, and instead of a fat, short-backed, short-legged animal, it became a long-legged, light-bodied beast, formed for running.

This specialization in the direction of speed at first proceeded very slowly, but at last, as the dangers to which the animals were subjected became more and more pressing, it took place rapidly, and as a consequence the last buffalo killed on the plains were extremely long-legged and rangy, and were very different in appearance—as they were in their habits—from the animals of twenty years ago.

Buffalo running was not a sport that required much skill, yet it was not without its dangers. Occasionally a man was killed by the buffalo, but deaths from falls and from bursting guns were more common. Many curious stories of such accidents are told by the few surviving old-timers whose memory goes back fifty years, to the time when flint-lock guns were in use. A mere fall from a horse is lightly regarded by the practised rider; the danger to be feared is that in such a fall the horse may roll on the man and crush him. Even more serious accidents occurred when a man fell upon some part of his equipment, which was driven through his body. Hunters have fallen in such a way that their whip-stocks, arrows, bows, and even guns, have been driven through their bodies. The old flint-lock guns, or "fukes," which were loaded on the run, with powder poured in from the horn by guess, and a ball from the mouth, used frequently to burst, causing the loss of hands, arms, and even lives.

While most of the deaths which occurred in the chase resulted from causes other than the resistance of the buffalo, these did occasionally kill a man. A curious accident happened in a camp of Red River half-breeds in the early seventies. The son of an Iroquois half-breed, about twenty years old, went out one day with the rest of the camp to run buffalo. At night he did not return, and the next day all the men went out to search for him. They found the horse and the arms, but could not find the man, and could not imagine what had become of him. About a year later, as the half-breeds were hunting in another part of the country, a cow was seen which had something unusual on her head. They chased and killed her, and found that she had on her head the pelvis of a man, one of the horns having pierced the thin part of the bone, which was wedged on so tightly that they could hardly get it off. Much of the hair on the head, neck, and shoulders of the cow was worn off short, and on the side on which the bone was, down on the neck and shoulders, the hair was short, black, and looked new, as if it had been worn entirely off the skin, and was just beginning to grow out again. It is supposed that this bone was part of the missing young man, who had been hooked by the cow, and carried about on her head until his body fell to pieces.

My old and valued friend Charles Reynolds, for years chief of scouts at Fort Lincoln, Dakota, and who was killed by the Sioux in the Custer fight in 1876, told me of the death of a hunting partner of his, which shows how dangerous even a dying buffalo may be. The two men had started from the railroad to go south and bring in a load of meat. On finding a bunch of buffalo, they shot down by stalking what they required, and then on foot went up to the animals to skin them. One cow, lying on her side, was still moving a little convulsively, but dying. The man approached her as if about to cut her throat, but when he was within a few feet of her head, she sprang to her feet, rushed at him, struck him in the chest with her horns, and then fell dead. Charley ran up to his partner, and to his horror saw that the cow's horn had ripped him up from the belly to the throat, so that he could see the heart still expanding and contracting.

Charley buried his partner there, and returning to the town, told his story. He was at once arrested on the charge that he had murdered his companion, and was obliged to return to the place and to assist in digging up the body to satisfy the suspicious officials of the truth of his statements.

In the early days, when the game was plenty, buffalo-running was exhilarating sport. Given a good horse, the only other requisite to success was the ability to remain on his back till the end of the chase. No greater degree of skill was needed than this, and yet the quick motion of the horse, the rough ground to be traversed, and the feeling that there was something ahead that must be overtaken and stopped, made the ride attractive. There was the very slightest spice of danger; for while no one anticipated a serious accident, it was always possible that one's horse might step into a badger-hole, in which case his rider would get a fall that would make his bones ache.

The most exciting, and by far the most interesting, hunts in which I ever took part were those with the Indians of the plains. They were conducted almost noiselessly, and no ring of rifle-shot broke the stillness of the air, nor puff of smoke rose toward the still, gray autumn sky. The consummate grace and skill of the naked Indians, and the speed and quickness of their splendid ponies, were well displayed in such chases as these. More than one instance is recorded where an Indian sent an arrow entirely through the bodies of two buffalo. Sometimes such a hunt was signalized by some feat of daring bravado that, save in the seeing, was scarcely credible, as when the Cheyenne Big Ribs rode his horse close up to the side of a huge bull, and, springing on his back, rode the savage beast for some distance, and then with his knife gave him the death-stroke. Or a man might find himself in a position of comical danger, as did "The Trader" who was thrown from his horse on to the horns of a bull without being injured. One of the horns passed under his belt and supported him, and at the same time prevented the bull from tossing him. In this way he was carried for some distance on the animal's head, when the belt gave way and he fell to the ground unhurt, while the bull ran on. There were occasions when buffalo or horses fell in front of horsemen riding at full run, and when a fall was avoided only by leaping one's horse over the fallen animal. In the buffalo chase of old days it was well for a man to keep his wits about him; for, though he might run buffalo a thousand times without accident, the moment might come when only instant action would save him his life, or at least an ugly hurt.

In the early days of the first Pacific Railroad, and before the herds had been driven back from the track, singular hunting-parties were sometimes seen on the buffalo range. These hunters were capitalists connected with the newly constructed road, and some of them now for the first time bestrode a horse, while few had ever used firearms. On such a hunt, one well-known railroad director, eager to kill a buffalo, declined to trust himself on horseback, preferring to bounce over the rough prairie in an ambulance driven by an alarmed soldier, who gave less attention to the mules he was guiding than to the loaded and cocked pistol which his excited passenger was brandishing. These were amusing excursions, where a merry party of pleasant officers from a frontier post, and their guests, a jolly crowd of merchants, brokers, and railroad men from the East, started out to have a buffalo-hunt. With them went the post guide and a scout or two, an escort of soldiers, and the great blue army-wagons, under whose white tilts were piled all the comforts that the post could furnish—unlimited food and drink, and many sacks of forage for the animals. Here all was mirth and jest and good-fellowship, and, except that canvas covered them while they slept, the hunters lived in as much comfort as when at home. The killing of buffalo was to them only an excuse for their jolly outing amid novel scenes.

It was on the plains of Montana, in the days when buffalo were still abundant, that I had one of my last buffalo-hunts—a hunt with a serious purpose. A company of fifty or more men, who for weeks had been living on bacon and beans, longed for the "boss ribs" of fat cow, and when we struck the buffalo range two of us were deputed to kill some meat. My companion was an old prairie-man of great experience, and I myself was not altogether new to the West, for I had hunted in many territories, and had more than once been "jumped" by hostile Indians. Our horses were not buffalo-runners, yet we felt a certain confidence that if we could find a bunch and get a good start on them, we would bring in the desired meat. The troops would march during the day, for the commanding officer had no notion of waiting in camp merely for fresh meat, and we were to go out, hunt, and over-take the command at their night's camp.

The next day after we had reached the buffalo range, we started out long before the eastern sky was gray, and were soon riding off over the chilly prairie. The trail which the command was to follow ran a little north of east, and we kept to the south and away from it, believing that in this direction we would find the game, and that if we started them they would run north or northwest—against the wind, so that we could kill them near the trail. Until some time after the sun had risen, we saw nothing larger than antelope; but at length, from the top of a high hill, we could see, far away to the east, dark dots on the prairie, which we knew could only be buffalo. They were undisturbed too; for, though we watched them for some time, we could detect no motion in their ranks.

It took us nearly two hours to reach the low, broken buttes on the north side of which the buffalo were; and, riding up on the east-ernmost of these, we tried to locate our game more exactly. It was important to get as close as possible before starting them, so that our first rush might carry us into the midst of them. Knowing the capabil-ities of our horses, which were thin from long travel, we felt sure that if the buffalo should take the alarm before we were close to them, we could not overtake the cows and young animals, which always run in the van, and should have to content ourselves with old bulls. On the other hand, if we could dash in among them during the first few hun-dred yards of the race, we should be able to keep up with and select the fattest animals in the herd.

When we reached a point just below the crest of the hill, I stopped and waited, while my companion rode on. Just before he got to the top he too halted, then took off his hat and peered over the ridge, exam-ining so much of the prairie beyond as was now visible to him. His inspection was careful and thorough, and when he had made sure that nothing was in sight, his horse took a step or two forward and then stopped again, and the rider scanned every foot of country before him. The horse, trained as the real hunter's horse is always trained, understood what was required of him, and with pricked ears examined the prairie beyond with as much interest as did his rider. When the calf of Charley's right leg pressed the horse's side, two or three steps more were taken, and then a lifting of the bridle-hand caused another halt.

At length I saw my companion slowly bend forward over his horse's neck, turn, and ride back to me. He had seen the backs of two buffalo lying on the edge of a little flat hardly a quarter of a mile from where we stood. The others of the band must be still nearer to us. By riding along the lowest part of the sag which separated the two buttes, and then down a little ravine, it seemed probable that we could come within a few yards of the buffalo unobserved. Our preparations did not take long. The saddle cinches were loosened, blankets arranged, saddles put in their proper places and tightly cinched again. Cartridges were brought round to the front and right of the belt, where they would be convenient for reloading. Our coats, tied behind the saddle, were looked to, the strings which held them being tightened and securely retied. All this was not lost on our horses, which understood as well as we did what was coming. We skirted the butte, rode through the low sag and down into the little ravine, which soon grew deeper, so that our heads were below the range of vision of almost anything on the butte. Passing the mouth of the little side ravine, however, there came into full view a huge bull, lying well up on the hillside. Luckily his back was toward us, and, each bending low over his horse's neck, we rode on, and in a moment were hidden by the side of the ravine. Two or three minutes more, and we came to another side ravine, which was wide and commanded a view of the flat. We stopped before reaching this, and a peep showed that we were within a few yards of two old cows, a young heifer, and a yearling, all of them to the north of us. Beyond, we could see the backs of others, all lying down.

We jumped on our horses again, and setting the spurs well in, galloped up the ravine and up on the flat; and as we came into view, the nearest buffalo, as if propelled by a huge spring, were on their feet, and, with a second's pause to look, dashed away to the north. Scattered over the flat were fifty or seventy-five buffalo, all of which, by the time we had glanced over the field, were off, with heads bending low to the ground, and short, spiky tails stretched out behind. We were up even with the last of the cows, and our horses were running easily and seemed to have plenty of reserve power. Charley, who was a little ahead of me, called back: "They will cross the trail about a mile north of here. Kill a couple when we get to it." I nodded, and we went on. The herd raced forward over the rolling hills, and in what seemed a very short time we rushed down a long slope on to a wide flat, in which was a prairie-dog town of considerable extent. We were on the very heels of the herd, and in a cloud of dust kicked up by their rapid flight. To see the ground ahead was impossible. We could only trust to our horses and our good luck to save us from falling. Our animals were doing better than we had supposed they could, and were going well and under a pull. I felt that a touch of the spurs and a little riding would bring us up even with the leaders of the buffalo. The pace had already proved too much for several bulls, which had turned off to one side and been passed by. As we flew across the flat, I saw far off a dark line and two white objects, which I knew must be our command. I called to my comrade, and, questioning by the sign, pointed at the buffalo. He nodded, and in a moment we had given free rein to our horses and were up among the herd. During the ride I had two or three times selected my game, but the individuals of the band changed positions so constantly that I could not keep track of them. Now, however, I picked out a fat two-year-old bull; but as I drew up to him he ran faster than before, and rapidly made his way toward the head of the band. I was resolved that he should not escape, and so, though I was still fifteen or twenty yards in the rear, fired. At the shot he fell heels over head directly across a cow which was running by his side and a little behind him. I saw her turn a somersault, and almost at the same instant heard Charley shoot twice in quick succession, and saw two buffalo fall. I fired at a fat young cow that I had pushed my pony up close to. At the shot she whirled, my horse did the same, and she chased me as hard as she could go for seventy-five yards, while I did some exceedingly vigorous spurring, for she was close behind me all the time. To do my horse justice, I think that he would have run as fast as he could, even without the spurs, for he appreciated the situation. At no time was there any immediate danger that the cow would overtake us; if there had been, I should have dodged her. Presently the cow stopped, and stood there very sick. When I rode back, I did not find it easy to get my horse near her; but another shot was not needed, and while I sat looking at her she fell over dead. The three buffalo first killed had fallen within a hundred yards of the trail where the wagons afterward passed, and my cow was but little farther away. The command soon came up, the soldiers did the butchering, and before long we were on the march again across the parched plain.

Of the millions of buffalo which even in our own time ranged the plains in freedom, none now remain. From the prairies which they used to darken, the wild herds, down to the last straggling bull, have disappeared. In the Yellowstone National Park, protected from destruction by United States troops, are the only wild buffalo which exist within the borders of the United States. These are mountain buffalo, and, from their habit of living in the thick timber and on the rough mountain-sides, they are only now and then seen by visitors to the park. It is impossible to say just how many there are, but from the best information that I can get, based on the estimates of reliable and conservative men, I conclude that the number was not less than four hundred in the winter of 1891–92. Each winter or spring the government scout employed in the park sees one or more herds of these buffalo, and as such herds are usually made up in part of young animals and have calves with them, it is fair to assume that they are steadily, if slowly, increasing. The report of a trip made in January, 1892, speaks of four herds seen in the Hayden Valley, which numbered respectively 78, 50, 110, and 15. Besides these, a number of scattering groups were seen at a distance, which would bring the number up to three hundred.

In the far northwest, in the Peace River district, there may still be found a few wood buffalo. They are seldom killed, and the estimate of their numbers varies from five hundred to fifteen hundred. This cannot be other than the merest guess, since they are scattered over many thousand square miles of territory which is without inhabitants, and for the most part unexplored.

On the great plains is still found the buffalo skull half buried in the soil and crumbling to decay. The deep trails once trodden by the marching hosts are grass-grown now, and fast filling up. When these most enduring relics of a vanished race shall have passed away, there will be found, in all the limitless domain once darkened by their feeding herds, not one trace of the American buffalo.

TIGE'S LION

ZANE GREY

Sportsmen who have hunted mountain lions are familiar with the details. The rock-ribbed ravines and spear-pointed pines, the patches of snow on the slopes, and the dry stone dust under the yellow cliffs with its pungent animal odor—these characterize the home of the big cat. The baying of the hounds, the cautious pursuit on foot or the long thrilling chase on horseback, ending before a dark cave or under a pine, and the "stand and deliver" with a heavy rifle—these are the features.

I have a story to tell of a hunt that was different.

The time was in May. With Buffalo Jones, the old plainsman, and his cowboys, I was camped on the northern rim of the Grand Canyon of Arizona, in what the Indians once named the Siwash. This heavily timbered plateau, bounded on three sides by the desert and on the fourth side by that strange delusive cleft called the canyon, is as wild and lonely, and as beautiful a place as was ever visited by man. Buckskin Mountain surmounts the plateau, and its innumerable breaks or ravines slope gently into the canyon. Here range thousands of deer and wild mustangs, and mountain lions live fat and unmolested.

On the morning of May 12, when Jones routed us out at five o'clock, as was his custom, a white frost, as deep as a light snow, clothed the forest. The air was nipping. An eager, crackling welcome came from the blazing campfire. Jim raked the hot coals over the lid of his oven. Frank and Lawson trooped in with the horses. Jones, as usual, had trouble with his hounds, particularly the ever-belligerent Tige.

Hounds in that remote section of Arizona retain a majority of their primitive instincts. Most of the time the meat they get they "rustle" for. So, taking the hard life into consideration, Jones' dogs were fairly well-behaved. Tige, a large-framed yellow bloodhound, was young, intractable, and as fierce as a tiger—whence his name. According to the cowboys, Tige was a cross between a locoed coyote and a maverick; in Jones' idea he had all the points of a great lion dog, only he needed his spirit curbed. Tige chased many a lion; he got tongue lashings and lashings of other kind, and even charge of fine shot; but his spirit remained untamed.

We had a captive lion in camp—one Jones had lassoed and brought in a few days before—and Tige had taken the matter as a direct insult to himself. Fight he would, and there was no use to club him. And on this morning when Jones slipped his chain he made for the lion again. After sundry knocks and scratches we dragged Tige to the campfire while we ate breakfast. Even then, with Jones' powerful grasp on his collar, he vented his displeasure and growled. The lion crouched close behind the pine and watched the hound with somber fiery eyes.

"Hurry, boys!" called Jones, in his sharp voice. "We'll tie up a lion this morning, sure as you're born. Jim, you and Lawson stick with us to-day. Yesterday, if we hadn't split, and lost each other, we'd have got one of those lions. If we get separated, keep yelling our signal."

Then he turned to me and shook his big finger: "Listen. I want you to hold in that black demon of a horse you're riding. He'll kill you if you are not careful. He hasn't been broke long. A year ago he was leading a band of wild mustangs over the mountain. Pull him in; hold him tight!"

"Which way?" asked Frank, as he swung into his saddle.

"I reckon it doesn't much matter," replied Jones, with his dry, grim chuckle. "We run across lion sign everywhere, don't we? Let's circle through the woods while the frost stays on."

We rode out under the stately silvered pines, down the long white aisles, with the rising sun tingeing the forest a delicate pink. The impatient hounds, sniffing and whining, trotted after Jones. They crossed fresh deer tracks with never a sign. Here and there deer, a species of mule deer almost as large as elk, bounded up the slopes. A mile or more from camp we ran over a lion trail headed for the mountain.

Sounder, the keenest hound we had, opened up first and was off like a shot. Tige gave tongue and leaped after him; then old Mose, with his short bark, led the rest of the pack. Our horses burst into action like a string of racers at the post. With Frank on his white mustang setting the pace, we drove through the forest glades swift as the wind.

"A hot trail, boys! Hi! Hi! Hi!" yelled Jones.

No need was there to inspire us. The music of the hounds did that. We split the cold air till it sang in our ears; we could scarcely get our breath, and no longer smelt the pine. The fresh and willing horses stretched lower and lower. The hounds passed out of sight into the forest, but their yelps and bays, now low, now clear, floated back to us. Either I forgot Jones' admonition or disregarded it, for I gave my horse, Satan, free rein and, without my realizing it at the time, he moved out ahead of the bunch. Compared to the riders in my rear I was a poor horseman, but as long as I could stick on, what did I care for that? Riding Satan was like sailing on a feather in a storm. Something wild in my blood leaped. My greatest danger lay in the snags and branches of the pines. Half the time I hugged Satan's neck to miss them. Many a knock and a brush I got. Looking backward once I saw I was leaving my companions, and grimly recalling former chases, in the finish of which I had not shown, I called to Satan.

"On! On! On, old fellow! This is our day!"

Then it seemed he had not been running at all. How he responded! His light, long powerful stride was a beautiful thing. The cold, sweet pine air, cutting between my teeth, left a taste in my mouth, and it had the exhilaration of old wine. I rejoiced in the wildness of movement and the indescribable blurred black and white around me; in sheer madness of sensorial perception I let out ringing yells. It was as if I were alone in the woods; it was all mine, and there was joy of chase, of action and of life.

The trail began to circle to the southwest, and in the next mile turned in the direction from which it had come. This meant the lion had probably been close at hand when we struck his trail, and hearing the hounds he had made for the canyon. Down the long, slightly swelling slope Satan thundered, and the pines resembled fence-pickets from a coasting sled. Often I saw gray, bounding flashes against the white background, and knew I had jumped deer. I wondered if any of the hounds were at fault, for sometimes they became confused at the crossing of a fresher scent. Satan kept a steady gait for five miles down the forest slope, and then raced out of the pines into a growth of scrubby oak. I knew I was not now far from the rim of the canyon, and despaired of coming up with the lion. Suddenly I realized I was not following a trail, as the frost had disappeared in the open. Neither did I hear the baying of the hounds. I hauled Satan up and, listening, heard no sound.

"Waa-hoo! Waa-hoo!" I yelled our signal cry. No answer came: only the haunting echo. While I was vainly trying to decide what to do, the dead silence was sharply broken by the deep bay of a hound. It was Tige's voice. In another second I had Satan plunging through the thicket of short oaks. Soon we were among the piñons near the rim of the canyon. Again I reined Satan to a standstill. From this point I could see out into the canyon, and as always, even under the most exciting circumstances, I drew a sharp breath at the wonder, the mystery, the sublimity of the scene. The tips of yellow crags and gray mesas and red turrets rose out of the blue haze of distance. The awful chasm, eighteen miles wide and more than a mile deep, stretched away clear and vividly outlined in the rare atmosphere for a hundred miles. The canyon seemed still wrapped in slumber, and a strange, vast silence that was the silence of ages, hung over the many-hued escarpments and sculptured domes.

Tige's bay, sounding close at hand, startled me and made Satan jump. I slid to the ground, and pulling my little Remington from the saddle, began hunting in the piñons for the hound.

Presently I sighted him, standing with his front paws against a big piñon. Tige saw me, wagged his tail, howled and looked up. Perhaps twenty feet from the ground a full-grown lion stood on branches that were swaying with his weight. He glared down at Tige and waved his long tail. He had a mean face, snarling, vicious. His fat sides heaved and I gathered he was not used to running, and had been driven to his limit.

"Tige, old boy, you're the real thing!" I yelled. "Keep him there!" For an instant I fingered the safety catch on my automatic. I did not much fancy being alone with that old fellow. I had already seen a grim, snarling face and outstretched claws in the air before my eyes—and once was enough! Still I did not want to kill him. Finally I walked cautiously to within fifty feet of him, and when he showed resentment in a slowly crouching movement I hastily snapped a picture of him. Hardly had I turned the film round when he leaped from the tree and bounded away. Knowing he would make for the rim and thus escape I dropped my camera and grabbed up the rifle. But I could not cut loose on him, because Tige kept nipping him, and I feared I might shoot the hound. Tige knew as well as I the intention of the lion and—brave fellow!—he ran between the beast and the canyon and turned him towards the woods. At this great work on the part of Tige I yelled frantically and dashed for my horse. Though the lion had passed close, Satan had not moved from his tracks.

"Hi! Hi! Hi! Take him, Tige!" I screamed, as the black launched out like an arrow.

On the open flat I spied Tige and his quarry, resembling yellow flashes in the scrub oak; and twice the hound jumped the lion. I swore in my teeth. The brave and crazy dog was going to his death. Satan fairly crashed through the thicket and we gained. I saw we were running along a cut-in from the main rim wall, and I thought the lion was making for a break where he could get down. Suddenly I saw him leap high into a pine on the edge of the forest. When I came up Tige was trying to climb the tree.

"Tige, old boy, I guess Jones had you sized up right," I cried, as I dismounted. "If that brute jumps again it will be his last."

At this moment I heard a yell, and I sent out three "Waa-hoos," which meant "come quickly!" In a few moments Sounder burst out of the forest, then Don, then Mose. How they did yelp! I heard the pounding of hoofs, more yells, and soon Frank dashed into the open, followed by the others. The big tawny lion was in plain sight, and as each hunter saw him a wild yell pealed out.

"Hi! Hi! There he is! Tige, you're the stuff!" cried Jones, whirling off his horse. "You didn't split on deer trails, like the rest of these blasted long-eared canines. You stuck to him, old dog! Well, he's your lion. Boys, spread out now and surround the tree. This is a good tree and I hope we can hold him here. If he jumps he'll get over the rim, sure. Make all the racket you can, and get ready for work when I rope him."

Sounder, Mose, Ranger and Don went wild while Jones began climbing the tree, and as for Tige, he went through antics never before seen in a dog. Jones climbed slowly, laboriously, with his lasso trailing behind him, his brawny arms bare. How grim and cool he looked! I felt sorry for the lion.

"Look out!" called Jim. "Shore thet lion means biz."

"Jones, he's an old cuss, an' won't stand no foolin'," said Frank.

The old buffalo hunter climbed just the same, calmly and deliberately, as if he were unaware of danger.

Lawson, who was afraid of nothing on earth except lions, edged farther and farther from under the pine. The lion walked back up the limb he had gone down, and he hissed and growled. When Jones reached the first fork, the lion spat. His eyes emitted flames; his sharp claws dug into the bark of the limb; he began to show restlessness and fear. All at once he made a quick start, apparently to descend and meet Jones. We yelled like a crew of demons, and he slipped back a bit.

"Far enough!" yelled Frank, and his voice rang.

"Cut me a pole," called Jones.

In a twinkling Frank procured a long sapling and handed it up. Jones hung the noose of his lasso on it, and slowly extended it toward the lion. I snapped a picture here, and was about to take another when Jim yelled to me.

"Here, you with the rifle! Be ready. Shore we'll have hell in a minute."

Hell there was, in less time. With the dexterity of a conjuror Jones slipped the noose over the head of the lion and tightened it. Spitting furiously the lion bit, tore and clawed at the rope.

"Pull him off, boys! Now! Hurry, while the rope is over that short limb. Then we'll hang him in the air for a minute while I come down and lasso his paws. Pull! Pull!"

The boys pulled with all their might but the lion never budged.

"Pull him off, dang it! Pull!" impatiently yelled Jones, punching the lion with the pole.

But the powerful beast would not be dislodged. His long body lengthened on the limb and his great muscles stood out in ridges. There was something grand in his defiance and his resistance. Suddenly Jones grasped the lasso and slid down it, hand over hand.

I groaned in my spirit. What a picture to miss! There I was with a rifle, the only one in the party, and I had to stand ready to protect life if possible—and I had to watch a rare opportunity, one in a lifetime, pass without even a try. It made me sick.

The men strained on the lasso, and shouted; the hounds whined, quivered and leaped into the air; the lion hugged the branch with his brawny paws.

"Throw your weight on the rope," ordered Jones.

For an instant the lion actually held the men off the ground; then with a scratching and tearing of bark he tumbled. But Jones had not calculated on the strength of the snag over which he expected to hang the lion. The snag was rotten; it broke. The lion whirled in the air. Crash! He had barely missed Lawson.

In a flash the scene changed from one of half-comic excitement to one of terrible danger and probably tragedy. There was a chorus of exclamation, and snarls and yelps, all coming from a cloud of dust. Then I saw a yellow revolving body in the midst of furry black whirling objects. I dared not shoot for fear of hitting my friends. Out of this snarling melee the lion sprang towards freedom. Jones pounced upon the whipping lasso, Frank and Jim were not an instant behind him, and the dogs kept at the heels of the lion. He turned on them like an exploding torpedo; then, giving a tremendous bound, straightened the lasso and threw the three men flat on their faces. But they held on.

Suddenly checked, the lion took a side jump bringing the tight lasso in connection with Lawson's flying feet. The frightened fellow had been trying to get out of the way. The lasso tripped him, giving him a hard fall. I tried to bring my rifle to bear just as the lion savagely turned on Lawson. But the brute was so quick, the action of the struggling men so confused and fast that it was impossible. I heard Jones bawl out some unintelligible command; I heard Lawson scream; I saw the flaming-eyed brute, all instinct with savage life, reach out with both huge paws.

It was at this critical instant that Tige bowled pell-mell into the very jaws of the lion. Then began a terrific wrestling combat. The lasso flew out of the hands of Frank and Jim, but the burly Jones, like his great dog, held on. Tige and the lion, fighting tooth and claw, began to roll down the incline. Jones was pulled to his feet, thrown flat again and dragged.

"Grab the rope!" he roared.

But no one could move. Jones rose to his knees, then fell, and lost the lasso.

Hound and lion in a savage clutch of death whirled down, nearer and nearer to the rim wall of the canyon. As they rolled I heard the rend and tear of hide. I knew Tige would never let go, even if he could, and I opened up with the automatic.

I heard the spats of the bullets, and saw fur, blood and gravel fly. On the very verge of the precipice the lion stretched out convulsively. Tige clung to his neck with a grim hold. Then they slipped over the wall.

Silence for a long second—then crash! There came up the rattle of stones, silence for a palpitating second—then crash! It was heavier, farther down and followed by a roar of sliding stones. Silence for a long, long moment. Finally a faint faraway sound which died instantly. The lion king lay at the foot of his throne and Tige lay with him.

RED LETTER DAYS IN BRITISH COLUMBIA

LIEUTENANT TOWNSEND WHELEN

In the month of July, 1901, my partner, Bill Andrews, and I were at a small Hudson Bay post in the northern part of British Columbia, outfitting for a long hunting and exploring trip in the wild country to the North. The official map showed this country as "unexplored," with one or two rivers shown by dotted lines. This map was the drawing card which had brought us thousands of miles by rail, stage and pack train to this out-of-the-way spot. By the big stove in the living room of the factor's house we listened to weird tales of this north country, of its enormous mountains and glaciers, its rivers and lakes and of the quantities of game and fish. The factor told us of three men who had tried to get through there in the Klondike rush several years before and had not been heard from yet. The trappers and Siwashes could tell us of trails which ran up either side of the Scumscum, the river on which the post stood, but no one knew what lay between that and the Yukon to the north.

We spent two days here outfitting and on the morning of the third said goodbye to the assembled population and started with our pack train up the east bank of the Scumscum. We were starting out to live and travel in an unknown wilderness for over six months, and our outfit may perhaps interest my readers: We had two saddle horses, four pack horses and a dog. A small tent formed one pack cover. We had ten heavy army blankets, which we used for saddle blankets while traveling, they being kept clean by using canvas sweat pads under them. We were able to pack 150 pounds of grub on each horse, divided up as nearly as I can remember as follows: One hundred and fifty pounds flour, 50 pounds sugar, 30 pounds beans, 10 pounds rice, 10 pounds dried apples, 20 pounds prunes, 30 pounds corn meal, 20 pounds oatmeal, 30 pounds potatoes, 10 pounds onions, 50 pounds bacon, 25 pounds salt, 1 pound pepper, 6 cans baking powder, 10 pounds soap, 10 pounds tobacco, 10 pounds tea, and a few little incidentals weighing probably 10 pounds. We took two extra sets of shoes for each horse, with tools for shoeing, 2 axes, 25 boxes of wax matches, a large can of gun oil, canton flannel for gun rags, 2 cleaning rods, a change of underclothes, 6 pairs of socks and 6 moccasins each, with buckskin for resoling, toilet articles, 100 yards of fishing line, 2 dozen fish hooks, an oil stove, awl, file, screwdriver, needles and thread, etc.

For cooking utensils we had 2 frying pans, 3 kettles to nest, 2 tin cups, 3 tin plates and a gold pan. We took 300 cartridges for each of our rifles. Bill carried a .38-55 Winchester, model '94, and I had my old .40-72 Winchester, model '95, which had proved too reliable to relinquish for a high-power small bore. Both rifles were equipped with Lyman sights and carefully sighted. As a precaution we each took along extra front sights, firing pins and main-springs, but did not have a chance to use them. I loaded the ammunition for both rifles myself, with black powder, smokeless priming, and lead bullets. Both rifles proved equal to every emergency.

Where the post stood the mountains were low and covered for the most part with sage brush, with here and there a grove of pines or quaking aspen. As our pack train wound its way up the narrow trail above the river bank we saw many Siwashes spearing salmon, a very familiar sight in that country. These gradually became fewer and fewer, then we passed a miner's cabin and a Siwash village with its little log huts and its hay fields, from which grass is cut for the winter consumption of the horses. Gradually all signs of civilization disappeared, the mountains rose higher and higher, the valley became a canon, and the roar of the river increased, until finally the narrowing trail wound around an outrageous corner with the river a thousand feet below, and looming up in front of us appeared a range of snow-capped mountains, and thus at last we were in the haven where we would be.

That night we camped on one of the little pine-covered benches above the canon. My, but it was good to get the smell of that ever-lasting sage out of our nostrils, and to take long whiffs of the balsam-ladened air! Sunset comes very late at this latitude in July, and it was an easy matter to wander up a little draw at nine in the evening and shoot the heads of three grouse. After supper it was mighty good to lie and smoke and listen to the tinkle of the horse bells as they fed on the luscious mountain grass. We were old campmates, Bill and I, and it took us back to many trips we had had before, which were, however, to be surpassed many times by this one. I can well remember how as a boy, when I first took to woods loafing, I used to brood over a little work which we all know so well, entitled, "Woodcraft," by that grand old man, "Nessmuk," and particularly that part where he relates about his eight-day tramp through the then virgin wilderness of Michigan. But here we were, starting out on a trip which was to take over half a year, during which time we were destined to cover over 1,500 miles of unexplored mountains, without the sight of a human face or an axe mark other than our own.

The next day after about an hour's travel, we passed the winter cabin of an old trapper, now deserted, but with the frames for stretching bear skins and boards for marten pelts lying around—betokening the owner's occupation. The dirt roof was entirely covered with the horns of deer and mountain sheep, and we longed to close our jaws on some good red venison. Here the man-made trails came to an end, and henceforth we used the game trails entirely. These intersect the country in every direction, being made by the deer, sheep and caribou in their migrations between the high and low altitudes. In some places they were hardly discernible, while in others we followed them for days, when they were as plainly marked as the bridle paths in a city park. A little further on we saw a whole family of goats sunning themselves on a high bluff across the river, and that night we dined on the ribs of a fat little spike buck which I shot in the park where we pitched our tent.

To chronicle all the events which occurred on that glorious trip would, I fear, tire my readers, so I will choose from the rich store certain ones which have made red-letter days in our lives. I can recollect but four days when we were unable to kill enough game or catch enough fish to keep the table well supplied, and as luck would have it, those four days came together, and we nearly starved. We had been camped for about a week in a broad wooded valley, having a glorious loaf after a hard struggle across a mountain pass, and were living on trout from a little stream alongside camp, and grouse which were in the pine woods by the thousands. Tiring of this diet we decided to take a little side trip and get a deer or two, taking only our three fattest horses and leaving the others behind to fatten up on the long grass in the valley, for they had become very poor owing to a week's work high up above timber line. The big game here was all high up in the mountains to escape the heat of the valley. So we started one morning, taking only a little tea, rice, three bannocks, our bedding and rifles, thinking that we would enjoy living on meat straight for a couple of days. We had along with us a black mongrel hound named Lion, belonging to Bill. He was a fine dog on grouse but prone to chase a deer once in a while.

About eight miles up the valley could be seen a high mountain of green serpentine rock and for many days we had been speculating on the many fine bucks which certainly lay in the little ravines around the base, so we chose this for our goal. We made the top of the mountain about three in the afternoon, and gazing down on the opposite side we saw a little lake with good horse feed around it and determined to camp there. About half way down we jumped a doe and as it stood on a little hummock Bill blazed away at it and undershot. This was too much for Lion, the hound, and he broke after the deer, making the mountainside ring with his baying for half an hour. Well, we hunted all the next day, and the next, and never saw a hair. That dog had chased the deer all out of the country with his barking.

By this time our little grub-stake of rice, bannocks and tea was exhausted, and, to make things worse, on the third night we had a terrific hail storm, the stones covering the ground three inches deep. Breakfast the next morning consisted of tea alone and we felt pretty glum as we started out, determining that if we did not find game that day we would pull up stakes for our big camp in the valley. About one o'clock I struck a fresh deer trail and had not followed it long before three or four others joined it, all traveling on a game trail which led up a valley. This valley headed up about six miles from our camp in three little ravines, each about four miles long. When I got to the junction of these ravines it was getting dark and I had to make for camp. Bill was there before me and had the fire going and some tea brewing, but nothing else. He had traveled about twenty miles that day and had not seen a thing. I can still see the disgusted look on his face when he found I had killed nothing. We drank our tea in silence, drew our belts tighter and went to bed.

The next morning we saddled up our horses and pulled out. We had not tasted food for about sixty hours and were feeling very faint and weak. I can remember what an effort it was to get into the saddle and how sick and weak I felt when old Baldy, my saddle horse, broke into a trot. Our way back led near the spot where I had left the deer trail the night before, and we determined to ride that way hoping that perhaps we might get a shot at them. Bill came first, then Loco, the pack horse, and I brought up the rear. As we were crossing one of the little ravines at the head of the main valley Loco bolted and Bill took after him to drive him back into the trail. I sat on my horse idly watching the race, when suddenly I saw a mouse-colored flash and then another and heard the thump, thump of cloven feet. Almost instantly the whole ravine seemed to be alive with deer. They were running in every direction. I leaped from my horse and cut loose at the nearest, which happened to be a doe. She fell over a log and I could see her tail waving in little circles and knew I had her. Then I turned on a big buck on the other side of the ravine and at the second shot he stumbled and rolled into the little stream. I heard Bill shooting off to the left and yelled to him that we had enough, and he soon joined me, saying he had a spike buck down. It was the work of but a few minutes to dress the deer and soon we had a little fire going and the three livers hanging in little strips around it. Right here we three, that is, Bill, the dog and myself, disposed of a liver apiece, and my! how easily and quickly it went—the first meat in over a week. Late that night we made our horse camp in the lower valley, having to walk all the way as our horses packed the meat. The next day was consumed entirely with jerking meat, cooking and eating. We consumed half the spike buck that day. When men do work such as we were doing their appetites are enormous, even without a fast of four days to sharpen them up.

One night I well remember after a particularly hard day with the pack train through a succession of wind-falls. We killed a porcupine just before camping and made it into a stew with rice, dough balls, onions and thick gravy, seasoned with curry. It filled the kettle to within an inch of the top and we ate the whole without stopping, whereat Bill remarked that it was enough for a whole boarding-house. According to the catalogue of Abercrombie and Fitch that kettle held eight quarts.

We made it the rule while our horses were in condition, to travel four days in the week, hunt two and rest one. Let me chronicle a day of traveling; it may interest some of you who have never traveled with a pack train. Arising at the first streak of dawn, one man cooked the breakfast while the other drove in the horses. These were allowed to graze free at every camping place, each horse having a cow bell around its neck, only Loco being hobbled, for he had a fashion of wandering off on an exploring expedition of his own and leading all the other horses with him. The horses were liable to be anywhere within two miles of camp, and it was necessary to get behind them to drive them in. Four miles over these mountains would be considered a pretty good day's work in the East. Out here it merely gave one an appetite for his breakfast. If you get behind a pack of well-trained horses they will usually walk right straight to camp, but on occasions I have walked, thrown stones and cussed from seven until twelve before I managed to get them in. Sometimes a bear will run off a pack of horses. This happened to us once and it took two days to track them to the head of a canon, fifteen miles off, and then we had to break Loco all over again.

Breakfast and packing together would take an hour, so we seldom got started before seven o'clock. One of us rode first to pick out the trail, then followed the four pack horses and the man in the rear, whose duty it was to keep them in the trail and going along. Some days the trail was fine, running along the grassy south hillsides with fine views of the snowcapped ranges, rivers, lakes and glaciers; and on others it was one continual struggle over fallen logs, boulders, through ice-cold rivers, swifter than the Niagara rapids, and around bluffs so high that we could scarcely distinguish the outlines of the trees below. Suppose for a minute that you have the job of keeping the horses in the trail. You ride behind the last horse, lazily watching the train. You do not hurry them as they stop for an instant to catch at a whiff of bunch grass beside the trail. Two miles an hour is all the speed you can hope to make. Suddenly one horse will leave the trail enticed by some par-ticularly green grass a little to one side, and leaning over in your saddle you pick up a stone and hurl it at the delinquent, and he falls into line again. Then everything goes well until suddenly one of the pack horses breaks off on a faint side trail going for all he is worth. You dig in your spurs and follow him down the mountain side over rocks and down timber until he comes to a stop half a mile below in a thicket of quaking aspen. You extricate him and drive him back. The next thing you know one of the horses starts to buck and you notice that his pack is turning; then everything starts at once. The pack slides between the horse's legs, he bucks all the harder, the frying pan comes loose, a side pack comes off and the other horses fly in every direction. Perhaps in an hour you have corralled the horses, repacked the cause of your troubles and are hitting the trail again. In another day's travel the trail may lead over down timber and big boulders and for eight solid hours you are whipping the horses to make them jump the obstructions, while your companion is pulling at the halters.

Rustling with a pack train is a soul-trying occupation. Where pos-sible we always aimed to go into camp about three in the afternoon.

Then the horses got a good feed before dark—they will not feed well at night—and we had plenty of time to make a comfortable camp and get a good supper. We seldom pitched our tent on these one-night camps unless the weather looked doubtful, preferring to make a bed of pine boughs near the fire. The blankets were laid on top of a couple of pack sheets and the tent over all.

For several days we had been traveling thus, looking for a pass across a long snow-capped mountain range which barred our way to the north. Finally we found a pass between two large peaks where we thought we could get through, so we started up. When we got up to timber-line the wind was blowing so hard that we could not sit on our horses. It would take up large stones the size of one's fist and hurl them down the mountain side. It swept by us cracking and roaring like a battery of rapid-fire guns. To cross was impossible, so we back-tracked a mile to a spot where a little creek crossed the trail, made camp and waited. It was three days before the wind went down enough to allow us to cross.

The mountain sheep had made a broad trail through the pass and it was easy to follow, being mostly over shale rock. That afternoon, descending the other side of the range, we camped just below timber line by a little lake of the most perfect emerald hue I have ever seen. The lake was about a mile long. At its head a large glacier extended way up towards the peaks. On the east was a wall of bright red rock, a thousand feet high, while to the west the hillside was covered with dwarf pine trees, some of them being not over a foot high and full-grown at that. Below our camp the little stream, the outlet of the lake, bounded down the hillside in a succession of waterfalls. A more beautiful picture I have yet to see. We stayed up late that night watching it in the light of the full moon and thanked our lucky stars that we were alive. It was very cold; we put on all the clothes we owned and turned in under seven blankets. The heavens seemed mighty near, indeed, and the stars crackled and almost exploded with the still silver mountains sparkling all around. We could hear the roar of the waterfalls below us and the bells of the horses on the hillside above. Our noses were very cold. Far off a coyote howled and so we went to sleep—and instantly it was morning.

I arose and washed in the lake. It was my turn to cook, but first of all I got my telescope and looked around for signs of game. Turning the glass to the top of the wooded hillside, I saw something white moving, and getting a steady position, I made it out to be the rump of a mountain sheep. Looking carefully I picked out four others. Then I called Bill. The sheep were mine by right of discovery, so we traded the cook detail and I took my rifle and belt, stripped to trousers, moccasins and shirt, and started out, going swiftly at first to warm up in the keen mountain air. I kept straight up the hillside until I got to the top and then started along the ridge toward the sheep. As I crossed a little rise I caught sight of them five hundred yards ahead, the band numbering about fifty. Some were feeding, others were bedded down in some shale. From here on it was all stalking, mostly crawling through the small trees and bushes which were hardly knee-high. Finally, getting within one hundred and fifty yards, I got a good, steady prone position between the bushes, and picking out the largest ram, I got the white Lyman sight nicely centered behind his shoulder and very carefully and gradually I pressed the trigger. The instant the gun went off I knew he was mine, for I could call the shot exactly. Instantly the sheep were on the move. They seemed to double up, bunch and then vanish. It was done so quickly that I doubt if I could have gotten in another shot even if I had wished it. The ram I had fired at was knocked completely off its feet, but picked himself up instantly and started off with the others; but after he had run about a hundred yards I saw his head drop and turning half a dozen somersaults, he rolled down the hill and I knew I had made a heart shot. His horns measured 16½ inches at the base, and the nose contained an enormous bump, probably caused in one of his fights for the supremacy of the herd.

I dressed the ram and then went for the horses. Bill, by this time, had everything packed up, so after going up the hill and loading the sheep on my saddle horse, we started down the range for a region where it was warmer and less strenuous and where the horse feed was better. That night we had mountain sheep ribs—the best meat that ever passed a human's mouth—and I had a head worth bringing home. A 16½-inch head is very rare in these days. I believe the record head measured about 19 inches. I remember distinctly, however, on another hunt in the Lillooet district of British Columbia, finding in the long grass of a valley the half-decayed head of an enormous ram. I measured the pith of the skull where the horn had been and it recorded 18 inches. The horn itself must have been at least 21 inches. The ram probably died of old age or was unable to get out of the high altitude when the snow came.

We journeyed on and on, having a glorious time in the freedom of the mountains. We were traveling in a circle, the diameter of which was about three hundred miles. One day we struck an enormous glacier and had to bend way off to the right to avoid it. For days as we travelled that glacier kept us company. It had its origin way up in a mass of peaks and perpetual snow, being fed from a dozen valleys. At least six moraines could be distinctly seen on its surface, and the air in its vicinity was decidedly cool. Where we first struck it it was probably six miles wide and I believe it was not a bit less than fifty miles long. We named it Chilco glacier, because it undoubtedly drained into a large lake of that name near the coast. At this point we were not over two hundred miles from the Pacific Ocean.

As the leaves on the aspen trees started to turn we gradually edged around and headed toward our starting point, going by another route, however, trusting to luck and the careful map we had been making to bring us out somewhere on the Scumscum river above the post. The days were getting short now and the nights very cold. We had to travel during almost all the daylight and our horses started to get poor. The shoes we had taken for them were used up by this time and we had to avoid as much as possible the rocky country. We travelled fast for a month until we struck the headwaters of the Scumscum; then knowing that we were practically safe from being snowed up in the mountain we made a permanent camp on a hillside where the horsefeed was good and started to hunt and tramp to our hearts' delight, while our horses filled up on the grass. We never killed any more game than we could use, which was about one animal every ten days. In this climate meat will keep for a month if protected from flies in the daytime and exposed to the night air after dark.

We were very proud of our permanent camp. The tent was pitched under a large pine tree in a thicket of willows and quaking aspen. All around it was built a windbreak of logs and pine boughs, leaving in front a yard, in the center of which was our camp fire. The windbreak went up six feet high and when a fire was going in front of the tent we were as warm as though in a cabin, no matter how hard the wind blew. Close beside the tent was a little spring, and a half a mile away was a lake full of trout from fifteen pounds down. We spent three days laying in a supply of firewood. Altogether it was the best camp I ever slept in. The hunting within tramping distance was splendid. We rarely hunted together, each preferring to go his own way. When we did not need meat we hunted varmints, and I brought in quite a number of prime coyote pelts and one wolf. One evening Bill staggered into camp with a big mountain lion over his shoulders. He just happened to run across it in a little pine thicket. That was the only one we saw on the whole trip, although their tracks were everywhere and we frequently heard their mutterings in the still evenings. The porcupines at this camp were unusually numerous. They would frequently get inside our wind break and had a great propensity for eating our soap. Lion, the hound, would not bother them; he had learned his lesson well. When they came around he would get an expression on his face as much as to say, "You give me a pain."

The nights were now very cold. It froze every night and we bedded ourselves down with lots of skins and used enormous logs on the fire so that it would keep going all night. We shot some marmots and made ourselves fur caps and gloves and patched up our outer garments with buckskin. And still the snow did not come.

One day while out hunting I saw a big goat on a bluff off to my right and determined to try to get him for his head, which appeared through my telescope to be an unusually good one. He was about half a mile off when I first spied him and the bluff extended several miles to the southwest like a great wall shutting off the view in that direction. I worked up to the foot of the bluffs and then along; climbing up several hundred feet I struck a shelf which appeared to run along the face at about the height I had seen the goat. It was ticklish work, for the shelf was covered with slide rock which I had to avoid disturbing, and then, too, in places it dwindled to a ledge barely three feet wide with about five hundred feet of nothing underneath. After about four hundred yards of this work I heard a rock fall above me and looking up saw the billy leaning over an outrageous corner looking at me. Aiming as nearly as I could straight up I let drive at the middle of the white mass. There was a grunt, a scramble and a lot of rocks, and then down came the goat, striking in between the cliff and a big boulder and not two feet from me. I fairly shivered for fear he would jump up and butt me off the ledge, but he only gave one quiver and lay still. The 330-grain bullet entering the stomach, had broken the spine and killed instantly. He was an old grandfather and had a splendid head, which I now treasure very highly. I took the head, skin, fat and some of the meat back to camp that night, having to pack it off the bluff in sections. The fat rendered out into three gold-pans full of lard. Goat-fat is excellent for frying and all through the trip it was a great saving on our bacon.

Then one night the snow came. We heard it gently tapping on the tent, and by morning there was three inches in our yard. The time had come only too soon to pull out, which we did about ten o'clock, bidding good-bye to our permanent camp with its comfortable windbreak, its fireplace, table and chairs. Below us the river ran through a canon and we had to cross quite a high mountain range to get through. As we ascended the snow got deeper and deeper. It was almost two feet deep on a level on top of the range. We had to go down a very steep hog-back, and here had trouble in plenty. The horses' feet balled up with snow and they were continually sliding. A pack horse slid down on top of my saddle horse and started him. I was on foot in front and they knocked me down and the three of us slid until stopped by a fallen tree. Such a mess I never saw. One horse was on top of another. The pack was loose and frozen ropes tangled up with everything. It took us half an hour to straighten up the mess and the frozen lash ropes cut our hands frightfully. My ankle had become slightly strained in the mix-up and for several days I suffered agonies with it. There was no stopping—we had to hit the trail hard or get snowed in. One day we stopped to hunt. Bill went out while I nursed my leg. He brought in a fine seven-point buck.

Speaking of the hunt he said: "I jumped the buck in a flat of down timber. He was going like mad about a hundred yards off when I first spied him. I threw up the old rifle and blazed away five times before he tumbled. Each time I pulled I was conscious that the sights looked just like that trademark of the Lyman sight showing the running deer and the sight. When I went over to look at the buck I had a nice little bunch of five shots right behind the shoulder. Those Lyman sights are surely the sights for a hunting rifle." Bill was one of the best shots on game I ever saw. One day I saw him cut the heads off of three grouse in trees while he sat in the saddle with his horse walking up hill. Both our rifles did mighty good work. The more I use a rifle the more I become convinced of the truth of the saying, "Beware of the man with one gun." Get a good rifle to suit you exactly. Fix the trigger pull and sights exactly as you wish them and then stick to that gun as long as it will shoot accurately and you will make few misses in the field.

Only too soon we drove our pack-train into the post. As we rode up two men were building a shack. One of them dropped a board and we nearly jumped out of our skins at the terrific noise. My! how loud everything sounded to our ears, accustomed only to the stillness of those grand mountains. We stayed at the post three days, disposing of our horses and boxing up our heads and skins, and then pulled out for civilization. Never again will such experiences come to us. The day of the wilderness hunter has gone for good. And so the hunt of our lives came to an end.

THE ALASKAN GRIZZLY

HAROLD MCCRACKEN

The great Alaskan grizzly—the Kodiak brown bear (*Ursus midden-dorffi*) and its even larger Alaska Peninsula brother (*Ursus gyas*)—is probably as far famed as either the African lion or the Bengal tiger. And yet, probably less is known of its life history than of any of the other larger mammals. He is, nevertheless, a sort of fictitious by-word at the hearths of all those hunter-sportsmen who enjoy the savor of genuine hazard in their quest for sport and trophies. A beast whom most prefer to "talk" about hunting, rather than face in mortal combat. And his 1,000 to 2,000 pounds of brawn and power is unquestionably the embodiment of all that even the most adventurous care to seek. He is supreme in size, in brute power, as well as in physical dexterity, sagacity, and pernicious damnableness in the animal kingdom. And this, not in the mere belief of a casual observer, but weighed and tried on the scales of science. To go into details regarding the life history, the "whys" and "whens" and "hows" of his life career, would entail a goodly volume, which, though immensely interesting in every detail, would be far too cumbersome in such a place as this.

His home is that long, slightly curved arm that reaches out from the southwestern corner of Alaska, separating the North Pacific Ocean from the Bering Sea, and dabbling off in the spattered Aleutian Islands. The Alaska Peninsula is today one of the most wild, least visited and less known of all the districts on this continent.

But in reality, the Alaska Peninsula is, for the most part, a terribly wild Garden of Eden. Its waterways boast more fine fish than any other similar sized section of the globe; on its rounded undulating hills and tundra lands are great herds of caribou, the finest of edible flesh; it is carpeted with berry bushes; there are fine furred animals in abundance; millions of wildfowl, duck, geese, eiders, seals, sea lions; big bears—everything necessary for the welfare and happiness of primitive man. It is a truly primitive land.

While the great Alaska Peninsula bear is a carnivore, or flesh eater—and what applies to this bear also applies in many respects to his brothers, the sub- and sub-sub-species of other districts of Alaska—yet he has frequently and correctly been called "the great grass-eating bear" and also "the great fish-eating bear." All animals subsist in the manner and on the foods that demand the least efforts, hazard and inconvenience to their life and comforts. Thus the bears of the Alaska Peninsula have chosen fish and grass and berries as their main diet of food, varied with an occasional caribou, a seal, or meal from the carcass of a dead whale or walrus washed up on the beach. During most of the months of the year, the streams are choked with salmon, affording him an inexhaustible supply until well into the middle of the winter. And as hibernation is for the most part only an alternative for existing under winter conditions, when it is hard or sometimes impossible to get food, and as the Alaska Peninsula is in winter moderated by the warming Japan Current, making it a quite mild and livable heath for old Gyas, he is forced to spend but a relatively short period in the "long sleep." This increased activity, together with the abundance of fine food, accounts for the unusual size to which the bears of that district grow.

And he is very much aware of his size and strength; and the fact that he has had no outside natural enemy through the line of his ancestors has made him aggressive, haughty and overbearing, fearing nothing and crushing all that impedes his way.

Thus the Alaska Peninsula grizzly is to be found a most unscrupulous fighter, and his acquaintance with man and his high-powered rifles is as yet too short and limited to have impressed upon his brute mind that here is a most powerful mortal enemy. He usually charges when wounded, more than frequently when a female with very young cubs is suddenly surprised or attacked, and occasionally when watching a fresh "kill" or "cache," and surprised. And, if old Gyas decides to fight, woe betide our bold Nimrod unless he is a good shot and non-excitable, or accompanied by someone who possesses these valuable faculties. For a wounded grizzly will not stop for one to reload his gun, nor pause to be shot at until the vital spot is struck. He means blood! Fifty bullets that are not placed in the proper spot will not stop him; and you can't back out once he accepts your challenge. Not that one is certain of being charged by every Alaskan grizzly that he fells; I have had even females retreat until knocked down. But these cases are really the exception, and the experiences of practically all the old bear hunters of that district—I have known most of them—will bear me out in the statement that these Alaskan grizzlies almost invariably charge under the three circumstances I have cited. The natives of Alaska do not often go to look for these big bears. They have a great deal of respect for them—as all others who know them have.

We are at King Cove, a native village near the site of the once famous village of Belkovski, center of the sea otter hunting grounds of old. We are about 600 miles southwest of Kodiak, the nearest town of over fifteen white inhabitants; and very near the extreme western end of the Alaska Peninsula, and almost due north of Honolulu by location. And here, where the traveler is almost never seen, we will start out to hunt for the biggest of carnivora—start it by incidentally being shipwrecked, almost drowned and getting a foot severely frozen.

It was on the morning of Wednesday, November 1, 1916, that I left King Cove in a 28-foot covered-over powerboat with Captain Charlie Madsen. We headed for the Isanotski Straits, at the end of the peninsula, and the Bering Sea country, where I intended hunting Grant's Barren Ground caribou and the big grizzlies at several desirable localities near the end of the peninsula.

It was cloudy; looked like another snowstorm; but the wind being from the north, rave it might and the low hills of the mainland would protect us until we reached the end of the peninsula, where we could hunt bear and wait for more favorable winds. But the winds of the North are most fickle!

It was a most magnetic sight as we plied out towards the cape at the entrance of the bay, sending flock after flock of salt-water ducks flopping off over the swelling surface of the blue-green sea. An occasional seal could be seen plunging headlong into the water from the jut of a reef or an outcrop of the rocky shoreline. The hills were gray, dappled with the first settling snows of winter, and the clouds were heavy and leaden looking.

As we rounded the cape the swells became more pronounced, carrying a deep, rolling, green-sided trough. But our boat plied steadily on, plunging its nose fearlessly into the rising waves.

Breasting some five miles of rocky coastline, we rounded the second cape at the entrance to Cold (Morofski) Bay, which protrudes some twenty-five miles back into the peninsula, almost making what is to the west an island and what is to the east the end of the peninsula. As we had expected, the wind was raging out of the bay to seaward. But heading the boat's nose towards Thin Point, about ten miles distant, we started fighting our way to the protection of the opposite cape.

Madsen had been watching the sky with misgiving and shortly announced that the wind was changing to the southwest.

I naturally inquired what would be the best course to pursue, knowing that it undoubtedly meant more storm and that we would soon be in the thick of it.

"Cap" decided we would take a chance on reaching Thin Point before the wind had swung to the southwest and thrown the storm in our faces. Once behind the cape we would be safe.

But we were not halfway across when the wind, swinging out past the protection of the peninsula and clashing against the tide, was soon lashing the sea into a stormy havoc. Diving into one great swell, the wind toppled its crest over the boat, washing overboard the hatch-cover and pouring a volume of water into the hold upon our supplies and outfit. I got on deck and endeavored to get a piece of canvas nailed over the open hatchway before another big one should pour its volume into the boat, at the same time clinging as best I could to the pitching vessel.

In the midst of all this, and as if to impress more forcibly upon us our insignificance in this big affair, our engine stopped. Gas engines are hellish things anyhow, and always buck in just the wrong place. But one must act quickly in a case such as this, and almost before I knew it the boat's sail was up and we were racing back before the wind, toward the entrance to the bay we had not long left.

I took the rope and wheel, while Madsen endeavored to get the engine running again, though vainly.

But the wind was now coming in such gusts that each one nigh turned our boat onto its nose. It was also snowing and sleeting, almost hiding the outline of the coast.

A gust hit our sail, turning the boat clear on its side, taking water over the rail, and we narrowly escaped finding ourselves in the arms of Neptune himself. Madsen left the engine and decided we would run before the wind and tack into King Cove Bay.

We crossed the entrance to the bay, driven at top speed towards the opposite cape and line of rocky reefs.

Going as close to as safe, the sail was drawn in with an endeavor to throw it to the opposite side, thus turning the boat. But the wind was too strong and the sea too rough, and try as we might, we would only be driven helplessly on towards the reef where the waves were dashing their foam and spray high in the air. Then a big wave took the flopping sail, pulling the boat over onto its side until the canvas was torn from end to end. As a last resort the anchor was thrown out; this failed to catch sufficiently to hold us and was regained at great difficulty when we saw that hitting the reef was inevitable.

The first rock of the reef that the boat hit, jammed its head through the bottom of the hull and we clambered out into the big dory we were towing and started for shore through the narrow, raging channels in the reef. But this being an open boat, it soon swamped in the breakers and we were forced to take to the water and make shore as best we could. Swimming was impossible, but keeping our heads above the water as best we could, and riding the waves, we were soon washed up on the rocky shore, like half-drowned rats.

To build a fire was impossible for lack of material; we must wait until the boat washed over the reef and was driven ashore. So, wet and cold, and facing a biting snow and sleet and rain-pelleted wind, we walked back and forth over the rocks and waited.

Through all this, while we had been battling with the elements for our very lives, I had noticed with no small interest how very little the storming and havoc had inconvenienced the little creatures that made their homes in or on the sea. The ducks swam about, quacking, and apparently thoroughly enjoying their buoyant existence. So even storms at sea, it seemed, were a mere matter of relativity and part of the everyday life of those that made their home thereon.

Eventually the boat came ashore—it was fortunately high tide— and getting aboard we got out block and tackle, sunk our anchor as a deadman, and pulled the boat up as best we could. Supplies and everything were drenched and several planks in the hull were smashed.

When we had done all that we could we started for the village—a hard hike. It was well after dark when we reached the squatty barrabaras, or native dirt huts, of King Cove, and we were wet and tired and miserable—ready for a meal and the blankets.

As I began to thaw out, however, I found that part of my right foot had frozen—the leather boots I had been wearing having shrunk and stopped the circulation of blood, causing the freezing. I was laid up for over a week with my foot, though it took Madsen, with the assistance of several natives, somewhat longer to get the boat repaired and back to the village.

Such are but a bit of the "pleasures" that often come with hunting big bear at the western end of the Alaskan Peninsula.

I was especially fortunate in making a one-day bag of four of these Alaska Peninsula bears, a big female and her three yearling cubs, the latter being as large as quite mature Southern brown bears I have gotten.

Deciding to spend a day alone in the hills after caribou, I took the .30–40 Winchester—in consideration of the bear—and followed the beach of a lagoon or bay to its head about two and half miles from the village. From the head of the lagoon a valley rose at an easy pitch for about two miles to a low divide on the opposite side of which was a large valley extending out onto the Pacific. This was a very good place for caribou.

At the head of the lagoon I stopped to shoot some salt water ducks with a .22 Colt revolver, but had fired but a few shots when I was attracted by the bawling of a bear. Glancing in the direction of the sound, I saw a brown bear making a speedy, somewhat noisy, getaway up through the alders from where he had been no doubt eating salmon in the creek a few hundred yards up-valley from me. He was then a good five hundred yards distant and in the alders. I fired, hoping at least to turn him back down the hillside, but he made the top of the ridge and went over it out of sight. I started a speedy climb up through the alders towards the top, not far from where he went over. By the time I reached this, Mr. Ursus had gone down the other side and was making a "hiyu clattewa" along the opposite side of the valley. I started up the ridge toward an open space in the alders with the intent of hurrying down to the creek and descending it with hopes of heading the bear off or getting a shot at him while crossing a wide rock slide a few hundred yards below. But I had not gone a dozen steps when I saw three other bears coming along at a good pace on quite the same course that Number One had taken. This was somewhat more of a "bear party" than I had really anticipated inviting myself to!

I felt quite certain that they would cross a small saddle through which the previous one had passed, and I decided to wait until they had come out of this and were somewhat below me before chancing a shot. I was alone, I remembered.

Squatting down in the alders, I waited with gun ready and, I must say, nerves tense. The first one to come through the saddle was the old female, a big, high-shouldered brute that strode in a manner indicating it was looking for me every bit as much as I was waiting for it. She was followed by her other two yearlings—big fellows almost as tall and as broad as they were long. Being alone, and feeling that the female would undoubtedly fight, I deemed it most wise to play doubly safe.

Conditions were fortunately in my favor. The wind was from seaward, and the alders were heavy enough to conceal me from her none too good eyesight, and it would be difficult for her to determine from just which direction the report of my rifle came. The dispatching of the old one was of course my first move. The rest would be comparatively easy. I did not have an opportunity of a good shot, however, until the three had reached the creek bed and crossed and started up along the other side. I slipped into a heavy clump of alders and waited. She was not then, I was quite sure, aware of my whereabouts at least. She lumbered slowly along, yet ever watchful, I could see. Coming out in a little open space she stopped and made an apparent survey of the surrounding vicinity. I took a coarse bead and let drive at her shoulder. I could fairly hear the bullet slap into her. With a nasal bellow she wheeled and made a vicious swipe at the nearest yearling. I fired again, at which she wheeled and charged madly along the hillside opposite me. She went into a small ravine and in a moment came up into sight on one side and stopped, snout swaying high in the air to catch a scent of the danger. I steadied my aim and at the report she went down in a heap and rolled out of sight. "A bull's-eye!" I thought, and breathed a sigh of relief.

The two cubs had made off in the opposite direction, stopping occasionally to look about. I knocked down one of these at the second shot, breaking his back, though he raised on his forelegs and bawled for all he was worth. I was about to let him have another, when out of the ravine came Mrs. Ursus, mad and apparently as much alive as ever, although dragging her right foreleg. She scrambled through the alders straight to the bawling cub. Greatly surprised, and a little uneasy, I again let drive at her. She threw her head to one side, at the same time letting forth another nasal cry. At my next shot she wheeled completely around and charged along the mountainside for a short distance with head held high and every nerve strained to its utmost to locate the cause of her molestation—snarling and bawling in a manner that made me perspire uncomfortably. She was desperate and no doubt calling upon the souls of all her past ancestors to assist her in locating the peculiar new enemy. Then she charged back to the cub. Finally she made a dash almost straight in my direction.

One does not fully appreciate the thrills of real bear hunting until he has experienced just such circumstances as this. To be alone in such a case is a quite different matter from being in company—poor though it may be.

She at last came to a standstill, standing half sidelong to me, and I clamped the gold bead square on her neck and let drive. She went down, got up, and tearing a few alders up by the roots, unwillingly sank in a heap. She had finished her career as a big brown bear on the Alaska Peninsula.

The rest was quite easy and uneventful.

With the assistance of three natives I skinned the four, took the necessary measurements for mounting, and brought the pelts in by boat. The natives, however, made a second trip, bringing in every bit of the meat of all four, salting it down for winter use. The pelts were in fine condition and beautiful specimens, the large one measuring a full ten feet. They are now in the Ohio State Museum.

It was on Sunday, November 19, 1916, that I bagged the original "bearcat"—one of the largest bears ever killed on the continent.

We were hunting around the eastern side of Frosty Peak, a high volcanic mountain towering between Morzhovi and Morofski Bays and about ten miles from the Pacific. This is about twenty miles from King Cove, near the end of the peninsula, and a very good place for big bears. It was a big one that I wanted now; and though numerous tracks and one medium-sized bear were seen, none were bothered until the original "bearcat" was found. That took two days under Old Frosty.

I had previously been hunting Grant's Barren Ground caribou on the Bering Sea side of the peninsula and before we landed at the foot of Frosty Peak on our return there was a good twelve inches of snow on the ground. In places it had already drifted to a depth of five feet. Bear hunting was quite an easy matter—though a little unpleasant on account of the snow and cold—as it was a small matter to track the animals. As the streams were still open and full of salmon, but a small percentage of the bruins had sought their winter quarters, the pads of their big clawed feet having beaten paths along the iced shores of the stream where they came periodically to gorge themselves.

It was late afternoon of the second day under Frosty Peak that we found the fresh trail of our longed-for quarry. We had been investigating the broad alder-patched table of one of the valleys that cut up toward the pinnacle of Old Frosty. There were numerous tracks along the creek where the brownies had been feasting on the silver salmon, though no fresh ones of a really large bear. But as we came well up to the head of the valley we saw the well-distinguished trail of an unquestionably large bear where it had made its way up through the snow on the mountainside into a heavy growth of alders. This was at the very foot of the peak and in the highest growth of alders. Upon reaching the tracks we were well satisfied that they could have been made only by the paw and claw of just the bear that we were seeking. Although it was evident that he had been in no special hurry in making the climb, yet it was all that a six-foot man could possibly do to step from one track to the next.

To the left of the alder patch was a comparatively open track of rocky ground with only a spare patch of brush here and there. It was certain that he could not, if still in the thicket, escape in that direction without being noticed. But on the right there was a low ridge, the opposite side of which dipped down into a deep wide ravine. The alders extended to within a few yards of this ridge, and to see the other side it was necessary to mount to the top of it. Also, it was quite probable that the bear had already gone over this ridge and might then be high up in the canyon near to its hibernation quarters.

Being unable to locate the bear with my glasses, I decided to make a complete detour around the patch, to be assured whether or not he was still in there.

So leaving Charlie on the flat below, I took the two natives and started up through the alders on the trail of old Ursus. As soon as possible we mounted the ridge at the right and went along the extent of it to assure ourselves that the bear had not crossed. This he had not. But to make doubly sure that he was still in the alder patch, we went above and around it to complete the circle about the place. He was without question lying somewhere in that thicket.

Upon reaching the flat, and as a last resource, we fired several volleys up through the alders. Then one of the natives spotted him standing in a thick growth of the alders, where he had gotten up and was looking inquiringly down at us. We moved down opposite to him and I fired from the shoulder. He started off along the mountainside, like an animal that had just broken from its cage. Then I fired again. Mounting a little knoll in the open he peered dubiously down at us—in unmistakable defiance. I held on him full in the chest for my next shot, at which he let out a bellow and came for us. My shots had hit, though he had not so much as bit or clawed at the wound on either occasion— merely jumped slightly. He was then about 200 yards distant, though I was well aware of the short time that it would take him to cover that distance. And he was a big fellow—looked literally more like a load of hay than a bear, coming down the mountainside.

I had previously told the others not to shoot until I called for help, as I was anxious to fell this big brute single-handed. But on he came, and though try as I might, I could not stop him. My shots seemed to be taking no effect whatever. And then, when he had come about half the distance, I yelled "Shoot!" And I'd have liked to have done so long before. The four guns spoke simultaneously, but old Gyas still kept coming.

I squatted down in the snow, and resting my elbows on my knees, decided to take the long chance—a shot for the head. I was confident that Madsen could stop him before he reached us, and determined to take a chance shot of dropping him in a heap. The two natives, however, were not so confident and began to move backward, shooting as they went.

He turned an angle to cross a small ravine, and while he was mounting the opposite side at a decreased pace I held just forward of the snout. The first shot missed, as I saw a small flit of snow where it hit just in front of him. But at the second shot he dropped in a heap, falling on his belly with his nose run into the snow. After waiting for some moments to make certain he was beyond the trouble point, we climbed up through the alders to where he lay. The others stood by with guns ready while I went up and poked him with the end of my own gun. He was dead.

This had all taken but a few moments, though relatively it seemed a great deal longer.

He was indeed a big fellow—a genuine bearcat. We gutted him, and as it was then getting late, hit for camp. The next morning we went back to skin the animal—and no small task it was!

He had been hit twelve times, we found. Nine of the shots had entered the neck and shoulder and two in the head and one in the abdomen. One bullet had hit him squarely in the mouth, shattering the tops of his lower teeth on one side, piercing the tongue and lodging in the back of his throat. Four of the .30 caliber leads were retrieved from the shoulder, where they had not so much as reached the bone. The shot that stopped him struck well up on the brain box, but squarely enough to break the casing of the bone and penetrate the skull, though only a part of the lead entered the brain, the most of it spattering off in the fleshy part of the head. It was a lucky shot on an even more lucky day!

We estimated his live weight at from 1,600 to 1,800 pounds, and the skin at twelve feet in length. The actual measurements of the tanned skin, however, as made by Chas. A. Ziege, noted taxidermist of Spokane, Wash., are: eleven feet four inches maximum length, by ten feet six inches spread of fore legs. The skull, measured one year after killing, eighteen and one-quarter inches, or one-half inch under the world record, according to Washington, D. C., authorities.

THE PLURAL OF MOOSE IS MISE

IRWIN S. COBB

At the outset, when our expedition was still in the preparatory stages, we collectively knew a few sketchy details regarding the general architectural plan and outward aspect of the moose. One of us had once upon a time, years and years before, shot at or into—this point being debatable—a moose up in Maine. Another professed that in his youth he had seriously annoyed a moose with buckshot somewhere in Quebec. The rest of us had met the moose only in zoos with iron bars between us and him or in dining halls, where his head, projecting in a stuffed and mounted condition from the wall, gave one the feeling of dining with somebody out of the Old Testament. Speaking with regard to his family history, we understood he was closely allied to the European elk—the Unabridged told us that—and we gathered that, viewed at a distance, he rather suggested a large black mule with a pronounced Roman nose and a rustic hatrack sprouted out between his ears. Also, through our reading upon the subject, we knew that next to the buffalo he was the largest vegetarian in North America and, next to a man who believes in the forecast of a campaign manager on the eve of an election, the stupidest native mammal that we have. By hearsay we had been made aware that he possessed a magnificent sense of smell and a perfectly wonderful sense of hearing, but was woefully shy on the faculty of thought, the result being that while by the aid of his nose and his ear he might all day elude you, if then perchance you did succeed in getting within gunning range of him he was prone to remain right where he was, peering blandly at you and accommodatingly shifting his position so as to bring his shape broadside on, thereby offering a better target until you, mastering the tremors of eagerness, succeeded in implanting a leaden slug in one of his vital areas.

But, offhand, we couldn't decide what the plural of him was. Still if the plural of goose were geese and the plural of mouse were mice it seemed reasonable to assume that the plural of moose should be mise. Besides, we figured that when we had returned and met friends and told them about our trip it would sound more impressive, in fact more plural, to say that we had slain mise rather than that we had slaughtered moose. In the common acceptance of the term as now used, moose might mean one moose or a herd of them, but mise would mean at least a bag of two of these mighty creatures and from two on up to any imaginable number.

One mentally framed the conversation:

"Well, I hear you've been up in Canada moose hunting." This is the other fellow speaking. "Kill any moose?"

"Kill any moose? Huh, we did better than that—we killed mise."

So by agreement we arranged that mise it should be. This being settled we went ahead with plans for outfitting ourselves against our foray into the game country. We equipped ourselves with high-powered rifles, with patent bedding rolls, with fanciful conceits in high boots and blanket overcoats. We bought everything that the clerk in the shop, who probably had never ventured north of the Bronx in all the days of his sheltered life, thought we should buy, including wicked-looking sheath knives and hand axes to be carried in the belt, tomahawk fashion, and pocket compasses. Personally, I have never been able to figure out the exact value of a compass to a man adrift in a strange country. What is the use of knowing where north is if you don't know where you are? Nevertheless, I was prevailed upon to purchase a compass, along with upward of a great gross of other articles large and small which the clerk believed would be needful to one starting upon such an expedition as we contemplated.

On my account he did a deal of thinking. Not since the fall of 1917, when we were making the world safe for the sporting-goods dealers of America, could he have spent so busy and so happy an afternoon as the afternoon when I dropped in on him.

By past experience I should have known better than to permit myself to be swept off my feet by this tradesman's flood of suggestions and recommendations. Already I had an ample supply of khaki shirts that were endeared to me by associations of duck-hunting forays in North Carolina and chill evenings in an Adirondack camp and a memorable journey to Wyoming, where the sage hen abides. I treasured a pair of comfortable hunting boots that had gone twice to European battlefields and down into the Grand Canyon and up again and across the California desert, without ever breeding a blister or chafing a shin. Among my most valued possessions I counted an ancient shooting coat, wearing which I had missed quail in Kentucky, snipe on Long Island, grouse in Connecticut, doves in Georgia, and woodcock in New York State. Finally, had I but taken time for sober second consideration, I should have recalled that the guides I have from time to time known considered themselves properly accoutered for the chase when they put on the oldest suit of store clothes they owned and stuck an extra pair of wool socks in their pockets. But to the city-bred sportsman half the joy of going on a camping trip consists in getting ready for it. So eminent an authority as Emerson Hough is much given to warning the amateur sportsman against burdening himself with vain adornments, and yet I am reliably informed that the said Hough has a larger individual collection of pretty devices in canvas and leather than any person in this republic.

That clerk had a seductive way about him; he had a positive gift. Otherwise I suppose he would have been handling some line which practically sells itself, such as oil stocks or mining shares. Under the influence of his blandishments I invested in a sweater of a pattern which he assured me was being favored by the really prominent moose hunters in the current season, and a pair of corduroy hunting pants which, when walked in, gave off a pleasant swishing sound like a soft-shoe dancer starting to do a sand jig. I was particularly drawn to these latter garments as being the most vocal pants I had ever seen. As I said before, I bought ever and ever so many other things; I am merely mentioning some of the main items.

We assembled the most impassive group of guides in the whole Dominion—men who, filled with the spirit of the majestic wilds, had never been known publicly to laugh at the expense of a tender-footed stranger. They did not laugh at Harry Leon Wilson's conception of the proper equipment for a man starting upon such an excursion as this one. Wilson on being wired an invitation to go on a hunt for moose promptly telegraphed back that to the best of his recollection he had not lost any moose, but that if any of his friends had been so unfortunate or so careless as to mislay one he would gladly join in the quest for the missing. He brought along an electric flashlight, in case the search should be prolonged after nightfall, a trout rod and a camera. The guides did not laugh at Colonel Tillinghast Houston's unique notion of buying an expensive rifle and a hundred rounds of ammunition and then spending his days in camp sitting in a tent reading a history of the Maritime Provinces in two large volumes. They did not laugh at

Colonel Bozeman Bulger's overseas puttees or at Damon Runyon's bowie knife, or at Major McGeehan's eight-pound cartridge belt—it weighed more than that when loaded; I am speaking of it, net—or at Frank Stevens' sleeping cap or at Bill MacBeth's going-away haircut— the handiwork of a barber who was a person looking with abhorrence upon the thought of leaving any hair upon the human neck when it is so easy to shave all exposed surfaces smooth and clean from a point drawn across the back of the head at the level of the tops of the ears on down as far as the rear collar button. He must have been a lover of the nude in necks, that barber.

The guides did not laugh even at my vociferous corduroys, which at every step I took, went hist, hist, as though entreating their wearer to be more quiet so they might the better be heard.

By a series of relay journeys we moved up across the line into Quebec, thence back again below the boundary and across the state of Maine, thence out of Maine into New Brunswick and to the thriving city of St. John, with its justly celebrated reversible falls which, by reason of the eccentricities of the tide, tumble upstream part of the time and downstream part of the time, thence by steamer across that temperamental body of water known as the Bay of Fundy, and so on into the interior of Nova Scotia. If anywhere on this continent there is a lovelier spot than the southern part of Nova Scotia in mid-fall I earnestly desire that, come next October, someone shall take me by the hand and lead me to it and let me rave. It used to be the land of Evangeline and the Acadians; now it is the land of the apple. You ran out of the finnan-haddie belt in and around Digby into the wonderful valley of the apples. On every hand are apples—on this side of the right-of-way, orchards stretching down to the blue waters of one of the most beautiful rivers in America, on that side, orchards climbing up the flanks of the rolling hills to where the combing of thick timber comes down and meets them; and everywhere, at roadside, on the verges of thickets, in pastures and old fields, are seedlings growing singly, in pairs and in clumps. They told us that the valley scenically considered is at its best in the spring after the bloom bursts out upon the trees and the whole countryside turns to one vast pink and white bridal bouquet, but hardly can one picture it revealing itself as a more delectable vision than when the first frosts have fallen and every bough of every tree is studded with red and green and yellow globes and the scent of the ripened fruit rises like an incense of spices and wine.

The transition from the pastoral to the wilderness is abrupt. You leave Annapolis Royal in a motor car—that is, you do if you follow in our footsteps—and almost immediately you strike into the big game country. Not that the big game does not lap over into the settlements and even into the larger towns on occasion, for it does. It is recorded that on a certain day a full-grown moose—and a full-grown moose is almost the largest full-grown thing you ever saw—strolled through one of the principal streets of St. John and sought to enter—this being in the old sinful times—a leading saloon. A prominent lawyer of the same city told me that some four weeks before our arrival a woman client of his, living some two miles from the corporate limits, called him on the telephone at his office to ask his professional advice as to how legally she might go about getting rid of a bull moose which insisted on frequenting her orchard and frightening her children when they went to gather pippins. She felt, she said, that a lawyer was the proper person to seek in the emergency that had arisen, seeing that the closed season for moose was still on and it would be unlawful to take a shot at the intruder, so what she particularly desired to know was whether she couldn't have him impounded for trespass or something of that nature.

But such things as these do not happen every day. Probably a man could spend months on end in St. John without seeing the first of the above-mentioned animals rambling down the sidewalk in the manner of a young moose-about-town and trying to drop into the place where the saloon used to be, only to back out again, with chagrin writ large upon his features, upon discovering that the establishment in question had been transformed into a hat store.

To meet the moose where frequently he is and not merely where occasionally he is, one must go beyond the outlying orchards and on into the vasty expanse of the real moose country—hundreds of hundreds of miles of virgin waste, trackless except for game trails and portages across the ridges between waterways. It is a country of tamaracks and hemlocks, of maples and beech and birch, of berries and flowering shrubs, of bogs and barrens and swampy swales, of great granite boulders left behind by the glaciers when the world was young and thawing, of countless lakes and brawling white rapids and deep blue pools where, in the spawning season, the speckled trout are so thick that the small trout have to travel on the backs of the larger ones to avoid being crushed in the jam. I did not see this last myself; my authority for the statement is my friend the veracious lawyer of St. John. But I saw all the rest of it—the woods wearing the flaunting war-paint colors of the wonderful Canadian Indian summer—crimson of huckleberry, tawny of tamarack, yellow of birch, scarlet of maple; the ruffed grouse strutting, unafraid as barnyard fowl and, thanks be to a three-year period of protection, almost as numerous as sparrows in a city street; the signs of hoofed and padded creatures crossing and crisscrossing wherever the earth was soft enough to register the foot tracks of wild things.

And if you want to know how interior New Brunswick looked after Nova Scotia, you are respectfully requested to reread the foregoing paragraph, merely leaving out some of the lakes and most of the boulders.

On a flawless morning, in a motorboat we crossed a certain lake, and I wish I knew the language that might serve to describe the glory of the colors that ringed that lake around and were reflected to the last flame-tipped leaf and the last smooth white column of birchen trunk in its still waters, but I don't. I'll go further and say I can't believe Noah Webster had the words to form the picture, and he had more words than anybody up to the time William J. Bryan went actively into politics. As for myself, I can only say that these colors fairly crackled. There were hues and combinations of hues, shadings and contrasts such as no artist ever has painted and no artist will care to paint, either, for fear of being called a nature faker.

The scene shifts to our main camp. We have met our guides and have marveled at their ability to trot over steep up-and-down-hill portages carrying, each one of them, upon his back a load which no humane man would put on a mule, and have marveled still more when these men, having deposited their mountainous burdens at the farther end of the carry, go hurrying back across the ridge presently to reappear bearing upon their shoulders upturned canoes, their heads hidden inside the inverted interiors and yet by some magic gift peculiar to their craft, managing somehow to dodge the overhanging boughs of trees and without losing speed or changing gait to skip along from one slick round-topped boulder top to another.

Now we are in the deep woods, fifty miles from a railroad and thirty miles from a farmhouse. We sleep at night in canvas leantos, with log fires at our feet; we wash our faces and hands in the lake and make high resolves—which we never carry out—to take dips in that same frosty water; we breakfast at sun-up and sup at dusk in a log shanty set behind the cluster of tents, and between breakfast and supper we seek, under guidance, for fresh meat and dining-room trophies.

We have come too late for the calling season, it seems. In the calling season Mr. Moose desires female society, and by all accounts desires it mightily. So the guide takes a mean advantage of his social cravings. Generally afoot, but sometimes in a canoe, he escorts the gunner to a likely feeding ground or a drinking place and through a scroll of birch bark rolled up in a megaphone shape, he delivers a creditable imitation of the call of the flirtatious cow moose. There are guides who can sound the love note through their cupped hands, but most of the fraternity favor the birchen cornucopia. The sound—part lonely bleat, part plaintive bellow—travels across the silent reaches for an incredible distance. Once when the wind was right there is record of a moose call having been heard six miles away from where it was uttered, but in this case the instrumentalist was Louis Harlowe, a half-breed Micmac Indian, the champion moose caller of Nova Scotia and perhaps of the world.

In the bog where he is lying, or on the edge of the barren where he is feeding, the bull hears the pleading entreaty and thereby is most grossly deceived. Forgetting the caution which guides his course at other times, he hurries to where the deceiver awaits him, in his haste smashing down saplings, clattering his great horns against the tree boles, splashing through the brooks. And then when he bursts forth into the open, snorting and puffing and grunting, the hunter beholds before him a target which in that setting and with that background must loom up like a grain elevator. Yet at a distance of twenty yards or thirty, he has been known to miss the mark clean and to keep on missing it, while the vast creature stands there, its dull brain filled with wonder that the expected cow should not be where he had had every vocal assurance that she would be, and seemingly only mildly disturbed by the crashing voice of the repeater and by the unseen, mysterious things which pass whistling over his back or under his belly as the gun quivers in the uncertain grasp of the overanxious or mayhap the buckague-stricken sportsman.

Once though he has made up his sluggish mind that all is not well for him in that immediate vicinity, he vanishes into deep cover as silently as smoke and as suddenly as a wink.

The mating time comes in mid-September and lasts about a month, more or less; and since the open season does not begin until October the first, it behooves the hunter who wishes to bag his moose with the least amount of physical exertion to be in camp during the first two weeks of October, for after that the bull moose is reverting to bachelorhood again. He may answer the call, but the chances are that he will not.

A little later on, after the snows have come, one may trail him with comparative ease. Besides, he is browsing more liberally then and consequently is moving pretty consistently. But between the time when the leaves begin to fall and the time when the snow begins to fly he is much given to staying in the densest coverts he can find and doing the bulk of his grazing by night.

So he must be still-hunted, as the saying goes, and it was still-hunting that we were called upon to do. The guide takes his birch-bark horn along each morning when he starts out, carrying it under one arm and an axe under the other, and upon his back a pouch containing the ingredients for a midday lunch and the inevitable fire-blackened teapot, which he calls by the affectionate name of "kittle." He never speaks of stopping for lunch. When the sun stands overhead and your foreshortened shadow has snuggled up close beneath your feet like a friendly black puppy, he suggests the advisability of "biling a kittle," by which he means building a fire and making tea. So the pack between his shoulders is necessary but the moose call is largely ornamental; it is habit for him to tote it and tote it he does; but mainly he depends upon his eyes and his ears and his uncanny knowledge of the ways of the thing we aim to destroy.

Yes, they call it still-hunting and still-hunting it truly is so far as Louis Harlowe, the half-breed, or Sam Glode, the full-blooded Micmac, or Charley Charlton, the head guide, is concerned, as he goes worming his way through the undergrowth in his soft-soled moccasins, instinctively avoiding the rotted twig, the loose bit of stone and the swishy bough. But the pair of us, following in his footsteps, in our hard-bottomed, hobnailed boots, our creaky leather gear and our noisy waterproofed nether garments, cannot, by the wildest latitude in descriptive terminology, be called still-hunters. Carrying small avalanches with us, we slide down rocky slopes which the guide on ahead of us negotiated in pussyfooted style; and we blunder into undergrowth; and we trip over logs and we flounder into bogs and out of them again with loud, churning sounds. Going into second on a hillside we pant like switch engines. I was two weeks behind with my panting when I came out of Canada and at odd times now I still pant briskly, trying to catch up.

Reaching level ground we reverse gears and halt to blow. Toward mid-afternoon, on the homebound hike, our weary legs creak audibly at the joints and our tired feet blunder and fumble among the dried leaves. We create all the racket which, without recourse to bass drums or slide trombones, it is humanly possible for a brace of overdressed, city-softened sojourners to create in deep woods. And still our guide— that person so utterly lacking in a sense of humor—speaks of our endeavor as still-hunting. If an ethical Nova Scotian guide—and all professional guides everywhere, so far as I have observed, are most ethical—were hired to chaperon Sousa's band on a still-hunt through the wilderness and on the way Mr. Sousa should think up a new march full of oom-pahs and everything, and the band should practice it while cruising from bog to barren, the guide, returning to the settlements after the outing, would undoubtedly refer to it as a still-hunt.

In our own case, I trust that our eagerness in some measure compensated for our awkwardness. At least, we worked hard—worked until muscles that we never knew before we had achingly forced themselves upon our attention. Yes, if for the first day or two our exertion brought us no reward in the shape of antlered frontlets or great black pelts drying on the rocks at the canoe landing or savory moose steaks in the frying pan; if it seemed that after all we would have to content ourselves with taking home a stuffed guide's head or so; if twilight found us reuniting at the supper table each with tales of endless miles of tramping to our credit but no game, nevertheless and notwithstanding, the labor we spent was not without its plenteous compensations.

To begin with, there was ever the hope that beyond the next thicket or across the next swale old Mr. Sixty Inch Spread would be browsing about waiting for us to come stealing upon him with all the stealthy approach of a runaway moving van and blow him over. There was the joy of watching our guide trailing, he reading the woods as a scholar reads a book and seeing there plain as print what we never would have seen—the impress of a great splayed hoof in the yellowed moss, the freshly gnawed twigs of the moose wood, the scarred bark high up on a maple to show that here a bull had whetted his horns, the scuffed earth where a bear had been digging for grubs, the wallow a buck deer had made at a crossing. And when he told us that the moose had passed this way, trotting, less than an hour before, but that the deer's bed was at least two nights old, while the bear's scratching dated back for days, we knew that he knew. Real efficiency in any line carries its own credentials and needs no bolstering affidavits. There may be better eyes in some human head than the pair Louis Harlowe owns or than that equally keen pair belonging to Harry Allen, the dean of New Brunswick guides, but I have yet to see their owner, and I am quite sure that for woodcraft there are no better equipped men anywhere than the two I have named.

We couldn't decide which was the finer—the supper at night with a great log fire chasing back the dense shadows, and the baked beans and the talk and the crisp bacon and the innocent lies passing back and forth or the midday lunch out in the tangy, painted forest, miles and miles away from anywhere at all, with the chickadees and the snow-birds and the robins flittering about, waiting their chance to gather the crumbs they knew we would leave behind for them, and with the moose birds informally dropping in on us before ever the kettle had begun to sing.

Naturalists know the moose bird, I believe, as the Canada jay and over the line in the States they call him the venison hawk, but by any name he is a handsome, saucy chap, as smart as Satan and as impudent as they make 'em. The first thin wisp of your fire, rising above the undergrowth, is his signal. For some of the denizens of the wilder-ness it may be just twelve o'clock, but to him it's feeding time. Here he comes in his swooping flight, a graceful, slate-blue figure with his snowy bib and tucker like a trencherman prepared. And there, follow-ing close behind him, are other members of his tribe. There always is one in the flock more daring than the rest. If you sit quietly, this fellow will flit closer and closer, his head cocked on one side, uttering half-doubtful, half-confident cheeps until he is snatching up provender right under your feet or even out of your hand. His preference is for meat—raw meat for choice, but his taste is catholic; he'll eat anything. Small morsels he swallows on the spot, larger tidbits he takes in his bill and flies away with to hide in a nearby tree crotch. His friends watch him, and by the time he has returned for another helping they have stolen his cache, so that chiefly what he gets out of the burden of his thriftful industry is the exercise. I do not know whether this should teach us that it is better to strive to lay something against a rainy day and take a chance on the honesty of the neighbors or to seize our pleasure when and where we find it and forget the morrow. Aesop might be able to figure it out, but, being no Aesop, I must continue to register uncertainty.

Campfire suppers and high noon barbecues and glorious sunrises and shooting the rapids in the rivers and paddling across the blue lake, scaring up the black duck and the loons from before us, and all the rest of it, was fine enough in its way, but it was not killing the bull moose. So we hunted and we hunted. We dragged our reluctant feet through moose bogs—beaver meadows these are in the Adirondacks—and we ranged the high ground and the low. Cow moose we encountered frequently and calves aplenty. But the adult male was what we sought.

We had several close calls, or perhaps I should say he did. One of our outfit—nameless here because I have no desire to heap shame upon an otherwise well-meaning and always dependable companion—had been cruising through thick timber all day without seeing anything to fire at. Emerging into an open glade on a ridge above Little Red Lake, he was moved to try his new and virgin automatic at a target. So he loosed off at one of the big black crows of the North that was perched, like a disconsolate undertaker, with bunched shoulders and drooping head, on a dead tamarack fifty yards away. He did not hit Brother Corbie but he tore the top out of the tamarack snag. And then when he and the guide had rounded the shoulder of the little hill and descended to a swamp below they read in certain telltale signs a story which came near to moving the marksman to tears.

Moving up the slope from the other side the guide had been calling, a bull moose—and a whaling big one, to judge by his hoof marks—

had been stirred to inquire into the circumstances. He had quitted the swamp and had ambled up the hill to within a hundred yards of the crest when—as the guide deduced it—the sound of the shot just above caused him to halt and swing about and depart from that neighborhood at his very best gait. But for that unlucky rifle report he probably would have walked right into the enemy. My friend does not now feel toward crows as he formerly felt. He thinks they should be abolished.

An experience of mine was likewise fraught with the germs of a tragic disappointment. In a densely thicketed district, my guide, with a view to getting a view of the surrounding terrain above the tops of the saplings, scaled the steep side of a boulder that was as big as an icehouse and then beckoned to me to follow.

But as a scaler I am not a conspicuous success. By main strength and awkwardness I managed to clamber up. Just as I reached the top and put my rifle down so that I might fan breath into myself with both hands, my boot soles slipped off the uncertain surface and I slid off my perch into space. Wildly I threw out both arms in a general direction. My clutching fingers closed on a limb of a maple which overshadowed the rock and I swung out into the air twelve feet or so above the inhospitable earth, utterly unable to reach with my convulsively groping feet the nearermost juts of granite. For an agonized moment it seemed probable that the only thing that might break my fall would be myself. But I kept my presence of mind. I flatter myself that in emergencies I am a quick thinker. As I dangled there an expedient came to me. I let go gradually.

And then as I plumped with a dull sickening thud into the herbage below and lay there weaponless, windless and jarred I saw, vanishing into the scrub not a hundred feet away, the black shape of a big and startled moose. I caught one fleeting glimpse of an enormous head, of a profile which might have belonged to one of the major prophets, of a set of horns outspreading even as the fronded palm outspreads itself, of a switching tail and a slab-sided rump, and then the shielding bushes closed and the apparition was gone, and gone for keeps. For my part there was nothing to do but to sit there for a spell and cherish regrets. Under the circumstances, trailing a frightened bull moose would have been about as satisfactory as trailing a comet, and probably not a bit more successful as to results.

For the majority of the members of our troupe the duration of the hunt had a time limit. On the afternoon of the last day in camp two of the party strolled into the immediate presence of a fair-sized bull and, firing together, one of them put a slug of lead in a twitching ear which he turned toward them. It must have been his deaf ear, else he would have been aware of their approach long before. But one moose was singular and the achievement of the plural number was our ambition. So four of us crossed back into New Brunswick, where, according to all native New Brunswickers, the moose grow larger than they do in the sister province, Nova Scotians taking the opposing side and being willing to argue it at all times.

With unabated determination the gallant quartet of us hunted and hunted. Three big deer died to make holiday for us but the moose displayed a coyness and diffidence which might be accounted for only on the ground that they heard we were coming. Indeed they could not very well help hearing it.

Each morning under the influence of the frost the flaming frost colors showed a dimming hue. Day before yesterday they had been like burning brands, yesterday there were dulled embers, today smoldering coals; and tomorrow they would be as dead ashes. Each night the sun went down in a nimbus of cold gray clouds. There was a taste and a smell as of snow in the air. The last tardy robin packed up and went south; the swarms of juncos grew thicker; wedge-shaped flights of coot and black duck passed overhead, their bills all pointing toward the Gulf of Mexico. Then on the last day there fell a rain which turned to sleet and the sleet to snow—four inches of it—and in the snow on that last day the reward which comes—sometimes—to the persevering was ours.

To know the climactic sensation which filled the triumphant amateur you must first of all care for the outdoors and for big-game shooting, and in the second place you must have known the feeling of hope deferred, and in the third place you must have reached the eleventh hour, so to speak, of your stay in these parts with the anticipation you had been nurturing for all these weeks since the trip was first proposed still unrealized in your soul.

You and your camp mate and your guide were on the last lap of the journey back to camp; the sun was slipping down the western wall of the horizon; the shadows were deepening under the spruces; you rounded the shoulder of a ridge and stood for a moment at your guide's back looking across a fire-burned barren. He stiffened like a pointer on a warm scent and pointed straight ahead. Your eye followed where his finger aimed, and two hundred yards away you saw a dark blot against a background of faded tamarack—a bull standing head-on. You shot together, you and your companion. Apparently the animal swung himself about and started moving at the seemingly languid lope of the moose, which really is a faster gait than you would suppose until you measure the length of his stride. You kept on firing, both of you, as rapidly almost as you could pull the triggers of your automatics. Twice he shook himself and humped his hindquarters as though stung, but he did not check his speed. You emptied your magazine, five shots. Your mate's fifth shell jammed in the chamber, putting him out of the running for the moment. In desperate haste you fumbled one more shell into your rifle, and just as the fugitive topped a little rise before disappearing for good into the shrouding second growth you got your sight full on the mark and sent a farewell bullet whistling on its way. The black hulk vanished magically.

"That'll do," said your guide, grinning broadly. "You got 'im. But load up again before we go down there. He's down and down for keeps, I think, judgin' by the way he flopped, but he might get up again."

But he didn't get up again. You came on him where he lay, still feebly twitching, with two flesh wounds in his flanks and a third hole right through him behind the shoulders—a thousand pounds of meat, a head worth saving and mounting and bragging about in the years to come, a pelt as big as a double blanket and at last the accomplished plural of moose was mise.

So then you did what man generally does when language fails to express what he feels. You harked back sundry thousands of years and you did as your remote ancestors, the cave dweller, did when he slew the sabretoothed whatyoumaycallhim. About the carcass of your kill you executed a war dance; at least you did if you chambered the emotions which filled the present writer to the choking point.

And then the next day, back in the settlements, when you reunited with the two remaining members of the outfit who had been in camp eight miles away from the camp where you stayed, and when you learned that now there was a total tally of three deceased beasties, the war dance was repeated, only this time it was a four-handed movement instead of a solo number.

BRANT SHOOTING ON GREAT SOUTH BAY

EDWIN MAIN POST

Thirty years ago this spring my wise father built a flat-bottomed sloop, forty-five feet long on the keel and seventeen feet wide, with an enclosed cabin that has square windows instead of portholes, and head room of six feet all over it. This cabin is twenty-one feet long, and consists of one large room with four wide berths, and a toilet room and a kitchen on either side of the centerboard at the forward end. Forward of the cabin beneath the deck there are three berths for the crew, an icebox and a large place for the storage of provisions.

Father named the boat Macy after an old friend, and has had her continuously in commission since she was launched; and Andrew Sammis, her first captain, is still in charge—a bit gray now, but still the same careful and trustworthy skipper as of yore. With the opening of the ducking season in October she goes into what we call winter commission, and when the end of the season comes around she is hauled out, thoroughly overhauled and prepared for the summer work. A few years ago we built an overhanging stern on her and installed a gasoline engine, so that we are no longer the slaves of the wind god. The Macy's Baby, as the stool-boat that carries the battery* is called,

---

* (Editor's Note: Now illegal in waterfowling, the battery was a flat, raft-like boat in which a shooter would lie on his back and be almost invisible in a spread of decoys.)

is always at her stern, and this, with the addition of two skiffs and one or more dinkies for use in the ice, makes quite a formidable tow for the old boat. When we have more than a day or two to spend in quest of the wily duck, we send the Macy out early to get a good place, and have a catboat meet us at the dock to sail us over to her. Generally we catch a train that arrives at Babylon, Long Island, at half-past three o'clock, and we reach the dock ten minutes afterwards.

Lay aside for a few moments your troubles and worries and come with us to kill some brant. The Macy is awaiting us, anchored just off the dock, and we see our good George coming off in the little skiff to speedily set us on board.

As you board the skiff you will not have to ask George, "Are there any birds?" for he will say: "Brant? Why, there's five million of the cusses in Cedar Island Cove. We'll have some o' them critters and don't you forget it." Captain Andrew greets us with a cheery "Good day, gentlemen," as we reach the side, and you enter the cabin to find upon the table a pleasant welcome in the shape of a generous cocktail for each of us. My father's hearty toast, "Glad to see you on board, sir," makes you feel at home at once, and as you glance around at the comfortable quarters you see that my tales of luxury have not been exaggerated.

We promptly lay aside our "store clothes" and don our old shooting things, as the men get the anchor up and hoist the sail, and are soon in the cockpit enjoying the fresh air. Our progress is slow and stately, due to the flotilla behind us, but we have only about four miles to go. Notice now the third member of our crew, a big, tall, fair-haired man with a smile that never comes off. This is Ansel, a newcomer to the Macy in comparison with the skipper, for Ansel has been with us only twenty years. He is a very important personage, for he is the engineer, chef, mate, general utility man and fun-maker for us all. Hark! There is his voice now calling us to dinner.

You sit down before a smoking leg of lamb and dishes of vegetables, with an appetite to which you have been a stranger for a long time, and eat and eat of the good things before you until you are astonished at yourself. Topping off with some of the chef's famous pudding, and helping yourself to a good cigar from the box on the centerboard trunk, you are content. I take the wheel to let the men go below to eat their dinner, and by the time they have finished we arrive at the place where we will set out the battery in the morning. While Andrew and George are furling the sail and making all snug on deck for the night, Ansel is putting things to rights below, and we cover the table with a green cloth and sit down to pass the time at a card game.

At ten o'clock we begin a round of jackpots, and when that is over, we turn into our berths ready for an early call to breakfast. At four o'clock we are called, and by the time we are dressed the breakfast is piping hot on the table. We hurry through our meal to let the men eat theirs, and while they are fixing out the battery and stool, we take a bit of a nap.

The skipper calls us when he sees the men have the stool nearly all out, and you and I put on our sweaters and a dark coat, take our guns and shells, and get into the skiff, to be rowed to the battery. The battery, or "box," as it is more often termed, is set pretty well to the windward of the bulk of the decoys, with just enough of them around it to hide it from birds coming down on the head; and in getting in we pick our way carefully through the decoys and step from the skiff well over toward the center, so as not to get any water in the boxes. On the deck of the box we have twelve iron decoys that are cut off on the bottom, so as not to loom up higher than those on the water, and these we distribute around, heads to the wind, to make the box lay level. We each have a rubber cloth and an old sweater to lie on, and a cloth-covered rubber pillow for our heads. Adjusting these comfortably, we load our guns, cock them and place them against the side on our right hand, taking care to keep at least two inches of the barrels over the end of the box, so that in case of an accidental discharge there will be no hole blown in the box. Long experience in battery shooting has taught me that the longer the barrels of a gun are, the safer it is, and I heartily recommend thirty-two-inch barrels.

Being all ready, we lie down, with only our eyes above the level of the water, and await the coming of our quarry. Two men with sharp eyes can keep a pretty thorough watch, except just behind them, and birds coming from that quarter generally swing off to one side or the other of the stool so that they can set their wings and light among the decoys headed up to the wind. You, as the guest of honor, are in the left-hand box, and just as the sun is rising I see a bunch of brant coming in over the beach from the ocean where they have been roosting. I think they will pass near enough to see our stool, so we lie very close, and occasionally I call them. But the moment they see the stool—and you can always tell this, because they give a sort of dart up in the air and, if they are coming in, settle down again headed toward us—I make no further calls, but say to you: "They are coming in on your side. Lie perfectly still until I say 'Now!' and then give it to them."

It is one of the most inspiriting sights in the world to see a bunch of these lordly birds headed for the stool, and a great many people are deceived as to the distance they are off, on account of their great size—often losing a good chance by rising too quickly. I watch them with one eye above the edge of the box as they set their wings and come gracefully to the stool, and when they are in good range, I say "Now! Let's try 'em!" and we sit up with our guns in our hands and fire. As they are on your side and headed up to windward, you will get the best show, because I must shoot at the tail of the bunch and will not have as good a chance to catch a double as you. You can count on my killing right and left, however, and as my second bird starts to fall, I see you have three down.

"Well done, my friend. We are not going to be skunked today. There are five of them, anyhow."

We both reload our guns, and I take my cap in my hand and swing it until I see an answering signal from the Macy. This means that they are to come down in the skiff and pick up our game.

There are three things of great importance in battery shooting: the first to be able to kill when the bird is in range, the second to be able to call, and the third to know how to use the "flopper." It is a bundle of worn-out mittens, tied together with a bit of string, that I keep in my hand as we lie in wait for the game, and it is used to attract the attention of birds that are passing too far away to see the stool. As I am about to explain the use of this queer contrivance, I see a bunch of brant leading through the bay to the north of us, about a mile away. If they keep their present course they will pass us without seeing our stool. Something must be done to attract their attention. Quickly I flop the flopper up above the level of the box two or three times, carefully watching for any sign that the birds have noticed something. If there is no such sign, I flop again.

Ah, this time they have seen it, for they rise in the air and head toward us. Now we lie close, and they come straight for our stool. If I were to flop even once after they have seen the stool, they would be off like a shot—and it is just here that the science of using the flopper means so much. This time they head up on my side, and, when I give the word, we fire, you to kill two, while I am lucky enough to double with each barrel. When George arrives with the skiff and we tell him eleven brant are down, he smiles all over.

I call to George to bring father down when he comes out to pick up again, for your day would not be complete without an hour or two in the box with that peerless sportsman, who is today, at the age of seventy-seven, one of the best shots I have ever seen. We kill again, and George comes down with father. As I get into the boat, father steps into the box with agility equal to mine, and I leave you to an enjoyment that has been the dearest privilege in my life. We have scarcely reached the Macy when you swing again, and I take up the glasses to watch with interest your good work.

As noontide comes we get the Macy under way and drop down to the box, to reward you with a cocktail when you come aboard, and have all ready a smoking lunch of Ansel's best. After lunch we take turns in the battery, and, when the time comes to take up, we count a row of brant along the washer and find thirty-five. We return to Babylon in ample time for you to catch your train, and we do not let you go until you promise to come again.

For Shame, Minnesota!

It is time that sportsmen awoke to the fact that they have interests to be considered and protected as well as any other class of citizens. Now Minnesota proposes to follow the selfish and mistaken policy pursued by other states and impose a tax upon nonresident sportsmen. It is hoped that such a measure will meet with serious opposition.

—*FIELD & STREAM*, JANUARY, 1899.

BEAR HUNTING IN THE SMOKIES

HORACE KEPHART

"Git up, pup! You've scrounged right in hyur in front of the far [fire]. You Dred! Whut makes you so blamed contentious?"

Little John shoved both dogs into a corner, and strove to scrape some coals from under a beech forestick that glowed almost hot enough to melt brass.

"This is the wust coggled-up far I ever seen, to fry by. Bill, hand me some Old Ned from that suggin' o' mine."

A bearded hunchback reached his long arm to a sack that hung under our rifles, drew out a chunk of salt pork, and began slicing it with his jackknife. On inquiry I learned that "Old Ned" is merely slang for fat pork, but that "suggin" or "sujjit" (the u pronounced like oo in look) is true mountain dialect for a bag, valise or carryall, its etymology being something to puzzle over.

Four dogs growled at each other under a long bunk of poles and hay that spanned one side of our cabin. The fire glared out upon the middle of an unfloored and windowless room. Deep shadows clung to the walls and benches, charitably concealing much dirt and disorder left by previous occupants, much litter of our own contributing.

We were on a saddle of the divide, a mile above sea level, in a hut built years ago for temporary lodgment of cattlemen herding on the grassy "balds" of the Smokies. A sagging "shake" roof covered its two rooms and the open space between them that we called our "entry." The state line between North Carolina and Tennessee ran through this unenclosed hallway. The Carolina room had a puncheon floor and a clapboard table, also better bunks than its mate; but there had risen a stiff southerly gale that made the chimney smoke so abominably that we were forced to take quarters in the neighbor state.

Granville lifted the lid from a big Dutch oven and reported "Bread's done."

There was a flash in the frying-pan, a curse and a puff from Little John. The coffee-pot boiled over. We gathered about the hewn benches that served for tables, and sat à la Turc upon the ground. For some time there was no sound but the gale without and the munching of ravenous men.

"If this wind'll only cease afore mornin', we'll git us a bear tomorrow."

A powerful gust struck the cabin, by way of answer; a great roaring surged up from the gulf of Defeat, from Desolation, and from the other forks of Bone Valley—clamor of ten thousand trees struggling with the blast.

"Hit's gittin' wusser."

"Any danger of this roost being blown off the mountain?" I inquired.

"Hit's stood hyur twenty year through all the storms; I reckon it can stand one more night of it."

"A man couldn't walk upright outside the cabin," I asserted, thinking of the St. Louis tornado, in which I had lain flat on my belly, clinging to an iron post.

The hunchback turned to me with a grave face. "I've seed hit blow, here on top o' Smoky, till a hoss couldn't stand up agin it. You'll spy, tomorrow, that several trees has been wind-throwed and busted to kindlin'."

I recalled that "several," in the South, means many—"a good many," as our own tongues phrase it.

"Oh shucks, Bill Cope," put in "Doc" Jones, "whut do you-uns know about windstorms? Now, I've hed some experiencin' up hyur that'll do to tell about. You remember the big storm three year ago, come grass, when the cattle all huddled up atop o' each other and friz in one pile, solid."

Bill grunted an affirmative.

"Wal, sir, I was a-herdin', over at the Spencer Place, and was out on Thunderhead when the wind sprung up. There come one turrible vyg'rous blow that jest nacherally lifted the ground. I went up in the sky, my coat ripped off, and I went a-sailin' end-over-end."

"Yes?"

"Yes. About half an hour later, I lit spang in the mud way down yander in Tuckaleechee Cove—yes, sir; ten mile as the crow flies, and a mile deeper'n trout-fish swim."

There was silence for a moment. Then Little John spoke up: "I mind about that time, Doc, but I disremember which buryin'-ground they-all planted ye in."

"Planted! Me? Huh! But I had one tormentin' time findin' my hat!"

The cabin shook under a heavier blast.

"Old Wind-maker's blowin' liars out o' North Car'lina. Hang on to yer hat, Doc! Whoop! Hear 'em a-comin."

"Durn this blow, anyhow! No bear'll cross the mountain sich a night as this."

"Can't we hunt down on the Carolina side?" I asked.

"That's whar we're goin' to drive; but hit's no use if the bear don't come over."

"How is that? Do they sleep in one state and eat in the other?"

"Yes. You see, the Tennessee side of the mountain is powerful steep and laurely, so man nor dog cain't git over it in lots o' places: that's whar the bears den. But the mast, sich as acorns and beech and hickory nuts, is mostly on the Car'lina side; that's whar they hafter come to feed. So, when its blows like this, they stay at home and suck their paws."

"So we'll have to do, at this rate."

"I'll go see whut the el-e-ments looks like."

We arose from our squatting postures. John opened the little shake door, which swung violently backward as another gust of wind boomed against the cabin. Dust and hot ashes scattered in every direction. The dogs sprang up, one encroached upon another, and they flew at each other's throats. They were powerful beasts, dangerous to man as well as to the brutes they were trained to fight; but John was their master, and he soon booted them into surly subjection.

"The older dog don't ginerally raise no ruction; hit's the younger one that's ill," by which he meant vicious. "You Coaly, you'll git some o' that meanness shuck outen you if you tackle an old she-bear tomorrow!"

"Has the young dog ever fought a bear?"

"No, he don't know nothin'. But I reckon he'll pick up some larnin' in the next two, three days."

"Have those dogs got the Plott strain? I've been told that the Plott hounds are the best bear dogs in the country."

"Tain't so," snorted John. "The Plott curs are the best; that is, half hound, half cur—though what weuns call the cur, in this case, raelly comes from a big furrin dog that I don't rightly know the breed of. Fellers, you can talk as you please about a streak o' the cur spilin' a dog; but I know hit ain't so—not for bear fightin' in these mountains, whar you cain't foller up on hossback, but hafter do your own runnin'."

"What is the reason, John?"

"Wal, hit's like this: a plumb cur, of course, cain't foller a cold track—he jest runs by sight; and he won't hang—he quits. But, t'other way, no hound'll raelly fight a bear—hit takes a big severe dog to do that. Hounds has the best noses, and they'll run a bear all day and night, and the next day, too; but they won't never tree—they're afeared to close in. Now look at them dogs o' mine. A cur ain't got no dew-claws—them dogs has. My dogs can foller ary trail, same's hound; but they'll run right in on the varmint, snappin' and chawin' and worryin' him till he gits so mad you can hear his tuches pop half a mile. He cain't run away—he haster stop every bit and fight. Finally he gits so tarred [tired] and het up that he trees to rest hisself. Then we-uns ketches up and finishes him."

"Mebbe you-uns don't know that a dew-clawed dog is snakeproof—"

But somebody, thinking that dog talk had gone far enough, produced a bottle of soothing-syrup that was too new to have paid tax. Then we discovered that there was musical talent, of a sort, in Little John. He cut a pigeon-wing, twirled around with an imaginary banjo, and sang in a quaint minor:

> Did you ever see the devil,
> With his pitchfork and ladle,
> And his old iron shovel,
> And his old gourd head?
> O, I will go to meetin',
> And I will go to meetin',
> Yes, I will go to meetin',
> In an old tin pan.

Other songs followed, with utter irrelevance—mere snatches from "ballets" composed, mainly, by the mountaineers themselves, though some dated back to a long-forgotten age when the British ancestors of these Carolina woodsmen were battling with lance and long bow. It was one of modern and local origin that John was singing when there came a diversion from without—

> La-a-ay down, boys,
> Le's take a nap:
> Thar's goin' to be trouble
> In the Cumberland Gap—

Our ears were stunned by one sudden thundering crash. The roof rose visibly, as though pushed upward from within. In an instant we were blinded by moss and dried mud—the chinking blown from between the logs of our shabby cabin. Dred and Coaly cowered as though whipped, while "Doc's" little hound slunk away in the keen misery of fear. We men looked at each other with lowered eyelids and the grim smile that denotes readiness, though no special eagerness, for dissolution. Beyond the "gant-lot"* we could hear trees and limbs popping like pistol shots.

Then that tidal wave of air swept by. The roof settled again with only a few shingles missing. We went to "redding up." Squalls broke against the mountainside, hither and yon, like the hammer of Thor testing the foundations of the earth. But they were below us. Here, on top, there was only the steady drive of a great surge of wind; and speech was possible once more.

"Fellers, you want to mark whut you dream about, tonight: hit'll shore come true tomorrow."

---

* Gant-lot: a fenced enclosure into which cattle are driven after cutting them out from those of other owners. So called because the mountain cattle run wild, feeding only on grass and browse, and "they couldn't travel well to market when they were filled up on green stuff; so they're penned up to git gant and nimble."

"Yes: but you mustn't tell whut yer dream was till the hunt's over, or it'll spile the charm."

There ensued a grave discussion of dream lore, in which the illiterates of our party declared solemn faith. If one dreamt of blood, he would surely see blood the next day. Another lucky sign for a hunter was to dream of quarreling with a woman, for that meant a she-bear. It was favorable to dream of clear water, but muddy water meant trouble.

The wind died away. When we went out for a last observation of the weather we found the air so clear that the lights of Knoxville were plainly visible, in the north-northwest, thirty-two miles in an air line. Not another light was to be seen on earth, although in some directions we could scan for nearly a hundred miles. The moon shone brightly. Things looked rather favorable for the morrow, after all.

~~~~~~

"Brek-k-k-fust!"

I awoke to a knowledge that somebody had built a roaring fire and was stirring about. Between the cabin logs one looked out upon a starry sky and an almost pitch-dark world. What did that pottering vagabond mean by arousing us in the middle of the night? But I was hungry. Everybody half arose on elbows and blinked about. Then we got up, each after his fashion, except one scamp who resumed snoring.

"Whar's that brekfust you're yellin' about?"

"Hit's for you-uns to help git! I knowed I couldn't roust ye no other way. Here, you, go down to the spring and fetch water. Rustle out, boys; we've got to git a soon start if you want bear brains an' liver for supper."

The "soon start" tickled me into good humor.

Our dogs were curled together under the long bunk, having popped indoors as soon as the way was opened. Somebody trod on Coaly's tail. Coaly snapped Dred. Instantly there was action between the four.

It is interesting to observe what two or three hundred pounds of dog can do to a ramshackle berth with a man on top of it. Poles and hay and ragged quilts flew in every direction. Sleepy Matt went down in the midst of the melee, swearing valiantly. I went out and hammered ice out of the washbasin while Granville and John quelled the riot. Presently our frying-pans sputtered and the huge coffeepot began to get up steam.

"Wal, who dreamt him a good dream?"

"I did," affirmed the writer. "I dreamt that I had an old colored woman by the throat and was choking dollars out of her mouth—"

"Good la!" exclaimed four men in chorus. "You hadn't orter a-told."

"Why? Wasn't that a lovely dream?"

"Hit means a she-bear, shore as a cap-shootin' gun, but you've spiled it all by tellin'. Mebbe somebody'll git her today, but you won't—your chanct is ruined."

So the reader will understand why, in this veracious narrative, I cannot relate any heroic exploits of my own in battling with Ursus Major.

There was still no sign of rose color in the eastern sky when we sallied forth. The ground, to use a mountaineer's expression, was "all spewed up with frost." Rime crackled underfoot and our mustaches soon stiffened in the icy wind.

It was settled that Little John Cable and the hunchback Cope should take the dogs far down into Bone Valley and start the drive, leaving Granville, Doc, Matt, and myself to picket the mountain. I was given a stand about half a mile east of the cabin, and had but a vague notion of where the others went.

By jinks, it was cold! I built a fire between the buttressing roots of a big mountain oak, but still my toes and fingers were numb. This was the 25th of November, and we were at an altitude where sometimes frost forms in July. The other men were more thinly clad than I, and with not a stitch of wool beyond their stocking; yet they seemed to revel in the keen air. I wasted some pity on Cope, who had no underwear worthy of the name; but afterwards I learned that he would not have worn more clothes if they had been given to him. This fellow never owned a coat until after his marriage. It is literal fact that some of these mountaineers (women and children, as well as men) think nothing of running around barefooted for hours in snow that is ankle-deep. One of my neighbor's children went barefooted all one winter, when the thermometer several times went below zero Fahrenheit. Many a night my companions had slept out on the mountain without blanket or shelter, when the ground froze and every twig in the forest was coated with rime from the winter fog.

Away out yonder beyond the mighty bulk of Clingmans Dome, which, black with spruce and balsam, looked like a vast bear rising to contemplate the northern world, there streaked the first faint, nebulous hint of dawn. Presently the big bear's head was tipped with a golden crown flashing against the scarlet fires of the firmament, and the earth awoke.

A rustling some hundred yards below me gave signal that the gray squirrels were on their way to water. Out of a tree overhead popped a mountain "boomer" (red squirrel), and down he came, eyed me, and stopped.

Somewhere from the sky came a strange, half-human note, as of someone chiding: "Wal-lace, Wal-lace, Wat!" I could get no view for the trees. Then the thing sailed into sight—a raven—flexibly changing its voice to a deep-toned "Co-logne, Co-logne, Co-logne."

As the morning drew on, I let the fire die to ashes and basked lazily in the sun. Not a sound had I heard from the dogs. My hoodoo was working malignly. Well, let it work. I was comfortable now, and that old bear could go to any other doom she preferred. It was pleasant enough to lie here alone in the forest and be free! Aye, it was good to be alive, and to be far, far away from the broken bottles and old tin cans of civilization.

For many a league to the southward clouds covered all the valleys in billows of white, from which rose a hundred mountain tops, like islands in a tropic ocean. My fancy sailed among and beyond them, beyond the horizon's rim, even unto those far seas that I had sailed in my youth, to the old times and the old friends that I should never see again.

But a forenoon is long-drawn-out when one has breakfasted before dawn, and has nothing to do but sit motionless in the woods and watch and listen. I got to fingering my rifle trigger impatiently and wishing that a wild Thanksgiving gobbler might blunder into view. Squirrels made ceaseless chatter all around my stand. Large hawks shrilled by me within tempting range, whistling like spent bullets. A groundhog sat up on a log and whistled, too, after a manner of his own. He was so near that I could see his nose wiggle. A skunk waddled around for twenty minutes, and once came so close that I thought he would nibble my boot. I was among old mossy beeches, scaled with polyphori, and twisted into postures of torture by their battles with the storms. Below, among chestnuts and birches, I could hear the t-wee, t-wee of "joree-birds" (towhees), which winter in the valleys. Incessantly came the chip-chip-chip of ground squirrels, the saucy bark of the grays, and great chirruping among the "boomers."

Far off on my left a rifle cracked. I pricked up and listened intently, but there was never a yelp from a dog. Since it is a law of the chase to fire at nothing smaller than turkeys, lest big game be scared away, this shot might mean a gobbler. I knew that Matt Hyde, to save his soul, could not sit ten minutes on a stand without calling turkeys (and he could call them with his unassisted mouth better than anyone I ever heard perform with leaf or wing bone or any other contrivance).

Thus the slow hours dragged along. I yearned mightily to stretch my legs. Finally, being certain that no drive would approach my stand that day, I ambled back to the hut and did a turn at dinner-getting. Things were smoking, and smelt good, by the time four of our men turned up, all of them dog-tired and disappointed, but stoical.

"That pup Coaly chased off atter a wildcat," blurted John. "We held the old dogs together and let him rip. Then Dred started a deer. It was that old buck that everybody's shot at, and missed, this three year back. I'd believe he's a hant if 't wasn't for his tracks—they're the biggest I ever seen. He must weigh two hundred and fifty. But he's a foxy cuss. Tuk right down the bed o' Desolation, up the left prong of Roaring Fork, right through the Devil's Race-path (how a deer can git through thar I don't see!), crossed at the Meadow Gap, went down Eagle Creek, and by now he's in the Little Tennessee. That buck, shorely to God, has wings!"

We were at table in the Carolina room when Matt Hyde appeared. He was the worst tatterdemalion I had seen outside of a hobo camp, his lower extremities being almost naked. Sure enough, he bore a turkey hen.

"I was callin' a gobbler when this fool thing showed up. I fired a shoot as she riz in the air, but only bruk her wing. She made off on her legs like the devil whoppin' out fire. I run, an' she run. Guess I run her half a mile through all-fired thickets. She piped 'Quit—quit,' but I said 'I'll see you in hell afore I quit!' and the chase resumed. Finally I knocked her over with a birch stob, and here we are."

Matt ruefully surveyed his legs. "Boys," said he, "I'm nigh breachless."

None but native-born mountaineers could have stood the strain of another drive that day, for the country that Cope and Cable had been through was fearful, especially the laurel up Roaring Fork and Kill-peter Ridge. But the stamina of these withey little men was even more remarkable than their endurance of cold. After a slice of meat (about half what a Northern office man would eat), a chunk of half-baked johnny-cake, and a pint or so of coffee, they were as fresh as ever.

I had made the coffee strong, and it was good stuff that I had brought from home. After his first deep draught, Little John exclaimed: "Hah! boys, that coffee hits whar ye hold it!"

I thought that a neat compliment from a sharpshooter.

We took new stands; but the afternoon passed without incident to those of us on the mountain tops. I returned to camp about five o'clock, and was surprised to see three of our men lugging across the gant-lot a small female bear.

"Hyar's yer old black woman," shouted John.

"How's this? I didn't hear any drive."

"Thar wa'n't none."

"Then where did you get your bear?"

"In one of Steve Howard's traps, dum him! Boys, I wish we hed roasted the temper outen them trap springs, like we talked o' doin'."

"The bear was alive, wasn't it?"

"As live as a hot coal. See the pup's head!"

I examined Coaly, who looked sick. The flesh was torn from his lower jaw and hung down a couple of inches. Two holes in the top of his head showed where the bear's tusks had done their best to crack his skull.

"When the other dogs found her, he rushed right in. She hadn't been trapped more'n a few hours, and she larned Coaly somethin' about the bear business."

"Won't this spoil him for hunting hereafter?"

"Not if he has his daddy's and mammy's grit. We'll know by tomorrow whether he's a shore-enough bear dog; for I've larned now whar they're crossin'—seed sign a-plenty."

All of us were indignant at the setter of the trap. It had been hidden in a trail, with no sign to warn a man from stepping into it. In Tennessee, I was told, it is a penitentiary offense to set out a bear trap. We agreed that a similar law ought to be passed in North Carolina.

"It's only two years ago," said Granville, "that Jasper Millington, an old man living on the Tennessee side, started acrost the mountain to get work at the Everett mine. Not fur from where we are now he stepped into a bear trap that was hid in the leaves, like this one. It broke his leg, and he starved to death in it."

Despite our indignation meeting, it was decided to carry the trapped bear's hide to Howard, and for us to use only the meat as recompense for trouble, to say nothing of risk to life and limb. Such is the mountaineers' regard for property rights!

The animal we had ingloriously won was undersized, weighing a scant 175 pounds. The average weight of Smoky Mountain bears is not great, but occasionally a very large beast is killed. Matt Hyde told us that he killed one on the Welch Divide in 1901, the meat of which, dressed, without the hide, weighed 434 pounds, and the hide "squared eight feet" when stretched for drying.

We spent the evening in debate as to where the next drive should be made. Some favored moving six miles eastward to the old mining shack at Siler's Meadow and trying the head waters of Forney's Creek, around Rip Shin Thicket and the Gunstick Laurel, driving towards Clingmans Dome and over into the bleak gulf, southwest of the Sugarland Mountains, that I had named Godforsaken—a title that stuck. We knew there were bears in that region, though it was a desperately rough country to hunt in.

But John and the hunchback had found "sign" in the opposite direction. Bears were crossing from Little River in the neighborhood of Thunderhead and Briar Knob, coming up just west of the Devil's

Court House and "using" around Block House, Woolly Ridge, Bear Pen, and thereabouts. The motion carried, and we adjourned to bed.

We breakfasted on bear meat, the remains of our Thanksgiving turkey and wheat bread shortened with bear's grease until it was light as a feather, and I made tea. It was the first time that Little John ever saw "store tea." He swallowed some of it as if it had been boneset, under the impression that it was some sort of "yerb" that would be good for his insides.

"Wal, people," exclaimed Matt, "I 'low I've done growed a bit, after that mess of meat. Le's be movin'."

It was a hard trip for me, climbing up the rock approach to Briar Knob. You may laugh as you please about a lowlander's lungs feeling rarefaction at 5,000 or 5,500 feet, but in the very moist air of the Southern mountains, with fog (cloud) in the bargain, most newcomers do feel it for a few days.

The boys were anxious for me to get a shot. I was paying them nothing; it was share-and-share alike; but their neighborly kindness moved them to do their best for the "furriner."

So they put on me what was probably the best stand for the day. It was above the Fire Scald, a brûlé or burnt-over space on the steep southern side of the ridge between Briar Knob and Laurel Top, overlooking the grisly slope of Killpeter. Here I could both see and hear an uncommonly long distance, and if the bear went either east or west I would have timely warning.

I had shivered on the mountain top for a couple of hours, hearing only an occasional bark from the dogs, which had been working in the thickets a mile or so below me, when suddenly there burst forth the devil of a racket. On came the chase, right in my direction. Presently I could even distinguish the different notes—the deep bellow of old Dred, the houndlike baying of Rock and Coaly, and Little Towse's yelp.

I thought that the bear might chance the comparatively open space of the Fire Scald, because there were still some ashes on the ground which would dust the dogs' nostrils and tend to throw them off the scent. And such, I do believe, was his intention. But the dogs caught up with him. They nipped him fore and aft. Time after time he shook them off; but they were true bear dogs, and knew no such word as quit.

I took a last squint at my rifle sights, made sure there was a cartridge in the chamber, and then felt my ears grow as I listened. Suddenly the chase swerved at a right angle and took straight up the side of Saddle-back. Either the bear would tree, or he would try to smash on through to the low rhododendron of the Devil's Court House, where dogs who followed might break their legs. I girded myself and ran, "wiggling and wingling" along the main divide, and then came the steep pull up Briar Knob. As I was grading around the summit with all the lope that was left in me, I heard a rifle crack, half a mile down Saddle-back. Old Doc was somewhere in that vicinity. I halted to listen. Creation, what a rumpus! Then another shot. Then the war whoop of the South that we read about.

By and by, up they came, John and Cope and Doc, carrying the bear on a trimmed sapling. Presently Hyde joined us, then came Granville, and we filed back to camp, where Doc told his story:

"Boys, them dogs' eyes shined like new money. Coaly fit again, all right, and got his tail bit. The bear div down into a sink-hole with the dogs atop o' him. Soon's I could shoot without hittin' a dog, I let him have it. Thought I'd shot him through the head, but he fit on. Then I jumped down into the sink an' kicked him loose from the dogs, or he'd a-killed Coaly. Wal, sir, he wa'n't hurt a bit—the ball just glanced off his head. He riz and knocked me down with his left paw, an' walked right over me, an' lit up the ridge. The dogs treed him in a minute. I went to shoot up at him, but my new hulls fit loose in this old chamber and the one drap out, so the gun stuck. Had to git my knife out and fit hit. Then the dad-burned gun wouldn't stand roostered (cocked); the feather-spring had jumped out o' place. But I held back with my thumb, and killed him anyhow."

"Bears," said John, "is all left-handed. Ever note that? Hit's the left paw you want to look out fer. He'd a-knocked somethin' out o' yer head if thar'd been much in it, Doc."

And so, laughing and chaffing, we finished dinner.

The mountaineers have a curious way of sharing the spoils of the chase. A bear's hide is sold and the proceeds divided equally among the hunters, but the meat is cut up into as many pieces as there are partners in the chase; then one man goes indoors or behind a tree, and somebody at the carcass, laying his hand on a portion, calls out: "Whose piece is this?"

"Granville Calhoun's," cries the hidden man, who cannot see it.

"Whose is this?"

"Bill Cope's."

And so on down the line. Everybody gets what chance determines for him, and there can be no charge of unfairness.

The next morning John announced that we were going to get another bear.

"Night afore last," he said, "Bill dremp that he saw a lot o' fat meat lyin' on the table; an' it done come true. Last night I dremp one that never was known to fail. Now you'll see it!"

It did not look like it by evening. We all worked hard and endured much—standers as well as drivers—but not a rifle had spoken up to the time when, from my far-off stand, I yearned for a hot supper.

Away down in the rear I heard the snort of a locomotive, one of those cog-wheel affairs that are specially built for mountain climbing. With a steam-loader and three camps of a hundred men each, it was despoiling the Tennessee forest. Slowly, but inexorably, a leviathan was crawling into the wilderness to consume it.

Wearily I plodded back to camp. No one had arrived but Doc. The old man had been thumped rather severely in yesterday's scrimmage, but complained only of "a touch o' rheumatiz." Just how the latter had left his clothes in tatters he did not explain.

It was late when Matt and Granville came in. The crimson and yellow of sunset had turned to a faultless turquoise, and this to a violet afterglow; then suddenly night rose from the valleys and enveloped us.

About nine o'clock I went out on the Little Chestnut Bald and fired signals, but there was no answer. The last we had known of the drivers was that they had been beyond Thunderhead, six miles of hard travel to the westward. There was fog on the mountain. Then Granville and Matt took the lantern and set out for Briar Knob. Doc was too stiff for travel, and I, being at that time a stranger in the Smokies, would be of no use hunting amid clouds and darkness. Doc and I passed a dreary three hours. Finally, at midnight, my shots were answered, and soon the dogs came limping in. Dred had been severely bitten in the shoulders and Rock in the head. Coaly was bloody about the mouth, where his first day's wound had reopened. Then came the four men, empty-handed, it seemed, until John slapped a bear's "melt" (spleen) upon the table. He limped from a bruised hip.

"That bear went 'way around all o' you-uns. We follered him clar over to the Spencer Place, and then he doubled and come back on the fur side o' the ridge. He crossed through the laurel on the Devil's Court House and tuk down an almighty steep place. It was plumb night by that time. I fell over a rock clift twenty feet down, and if't hadn't been for the laurel I'd a-bruk some bones. I landed right in the middle of them, bear and dogs, fightin' like gamecocks. The bear clim a tree. Bill sung out 'Is it fur down that?' and I said 'Pretty fur.' 'Wal,

I'm a-comin',' says he; and with that he grabbed a laurel to swing hisself down by, but the stem bruk, and down he came suddent, to jine the music. Hit was so dark I couldn't see my gun barrel, and we wuz all tangled up in green briars as thick as plough-lines. I had to fire twicet afore he tumbled. Then Matt an' Granville come. The four of us tuk turn-about crawlin' up out o' thar with the bear on our back. Only one man could handle him at a time—and he'll go a good two hundred, that bear. We gutted him, and left him near the top, to fotch in the mornin'. Boys, this is the time I'd give nigh all I'm worth for half a gallon o' liquor—and I'd promise the rest!"

"You'd orter see what Coaly did to that varmint," said Bill. "He bit a hole under the fore leg, through hide and ha'r, clar into the holler, so that you can stick your hand in and seize the bear's heart."

"John, what was that dream?"

"I dremp I stole a feller's overcoat. Now d'ye see? That means a bear's hide."

Coaly, three days ago, had been an inconsequential pup; but now he looked up into my eyes with the calm dignity that no fool or braggart can assume. He had been knighted. As he licked his wounds he was proud of them. "Scars of battle, sir. You may have your swagger ribbons and prize collars in the New York dog show, but this for me!"

AN ELK HUNT AT TWO-OCEAN PASS

THEODORE ROOSEVELT

In September, 1891, with my ranch-partner, Ferguson, I made an elk-hunt in northwestern Wyoming among the Shoshone Mountains, where they join the Hoodoo and Absoraka ranges. There is no more beautiful game-country in the United States. It is a park land, where glades, meadows, and high mountain pastures break the evergreen forest; a forest which is open compared to the tangled density of the woodland farther north. It is a high, cold region of many lakes and clear rushing streams. The steep mountains are generally of the rounded form so often seen in the ranges of the Cordilleras of the United States; but the Hoodoos, or Goblins, are carved in fantastic and extraordinary shapes; while the Tetons, a group of isolated rock-peaks, show a striking boldness in their lofty outlines.

This was one of the pleasantest hunts I ever made. As always in the mountains, save where the country is so rough and so densely wooded that one must go a-foot, we had a pack-train; and we took a more complete outfit than we had ever before taken on such a hunt, and so travelled in much comfort. Usually when in the mountains I have merely had one companion, or at most a couple, and two or three pack-ponies; each of us doing his share of the packing, cooking, fetching water, and pitching the small square of canvas which served as tent. In itself packing is both an art and a mystery, and a skilful professional packer, versed in the intricaies of the "diamond hitch," packs with a speed which no non-professional can hope to rival, and fixes the side packs and top packs with such scientific nicety, and adjusts the doubles and turns of the lash-rope so accurately, that everything stays in place under any but the most adverse conditions. Of course, like most hunters, I can myself in case of need throw the diamond hitch after a fashion, and pack on either the off or near side. Indeed, unless a man can pack it is not possible to make a really hard hunt in the mountains, if alone, or with only a single companion. The mere fair-weather hunter, who trusts entirely to the exertions of others, and does nothing more than ride or walk about under favorable circumstances, and shoot at what somebody else shows him, is a hunter in name only. Whoever would really deserve the title must be able at a pinch to shift for himself, to grapple with the difficulties and hardships of wilderness life unaided, and not only to hunt, but at times to travel for days, whether on foot or on horseback, alone. However, after one has passed one's novitiate, it is pleasant to be comfortable when the comfort does not interfere with the sport; and although a man sometimes likes to hunt alone, yet often it is well to be with some old mountain hunter, a master of woodcraft, who is a first-rate hand at finding game, creeping upon it, and tracking it when wounded. With such a companion one gets much more game, and learns many things by observation instead of by painful experience.

On this trip we had with us two hunters, Tazewell Woody and Elwood Hofer, a packer who acted as cook, and a boy to herd the horses. Of the latter, there were twenty; six saddle-animals and fourteen for the packs—two or three being spare horses, to be used later in carrying the elk-antlers, sheep-horns, and other trophies. Like most hunters' pack-animals, they were either half broken, or else broken down; tough, unkempt; jaded-looking beasts of every color—sorrel, buckskin, pinto, white, bay, roan. After the day's work was over, they were turned loose to shift for themselves; and about once a week they strayed, and all hands had to spend the better part of the day hunting for them. The worst ones for straying, curiously enough, were three broken-down old "bear-baits," which went by themselves, as is generally the case with the cast-off horses of a herd. There were two sleeping-tents, another for the provisions,—in which we ate during bad weather,—and a canvas tepee, which was put up with lodge-poles, Indian fashion, like a wigwam. A tepee is more difficult to put up than an ordinary tent; but it is very convenient when there is rain or snow. A small fire kindled in the middle keeps it warm, the smoke escaping through the open top—that is, when it escapes at all; strings are passed from one pole to another, on which to hang wet clothes and shoes, and the beds are made around the edges. As an offset to the warmth and shelter, the smoke often renders it impossible even to sit upright. We had a very good camp-kit, including plenty of cooking-and eating-utensils; and among our provisions were some canned goods and sweetmeats, to give a relish to our meals of meat and bread. We had fur coats and warm clothes,—which are chiefly needed at night,—and plenty of bedding, including water-proof canvas sheeting and a couple of caribou-hide sleeping-bags, procured from the survivors of a party of arctic explorers. Except on rainy days I used my buckskin hunting-shirt or tunic; in dry weather I deem it, because of its color, texture, and durability, the best possible garb for the still-hunter, especially in the woods.

Starting a day's journey south of Heart Lake, we travelled and hunted on the eastern edge of the great basin, wooded and mountainous, wherein rise the head-waters of the mighty Snake River. There was not so much as a spotted line—that series of blazes made with the axe, man's first highway through the hoary forest,—but this we did not mind, as for most of the distance we followed well-worn elk-trails. The train travelled in Indian file. At the head, to pick the path, rode tall, silent old Woody, a true type of the fast-vanishing race of game hunters and Indian fighters, a man who had been one of the California forty-niners, and who ever since had lived the restless, reckless life of the wilderness. Then came Ferguson and myself; then the pack-animals, strung out in line; while from the rear rose the varied oaths of our three companions, whose miserable duty it was to urge forward the beasts of burden.

It is heart-breaking work to drive a pack-train through thick timber and over mountains, where there is either a dim trail or none. The animals have a perverse faculty for choosing the wrong turn at critical moments; and they are continually scraping under branches and squeezing between tree-trunks, to the jeopardy or destruction of their burdens. After having been laboriously driven up a very steep incline, at the cost of severe exertion both to them and to the men, the foolish creatures turn and run down to the bottom, so that all the work has to be done over again. Some travel too slow; others travel too fast. Yet one cannot but admire the toughness of the animals, and the surefootedness with which they pick their way along the sheer mountain sides, or among boulders and over fallen logs.

As our way was so rough, we found that we had to halt at least once every hour to fix the packs. Moreover, we at the head of the column were continually being appealed to for help by the unfortunates in the rear. First it would be "that white-eyed cayuse; one side of its pack's down!" then we would be notified that the saddle-blanket of the "lopeared Indian buckskin" had slipped back; then a shout "Look out for the pinto!" would be followed by that pleasing beast's appearance, bucking and squealing, smashing dead timber, and scattering its load to the four winds. It was no easy task to get the horses across some of the boggy places without miring; or to force them through the denser portions of the forest, where there was much down timber. Riding with a pack-train, day in and day out, becomes both monotonous and irritating, unless one is upheld by the hope of a game-country ahead, or by the delight of exploration of the unknown. Yet when buoyed by such a hope, there is pleasure in taking a train across so beautiful and wild a country as that which lay on the threshold of our hunting grounds in the Shoshones. We went over mountain passes, with ranges of scalped peaks on either hand; we skirted the edges of lovely lakes, and of streams with boulder-strewn beds; we plunged into depths of sombre woodland, broken by wet prairies. It was a picturesque sight to see the loaded pack-train stringing across one of these high mountain meadows, the motley colored line of ponies winding round the marshy spots through the bright green grass, while beyond rose the dark line of frowning forest, with lofty peaks towering in the background. Some of the meadows were beautiful with many flowers—goldenrod, purple aster, bluebells, white immortelles, and here and there masses of blood-red Indian pinks. In the park-country, on the edges of the evergreen forest, were groves of delicate quaking-aspen, the trees often growing to quite a height; their tremulous leaves were already changing to bright green and yellow, occasionally with a reddish blush. In the Rocky Mountains the aspens are almost the only deciduous trees, their foliage offering a pleasant relief to the eye after the monotony of the unending pine and spruce woods, which afford so striking a contrast to the hardwood forest east of the Mississippi.

For two days our journey was uneventful, save that we came on the camp of a squawman—one Beaver Dick, an old mountain hunter, living in a skin tepee, where dwelt his comely Indian wife and half-breed children. He had quite a herd of horses, many of them mares and colts; they had evidently been well treated, and came up to us fearlessly.

The morning of the third day of our journey was gray and lowering. Gusts of rain blew in my face as I rode at the head of the train. It still lacked an hour of noon, as we were plodding up a valley beside a rapid brook running through narrow willow-flats, the dark forest crowding down on either hand from the low foot-hills of the mountains. Suddenly the call of a bull elk came echoing down through the wet woodland on our right, beyond the brook, seemingly less than half a mile off; and was answered by a faint, far-off call from a rival on the mountain beyond. Instantly halting the train, Woody and I slipped off our horses, crossed the brook, and started to still-hunt the first bull.

In this place the forest was composed of the western tamarack; the large, tall trees stood well apart, and there was much down timber, but the ground was covered with deep wet moss, over which we trod silently. The elk was travelling up-wind, but slowly, stopping continually to paw the ground and thresh the bushes with his antlers. He was very noisy, challenging every minute or two, being doubtless much excited by the neighborhood of his rival on the mountain. We followed, Woody leading, guided by the incessant calling.

It was very exciting as we crept toward the great bull, and the challenge sounded nearer and nearer. While we were still at some distance the pealing notes were like those of a bugle, delivered in two bars, first rising, then abruptly falling; as we drew nearer they took on a harsh squealing sound. Each call made our veins thrill; it sounded like the cry of some huge beast of prey. At last we heard the roar of the challenge not eighty yards off. Stealing forward three or four yards, I saw the tips of the horns through a mass of dead timber and young growth, and I slipped to one side to get a clean shot. Seeing us, but not making out what we were, and full of fierce and insolent excitement, the wapiti bull stepped boldly toward us with a stately swinging gait. Then he stood motionless, facing us, barely fifty yards away, his handsome twelve-tined antlers tossed aloft, as he held his head with the lordly grace of his kind. I fired into his chest, and as he turned I raced forward and shot him in the flank; but the second bullet was not needed, for the first wound was mortal, and he fell before going fifty yards.

The dead elk lay among the young evergreens. The huge, shapely body was set on legs that were as strong as steel rods, and yet slender, clean, and smooth; they were in color a beautiful dark brown, contrasting well with the yellowish of the body. The neck and throat were garnished with a mane of long hair; the symmetry of the great horns set off the fine, delicate lines of the noble head. He had been wallowing, as elk are fond of doing, and the dried mud clung in patches to his flank; a stab in the haunch showed that he had been overcome in battle by some master bull who had turned him out of the herd.

We cut off the head, and bore it down to the train. The horses crowded together, snorting, with their ears pricked forward, as they smelt the blood. We also took the loins with us, as we were out of meat, though bull elk in the rutting season is not very good. The rain had changed to a steady downpour when we again got under way. Two or three miles farther we pitched camp, in a clump of pines on a hillock in the bottom of the valley, starting hot fires of pitchy stumps before the tents, to dry our wet things.

Next day opened with fog and cold rain. The drenched packanimals, when driven into camp, stood mopingly, with drooping heads and arched backs; they groaned and grunted as the loads were placed on their backs and the cinches tightened, the packers bracing one foot against the pack to get a purchase as they hauled in on the lash-rope. A stormy morning is a trial to temper; the packs are wet and heavy, and the cold makes the work even more than usually hard on the hands. By ten we broke camp. It needs between two and three hours to break camp and get such a train properly packed; once started, our day's journey was six to eight hours, making no halt. We started up a steep, pine-clad mountain side, broken by cliffs. My hunting-shoes, though comfortable, were old and thin, and let the water through like a sieve. On the top of the first plateau, where black spruce groves were strewn across the grassy surface, we saw a band of elk, cows and calves, trotting off through the rain. Then we plunged down into a deep valley, and, crossing it, a hard climb took us to the top of a great bare table-land, bleak and wind-swept. We passed little alpine lakes, fringed with scattering dwarf evergreens. Snow lay in drifts on the north sides of the gullies; a cutting wind blew the icy rain in our faces. For two or three hours we travelled toward the farther edge of the table-land. In one place a spike bull elk stood half a mile off, in the open; he travelled to and fro, watching us.

As we neared the edge the storm lulled, and pale, watery sunshine gleamed through the rifts in the low-scudding clouds. At last our horses stood on the brink of a bold cliff. Deep down beneath our feet lay the wild and lonely valley of Two-Ocean Pass, walled in on either hand by rugged mountain chains, their flanks scarred and gashed by precipice and chasm. Beyond, in a wilderness of jagged and barren peaks, stretched the Shoshones. At the middle point of the pass, two streams welled down from either side. At first each flowed in but one bed, but soon divided into two; each of the twin branches then joined the like branch of the brook opposite, and swept one to the east and one to the west, on their long journey to the two great oceans. They ran as rapid brooks, through wet meadows and willow-flats, the eastern to the Yellowstone, the western to the Snake. The dark pine forests swept down from the flanks and lower ridges of the mountains to the edges of the marshy valley. Above them jutted gray rock peaks, snow-drifts lying in the rents that seamed their northern faces. Far below us, from a great basin at the foot of the cliff, filled with the pine forest, rose the musical challenge of a bull elk; and we saw a band of cows and calves looking like mice as they ran among the trees.

It was getting late, and after some search we failed to find any trail leading down; so at last we plunged over the brink at a venture. It was very rough scrambling, dropping from bench to bench, and in places it was not only difficult but dangerous for the loaded pack-animals. Here and there we were helped by well-beaten elk-trails, which we could follow for several hundred yards at a time. On one narrow pine-clad ledge, we met a spike bull face to face; and in scrambling down a very steep, bare, rock-strewn shoulder the loose stones started by the horses' hoofs, bounding in great leaps to the forest below, dislodged two cows.

As evening fell, we reached the bottom, and pitched camp in a beau-tiful point of open pine forest, thrust out into the meadow. There was good shelter, and plenty of wood, water, and grass; we built a huge fire and put up our tents, scattering them in likely places among the pines, which grew far apart and without undergrowth. We dried our steam-ing clothes, and ate a hearty supper of elk-meat; then we turned into our beds, warm and dry, and slept soundly under the canvas, while all night long the storm roared without. Next morning it still stormed fitfully; the high peaks and ridges round about were all capped with snow. Woody and I started on foot for an all-day tramp; the amount of game seen the day before showed that we were in a good elk-country, where the elk had been so little disturbed that they were travelling, feeding, and whistling in daylight. For three hours we walked across the forest-clad spurs of the foot-hills. We roused a small band of elk in thick timber; but they rushed off before we saw them, with much smashing of dead branches. Then we climbed to the summit of the range. The wind was light and baffling; it blew from all points, veering every few minutes. There were occasional rain-squalls; our feet and legs were well soaked; and we became chilled through whenever we sat down to listen. We caught a glimpse of a big bull feeding up-hill, and followed him; it needed smart running to overtake him, for an elk, even while feeding, has a ground-covering gait. Finally we got within a hundred and twenty-five yards, but in very thick timber, and all I could see plainly was the hip and the after-part of the flank. I waited for a chance at the shoulder, but the bull got my wind and was off before I could pull trigger. It was just one of those occasions when there are two courses to pursue, neither very good, and when one is apt to regret whichever decision is made.

At noon we came to the edge of a deep and wide gorge, and sat down shivering to await what might turn up, our fingers numb, and our wet feet icy. Suddenly the love-challenge of an elk came pealing across the gorge, through the fine, cold rain, from the heart of the forest opposite. An hour's stiff climb, down and up, brought us nearly to him; but the wind forced us to advance from below through a series of open glades. He was lying on a point of the cliff-shoulder, surrounded by his cows; and he saw us and made off. An hour afterward, as we were trudging up a steep hill-side dotted with groves of fir and spruce, a young bull of ten points, roused from his day-bed by our approach, galloped across us some sixty yards off. We were in need of better venison than can be furnished by an old rutting bull; so I instantly took a shot at the fat and tender young ten-pointer. I aimed well ahead and pulled trigger just as he came to a small gully; and he fell into it in a heap with a resounding crash. This was on the birthday of my eldest small son; so I took him home the horns, "for his very own." On the way back that afternoon I shot off the heads of two blue grouse, as they perched in the pines.

That evening the storm broke, and the weather became clear and very cold, so that the snow made the frosty mountains gleam like silver. The moon was full, and in the flood of light the wild scenery round our camp was very beautiful. As always where we camped for several days, we had fixed long tables and settles, and were most comfortable; and when we came in at nightfall, or sometimes long afterward, cold, tired, and hungry, it was sheer physical delight to get warm before the roaring fire of pitchy stumps, and then to feast ravenously on bread and beans, on stewed or roasted elk venison, on grouse and sometimes trout, and flapjacks with maple syrup.

Next morning dawned clear and cold, the sky a glorious blue. Woody and I started to hunt over the great table-land, and led our stout horses up the mountain-side, by elk-trails so bad that they had to climb like goats. All these elk-trails have one striking peculiarity. They lead through thick timber, but every now and then send off short, well-worn branches to some cliff-edge or jutting crag, commanding a view far and wide over the country beneath. Elk love to stand on these lookout points, and scan the valleys and mountains round about.

Blue grouse rose from beside our path; Clarke's crows flew past us, with a hollow, flapping sound, or lit in the pine-tops, calling and flirting their tails; the gray-clad whisky-jacks, with multitudinous cries, hopped and fluttered near us. Snow-shoe rabbits scuttled away, the big furry feet which give them their name already turning white. At last we came out on the great plateau, seamed with deep, narrow ravines. Reaches of pasture alternated with groves and open forests of varying size. Almost immediately we heard the bugle of a bull elk, and saw a big band of cows and calves on the other side of a valley. There were three bulls with them, one very large, and we tried to creep up on them; but the wind was baffling and spoiled our stalk. So we returned to our horses, mounted them, and rode a mile farther, toward a large open wood on a hill-side. When within two hundred yards we heard directly ahead the bugle of a bull, and pulled up short. In a moment I saw him walking through an open glade; he had not seen us. The slight breeze brought us down his scent. Elk have a strong characteristic smell; it is usually sweet, like that of a herd of Alderney cows; but in old bulls, while rutting, it is rank, pungent, and lasting. We stood motionless till the bull was out of sight, then stole to the wood, tied our horses, and trotted after him. He was travelling fast, occasionally calling; whereupon others in the neighborhood would answer. Evidently he had been driven out of some herd by the master bull.

He went faster than we did, and while we were vainly trying to overtake him we heard another very loud and sonorous challenge to our left. It came from a ridge-crest at the edge of the woods, among some scattered clumps of the northern nut-pine or pinyon—a queer conifer, growing very high on the mountains, its multiforked trunk and wide-spreading branches giving it the rounded top, and, at a distance, the general look of an oak rather than a pine. We at once walked toward the ridge, up-wind. In a minute or two, to our chagrin, we stumbled on an outlying spike bull, evidently kept on the outskirts of the herd by the master bull. I thought he would alarm all the rest; but, as we stood motionless, he could not see clearly what we were. He stood, ran, stood again, gazed at us, and trotted slowly off. We hurried forward as fast as we dared, and with too little care; for we suddenly came in view of two cows. As they raised their heads to look, Woody squatted down where he was, to keep their attention fixed, while I cautiously tried to slip off to one side unobserved. Favored by the neutral tint of my buckskin hunting-shirt, with which my shoes, leggings, and soft hat matched, I succeeded. As soon as I was out of sight I ran hard and came up to a hillock crested with pin-yons, behind which I judged I should find the herd. As I approached the crest, their strong, sweet smell smote my nostrils. In another moment I saw the tips of a pair of mighty antlers, and I peered over the crest with my rifle at the ready. Thirty yards off, behind a clump of pinyons, stood a huge bull, his head thrown back as he rubbed his shoulders with his horns. There were several cows around him, and one saw me immediately, and took alarm. I fired into the bull's shoul-der, inflicting a mortal wound; but he went off, and I raced after him at top speed, firing twice into his flank; then he stopped, very sick, and I broke his neck with a fourth bullet. An elk often hesitates in the first moments of surprise and fright, and does not get really under way for two or three hundred yards; but, when once fairly started, he may go several miles, even though mortally wounded; therefore, the hunter, after his first shot, should run forward as fast as he can, and shoot again and again until the quarry drops. In this way many ani-mals that would otherwise be lost are obtained, especially by the man who has a repeating-rifle. Nevertheless the hunter should beware of being led astray by the ease with which he can fire half a dozen shots from his repeater; and he should aim as carefully with each shot as if it were his last. No possible rapidity of fire can atone for habitual carelessness of aim with the first shot.

The elk I thus slew was a giant. His body was the size of a steer's, and his antlers, though not unusually long, were very massive and heavy. He lay in a glade, on the edge of a great cliff. Standing on its brink we overlooked a most beautiful country, the home of all homes for the elk: a wilderness of mountains, the immense evergreen forest broken by park and glade, by meadow and pasture, by bare hill-side and barren table-land. Some five miles off lay the sheet of water known to the old hunters as Spotted Lake; two or three shallow, sedgy places, and spots of geyser formation, made pale green blotches on its wind-rippled surface. Far to the southwest, in daring beauty and majesty, the grand domes and lofty spires of the Tetons shot into the blue sky. Too sheer for the snow to rest on their sides, it yet filled the rents in their rough flanks, and lay deep between the towering pinnacles of dark rock.

That night, as on more than one night afterward, a bull elk came down whistling to within two or three hundred yards of the tents, and tried to join the horse herd. The moon had set, so I could not go after it. Elk are very restless and active throughout the night in the rutting season; but where undisturbed they feed freely in the daytime, resting for two or three hours about noon.

Next day, which was rainy, we spent in getting in the antlers and meat of the two dead elk; and I shot off the heads of two or three blue grouse on the way home. The following day I killed another bull elk, following him by the strong, not unpleasing, smell, and hitting him twice as he ran, at about eighty yards. So far I had had good luck, killing everything I had shot at; but now the luck changed, through no fault of mine, as far as I could see, and Ferguson had his innings. The day after I killed this bull he shot two fine mountain rams; and during the remainder of our hunt he killed five elk,—one cow, for meat, and four good bulls. The two rams were with three others, all old and with fine horns; Ferguson peeped over a lofty precipice and saw them coming up it only fifty yards below him. His two first and finest bulls were obtained by hard running and good shooting; the herds were on the move at the time, and only his speed of foot and soundness of wind enabled him to get near enough for a shot. One herd started before he got close, and he killed the master bull by a shot right through the heart, as it trotted past, a hundred and fifty yards distant.

As for me, during the next ten days I killed nothing save one cow for meat; and this though I hunted hard every day from morning till night, no matter what the weather. It was stormy, with hail and snow almost every day; and after working hard from dawn until nightfall, laboriously climbing the slippery mountain-sides, walking through the wet woods, and struggling across the bare plateaus and cliff-shoulders, while the violent blasts of wind drove the frozen rain in our faces, we would come in after dusk wet through and chilled to the marrow. Even when it rained in the valleys it snowed on the mountaintops, and there was no use trying to keep our feet dry. I got three shots at bull elk, two being very hurried snap-shots at animals running in thick timber, the other a running-shot in the open, at over two hundred yards; and I missed all three. On most days I saw no bull worth shooting; the two or three I did see or hear we failed to stalk, the light, shifty wind baffling us, or else an outlying cow which we had not seen giving the alarm. There were many blue and a few ruffed grouse in the woods, and I occasionally shot off the heads of a couple on my way homeward in the evening. In racing after one elk, I leaped across a gully and so bruised and twisted my heel on a rock that, for the remainder of my stay in the mountains, I had to walk on the fore part of that foot. This did not interfere much with my walking, however, except in going down-hill.

Our ill success was in part due to sheer bad luck; but the chief element therein was the presence of a great hunting-party of Shoshone Indians. Split into bands of eight or ten each, they scoured the whole country on their tough, sure-footed ponies. They always hunted on horseback, and followed the elk at full speed wherever they went. Their method of hunting was to organize great drives, the riders strung in lines far apart; they signalled to one another by means of willow whistles, with which they also imitated the calling of the bull elk, thus tolling the animals to them, or making them betray their whereabouts. As they slew whatever they could, but by preference cows and calves, and as they were very persevering, but also very excitable and generally poor shots, so that they wasted much powder, they not only wrought havoc among the elk, but also scared the survivors out of all the country over which they hunted.

Day in and day out we plodded on. In a hunting-trip the days of long monotony in getting to the ground, and the days of unrequited toil after it has been reached, always far outnumber the red-letter days of success. But it is just these times of failure that really test the hunter. In the long run, common-sense and dogged perseverance avail him more than any other qualities. The man who does not give up, but hunts steadily and resolutely through the spells of bad luck until the luck turns, is the man who wins success in the end.

After a week at Two-Ocean Pass, we gathered our pack-animals one frosty morning, and again set off across the mountains. A two-days' jaunt took us to the summit of Wolverine Pass, near Pinyon Peak, beside a little mountain tarn; each morning we found its surface skimmed with black ice, for the nights were cold. After three or four days, we shifted camp to the mouth of Wolverine Creek, to get off the hunting grounds of the Indians. We had used up our last elk-meat that morning, and when we were within a couple of hours' journey of our intended halting-place, Woody and I struck off on foot for a hunt. Just before sunset we came on three or four elk; a spike bull stood for a moment behind some thick evergreens a hundred yards off. Guessing at his shoulder, I fired, and he fell dead after running a few rods. I had broken the luck, after ten days of ill success.

Next morning Woody and I, with the packer, rode to where this elk lay. We loaded the meat on a pack-horse, and let the packer take both the loaded animal and our own saddle-horses back to camp, while we made a hunt on foot. We went up the steep, forest-clad mountain-side, and before we had walked an hour heard two elk whistling ahead of us. The woods were open, and quite free from undergrowth, and we were able to advance noiselessly; there was no wind, for the weather was still, clear, and cold. Both of the elk were evidently very much excited, answering each other continually; they had probably been master bulls, but had become so exhausted that their rivals had driven them from the herds, forcing them to remain in seclusion until they regained their lost strength. As we crept stealthily forward, the calling grew louder and louder, until we could hear the grunting sounds with which the challenge of the nearest ended. He was in a large wallow, which was also a lick. When we were still sixty yards off, he heard us, and rushed out, but wheeled and stood a moment to gaze, puzzled by my buckskin suit. I fired into his throat, breaking his neck, and down he went in a heap. Rushing in and turning, I called to Woody, "He's a twelve-pointer, but the horns are small!" As I spoke I heard the roar of the challenge of the other bull not two hundred yards ahead, as if in defiant answer to my shot.

Running quietly forward, I speedily caught a glimpse of his body. He was behind some fir-trees about seventy yards off, and I could not see which way he was standing, and so fired into the patch of flank which was visible, aiming high, to break the back. My aim was true, and the huge beast crashed down-hill through the evergreens, pulling himself on his fore legs for fifteen or twenty rods, his hind quarters trailing. Racing forward, I broke his neck. His antlers were the finest I ever got. A couple of whisky-jacks appeared at the first crack of the rifle with their customary astonishing familiarity and heedlessness of the hunter; they followed the wounded bull as he dragged his great carcass down the hill, and pounced with ghoulish blood-thirstiness on the gouts of blood that were sprinkled over the green herbage.

These two bulls lay only a couple of hundred yards apart, on a broad game-trail, which was as well beaten as a good bridle-path.

We began to skin out the heads; and as we were finishing we heard another bull challenging far up the mountain. He came nearer and nearer, and as soon as we had ended our work we grasped our rifles and trotted toward him along the game-trail. He was very noisy, uttering his loud, singing challenge every minute or two. The trail was so broad and firm that we walked in perfect silence. After going only five or six hundred yards, we got very close indeed, and stole forward on tiptoe, listening to the roaring music. The sound came from a steep, narrow ravine, to one side of the trail, and I walked toward it with my rifle at the ready. A slight puff gave the elk my wind, and he dashed out of the ravine like a deer; but he was only thirty yards off, and my bullet went into his shoulder as he passed behind a clump of young spruce. I plunged into the ravine, scrambled out of it, and raced after him. In a minute I saw him standing with drooping head, and two more shots finished him. He also bore fine antlers. It was a great piece of luck to get three such fine bulls at the cost of half a day's light work; but we had fairly earned them, having worked hard for ten days, through rain, cold, hunger, and fatigue, to no purpose. That evening my home-coming to camp, with three elk-tongues and a brace of ruffed grouse hung at my belt, was most happy.

Next day it snowed, but we brought a pack-pony to where the three great bulls lay, and took their heads to camp; the flesh was far too strong to be worth taking, for it was just the height of the rut.

This was the end of my hunt; and a day later Hofer and I, with two pack-ponies, made a rapid push for the Upper Geyser Basin. We travelled fast. The first day was gray and overcast, a cold wind blowing strong in our faces. Toward evening we came on a bull elk in a willow thicket; he was on his knees in a hollow, thrashing and beating the willows with his antlers. At dusk we halted and went into camp, by some small pools on the summit of the pass north of Red Mountain.

The elk were calling all around us. We pitched our cozy tent, dragged great stumps for the fire, cut evergreen boughs for our beds, watered the horses, tethered them to improvised picket-pins in a grassy glade, and then set about getting supper ready. The wind had gone down, and snow was falling thick in large, soft flakes; we were evidently at the beginning of a heavy snowstorm. All night we slept soundly in our snug tent. When we arose at dawn there was a foot and a half of snow on the ground, and the flakes were falling as fast as ever. There is no more tedious work than striking camp in bad weather; and it was over two hours from the time we rose to the time we started. It is sheer misery to untangle picket-lines and to pack animals when the ropes are frozen; and by the time we had loaded the two shivering, wincing pack-ponies, and had bridled and saddled our own riding-animals, our hands and feet were numb and stiff with cold, though we were really hampered by our warm clothing. My horse was a wild, nervous roan, and as I swung carelessly into the saddle, he suddenly began to buck before I got my right leg over, and threw me off. My thumb was put out of joint. I pulled it in again, and speedily caught my horse in the dead timber. Then I treated him as what the cowboys call a "mean horse," and mounted him carefully, so as not to let him either buck or go over backward. However, his preliminary success had inspirited him, and a dozen times that day he began to buck, usually choosing a down grade, where the snow was deep, and there was much fallen timber.

All day long we pushed steadily through the cold, blinding snow-storm. Neither squirrels nor rabbits were abroad; and a few Clarke's crows, whisky-jacks, and chickadees were the only living things we saw. At nightfall, chilled through, we reached the Upper Geyser Basin. Here I met a party of railroad surveyors and engineers, coming in from their summer's field-work. One of them lent me a saddle-horse and a pack-pony, and we went on together, breaking our way through the snow-choked roads to the Mammoth Hot Springs, while Hofer took my own horses back to Ferguson.

I have described this hunt at length because, though I enjoyed it particularly on account of the comfort in which we travelled and the beauty of the land, yet, in point of success in finding and killing game, in value of trophies procured, and in its alternations of good and bad luck, it may fairly stand as the type of a dozen such hunts I have made. Twice I have been much more successful; the difference being due to sheer luck, as I hunted equally hard in all three instances. Thus on this trip I killed and saw nothing but elk; yet the other members of the party either saw, or saw fresh signs of, not only blacktail deer, but sheep, bear, bison, moose, cougar, and wolf. Now in 1889 I hunted over almost precisely similar country, only farther to the northwest, on the boundary between Idaho and Montana, and, with the exception of sheep, I stumbled on all the animals mentioned, and white goat in addition, so that my bag of twelve head actually included eight species—much the best bag I ever made, and the only one that could really be called out of the common. In 1884, on a trip to the Bighorn Mountains, I killed three bear, six elk and six deer. In laying in the winter stock of meat for my ranch I often far excelled these figures as far as mere numbers went; but on no other regular hunting trip, where the quality and not the quantity of the game was the prime consideration, have I ever equalled them; and on several where I worked hardest I hardly averaged a head a week. The occasional days or weeks of phenomenal luck, are more than earned by the many others where no luck whatever follows the very hardest work. Yet, if a man hunts with steady resolution he is apt to strike enough lucky days amply to repay him.

On this Shoshone trip I fired fifty-eight shots. In preference to using the knife I generally break the neck of an elk which is still struggling; and I fire at one as long as it can stand, preferring to waste a few extra bullets, rather than see an occasional head of game escape. In consequence of these two traits the nine elk I got (two running at sixty and eighty yards, the others standing, at from thirty to a hundred) cost me twenty-three bullets; and I missed three shots—all three, it is but fair to say, difficult ones. I also cut off the heads of seventeen grouse, with twenty-two shots; and killed two ducks with ten shots—fifty-eight in all. On the Bighorn trip I used a hundred and two cartridges. On no other trip did I use fifty.

To me still-hunting elk in the mountains, when they are calling, is one of the most attractive of sports, not only because of the size and stately beauty of the quarry and the grand nature of the trophy, but because of the magnificence of the scenery, and the stirring, manly, exciting nature of the chase itself. It yields more vigorous enjoyment than does lurking stealthily through the grand but gloomy monotony of the marshy woodland where dwells the moose. The climbing among the steep forest-clad and glade-strewn mountains is just difficult enough thoroughly to test soundness in wind and limb, while without the heart-breaking fatigue of white goat hunting. The actual grapple with an angry grisly is of course far more full of strong, eager pleasure; but bear hunting is the most uncertain, and usually the least productive, of sports.

As regards strenuous, vigorous work, and pleasurable excitement the chase of the bighorn alone stands higher. But the bighorn, grand beast of the chase though he be, is surpassed in size, both of body and of horns, by certain of the giant sheep of Central Asia; whereas the wapiti is not only the most stately and beautiful of American game— far more so than the bison and moose, his only rivals in size—but is also the noblest of the stag kind throughout the world. Whoever kills him has killed the chief of his race; for he stands far above his brethren of Asia and Europe.

BOB WHITE,
DOWN 'T ABERDEEN

NASH BUCKINGHAM

Andrew's letter was characteristic. "Entirely all right and welcome to include the Gentleman from Boston. Never mind the Yankee strain in his breeding. If he proves a good shot and able to negotiate a few of Colonel Lauderdale's 75–90 h.p. toddies, the Rebels will stand for his pedigree, and even though it leaks out that he's a Republican, why our game laws will protect him. I know a place where the birds are holding a convention. Down across the river, about eight miles from here, in a sandy-loam and pine-hill country full of sedge, pea patches and sorghum. I have a fine old friend there. He runs a water mill, but the last man he killed was a Prohibitionist. Grinds his own flour and believe me, boy, he is a biscuit maker. If you don't choose goggle-eyed hen eggs (from contented hens) about twice the size of fifty-dollar gold pieces, and can't choke down real all-pork sausage and baked hams, why bring along your own sum'p'n t'eat. The plug gets in so late that you all may have to go to the hotel for the night but Johnny'll move your outfit out to the house next day. Couldn't do much with Johnny after dark anyhow. There's a ghost scare on down here. A phantom called Mother Hubbard is working around the streets and Johnny claims that she 'done run sev-ul uv his frens' right on to degradation.' Fat chance to get him to hang around till midnight!"

How pleasant the recollection that drifted back a twelvemonth in prospective enjoyment of another visit! We were sitting again in comfortable cane-bottomed rockers on the wide veranda of the High Private's ancestral home. From crevices of the lofty, iron-capped columns clung villages of nests, in and out of which twittered the sparrows, bent either upon warlike sally against shrill encroaching jays or engaged in piercing squabbles relating to matters of domestic retention. It was Sunday afternoon on the Old Home Place, in the sweet purpling of a brave autumnal day. From down Matubba road the puffity-pant of the cotton gin was hushed. No crop wagons creaked past in swirls of Indian summer dust with their sputtering crackle of long blacksnake whips, uncoiling over the sodgerin' back and along sleek ribs of "jughaids." There was no jocose lingo of the mule curse; no bare-fanged country dogs, entrenched beneath the wagons. It was the time of year when flashing dawns melted away the tinge of frost scrolls from russet woodland; when gaud and arrogance of capricious color gave riotous defiance to the approach of sombrous winter. Black fingers twinkled among the hoary yield of cotton bolls; 'possum and coon throve in the bottoms; darky chants rose to exultant pitch with divers harbingers of peace and plenty. Doomed by ripe fatness and assaults with stick and stone, luscious persimmons plumped to earth and schoolboy stomachs. "Egg-bustin" puppies raced abroad, causing Brer Rabbit to hoist subject-to-change-without-notice signs. Canvas-coated hunters rode afield; lithe pointers and setters searched hill and dale for Bob Whites that leaped roaring from embrowning covert. And then—

I glanced mournfully through an office window into the forbidding bleakness of our latest cold snap. Surely, I reflected, it was a fine day for a murder or to set a hen. But, to the Gentleman from Boston, languishing at his hotel, I broke the glad tidings of our invitation, and grouchily set about waiting a squarer deal from the elements. Next day dawned clear as a bell. I had just spread the sporting section when Andrew called over Long Distance. At five that afternoon we cast off, aboard the "Plug," an abused little red-in-the-face train with a seven-hour-or-more-trip staring us straight in the stomach. Fast trains chased us into sidings and burly freights hooted us into submission, leaving the poor Plug to scramble home out of breath, practically discouraged and ready to give up. It was past midnight when we finally boomed across the Tombigbee, did a "gran' right an' left" in the switching line and bumped into the silent and aristocratic town of Aberdeen, Mississippi.

Two night-owl porters for rival hotels quarreled bitterly over our bags, one darky threatening to "part yo' hair, niggah, ef yo' doan turn loose dat grip-sack; don' yo' see dat fine-lookin' white man from Memphis don' want to stop at nobody's house 'cep mine?" This sable and subtle flattery had an effect of quelling the incipient riot, so we hastened uptown, registered at the comfortable Clopton House and dug far into our warm beds.

Morning came with reverse English on the fair weather. Leaden, blowy skies, an icy wind that promised chilly creeps and deeply gashed gumbo roads frozen into treacherous depths. Andrew was on hand early and regretted that it would be practically impossible to reach his selected territory. "But," said he, "we'll take in some ground I shot over last week and find all the birds we're lookin' for."

Breakfast over, the steeds were led up; Andrew whistled for Flash and Jim and we were off. The horse allotted the Gentleman from Boston was of dignified personality and winning ways, but the brute I drew was a "low-life" pure and simple. Scarcely had I a leg up, when, for the edification of a morbidly curious public, the wretch came undone right there on Main street. The idea of a regular, everyday Southern horse trying to sunfish and timberline rather surprised me, to say the least, and for a moment, just a moment, I had a good notion to hang my spurs in him and accompany the scratching with a tremendous beating over the head with my hat and a lot of yelling thrown in or off. But I had no spurs, so kept my hat out of the ring, clung to my weapon and pulled leather until Seldom-Fed quit hogging.

Our trek led through the stately old burg past the huge courthouse, crumbly with its struggle against the years, reminiscent of impassioned oratory and bitter but courtly legal battles. At intervals we glimpsed through spacious boundaries of wintered cedar hedge, oak, and locust, old-fashioned homes of singular and comforting beauty. Some, with their broad porches and superb lines of colonial paneling drooping into an almost sagging dilapidation of wartime impoverishment; others bespeaking an eloquent survival and defiance of time.

Leaving town we struck off into a bottom land of down corn and thicket. Out of the north a freezing, stinging wind wrung tears from our eyes with its biting whip. At the first ditch Andrew broke ice, wet our dogs' feet and applied a coating of tannic acid. A moment later, when cast off, they headed up through a corn field. Almost in the same breath it seemed, they froze on a point at an impenetrable thicket bordering a wide pond. We were more than glad to dismount and hurry toward the find. Approaching, we saw the birds flush wild and sweep across the pond into some briar tangles. We skirted the marsh, and, shooting in turn, managed to start the ball rolling with five singles. Leading our mounts, for walking proved far more preferable than facing the wind, we plugged through a creek bottom. We were joined here by a strange pointer belonging, Andrew said, to a gentleman in Aberdeen. "Flight" had evidently observed the departure of our safari, and being of congenial trend, had taken up the trail. Rounding a thicket clump we discovered Jimmy holding staunchly, with Flash backing as though his very life depended upon it. The new dog celebrated his arrival by pausing a second, as though to contemplate the picture, then dashed in, sending birds in every direction. The Gentleman from Boston accomplished a neat double, Andrew singled, but I was too far away to do much of anything save cuss and watch down a single or two. Andrew had Flash and Jim retrieve, then turned and eyed the guilt-stricken Flight with narrowed lids. Placing his gun against a convenient bush, he ripped a substantial switch from a sapling and grittingly invited the hapless one approach. This he did, in fawning, contrite hesitation, while the other dogs loafed in to enjoy the circus and give him the laugh. A moment later his cries rent the air, but the whaling had its effect—he flushed no more that day and attended strictly to business. At the horses we found Joe Howard, Andrew's cousin, who brought with him his good pointer, Ticket. Joe had ridden from his home two miles beyond town and reported tough sledding.

Fording a slushy bayou, we rode a short distance before seeing Flash, rigid as a poker, pointing in a ravine. Tick and Jim flattened on sight and Flight, with vivid memory of his recent dressing down, sprawled when Andrew's sharp warning reached him. A huge bevy buzzed from the sedge. "Blam-blam and blooie-blooie" ensued, with the result that each man tucked away a pair of birds in his coat. The singles went "home-free" by winging it across an ice-gorged back water. Farther on, Flight re-established himself somewhat in our good graces by a ripping find. It was ludicrous to see the fellow roll his protruding eyes and warn off the covetous Ticket who wormed a bit too near in an effort to assist. But best of all a glorious sun burned a blazing way through the clouds and cheered up everything.

In higher country, following the direction taken by some split-covey singles we saw Flight and Flash standing perhaps forty feet apart at the edge of a dense timber bottom. Thinking they had spotted some truants we separated; the Boston Boy and I going to Flash while Joe and Andrew pinned their faith to Flight's fancy. To our amazement two clustrous bevies roared from the clover almost simultaneously. Ed and I dropped four from our rise, while Joe and Andrew drew equal toll from theirs. For the next half hour we enjoyed the most magnificent of all shooting—single birds scattered in hedge boundaries and along the leaf-strewn files of the timber. We kicked about here and there, joking, laughing, betting on shots, taking turns as the dogs ranged stealthily ahead, pointing, it seemed, almost every moment. Occasionally, when a bird lay low or flushed wild some smooth chap, made a getaway, but we begrudged not one of these his escape. Finally, with bulging pockets we returned to the horses.

At a free-flowing artesian well Joe and Andrew produced capacious saddle pockets and unwound savory bundles. Their contents would have made the weariest Fletcherite drool at the mouth and forget his number of chews. There was cold quail and crisp "beat" biscuit. Then came "hog-haid" sandwiches and meaty spareribs, home-made pickles and hard-boiled eggs. And to top off came a jam cake and a chocolate one, the latter inlaid with marshmallow sauce and studded with walnut and pecan hearts.

Nothing disturbed the noon stillness save grunts of purest satisfaction serene and an occasional yell of "Aw, git away f'um here, dawg." After lunch came a pipe for the others and a "touch" by an old colored mammy who came like Rebekah to the Well, with her pitcher and a hard-luck story of the burned cabin. We each shelled out "two bits," and in addition to this purse a fat cane-cutter rabbit that Joe had bowled over surreptitiously sent her on her way rejoicing.

Climbing into our saddles we rode down through the spongy accretions of the bottoms, across a wide slough and out into a vast section of waste or "ole po' land" as Andrew termed it. A short way on Jim was discovered gazing rapturously into a plum thicket. We saw the birds go up and wing past, settling across a drainage ditch. One of the dogs had evidently come along down wind and frisked Jim out of a point, for he was very much embarrased. Then in rapid succession the dogs found birds seemingly right and left. Three big gangs were turned up within a radius of ten acres. It was glorious sport and the afternoon wore away almost without our knowledge. What with a puffy kill here, a miss there and the ever-recurring thrill when some tireless dog whirled into discovery, we were almost glad to gather up our reins and hit off toward the line of greening hills that marked the direction of our circle home.

In a short while we splashed across an expanse of meadow and began climbing through sedge-strewn valleys and steep ridges of pine forest. Shadows were lengthening among the trees and our horses' steps were muffled in the needle bedding underfoot. In an opening we halted and look away across the lowlands of our morning to where Aberdeen lay brooding in the peace and quiet of tranquil, fading sunshine. The piercing blast had softened with the chill of falling night. It seemed a thousand miles to the warmth of indoors and the delight of complete well-fed weariness. The faithful dogs had as yet evinced no signs of fatigue, in fact they were splitting the grass at top speed. Just as we reached the Gillespie place boundary fence Jimmy paused at a dry ditch along the road, sniffed, and then with head in air, walked forward as though treading on eggs.

"He's got his Sunday clothes on ag'in, ain't he?" asked Andrew, his face lighting with pardonable pride and a lean expansive grin. "But I believe we've all got pretty durn near the limit."

"Les'try 'em jus' one mo' fair fall," replied Joe, "it would be a shame to put one over on Jim dog after all his trouble."

"Satisfactory to me," pronounced Andrew. "Light down, gents, and bust a few night caps"—shoving two shells into his stubby Parker. Here Jimmy broke his point and tiptoed gingerly after the running birds. Then, out over the brink boiled a veritable beehive of quail. Ensued a miniature sham battle, followed by shouts of "I got two" and counter claims of "I killed that one" and "Fetch daid, suh." Discipline was forgotten for the nonce, but matters were adjusted when the dogs brought in enough birds to credit each man with a clean, undisputed double. "Better count up here," said Joe, "I've gotta leave you lads at the nex' gate." So the tally began, with low murmurings as each chap pulled bird after bird from his multipocketed coat.

"The limit here," announced Andrew, finishing first.

"For the first time in my young life a limit," chortled the Boston Boy.

"Another victory for the untrammeled Democracy," said Joe.

"Sufficiency here," I confessed.

At a padlocked gate, down the road, Joe took leave of us with a parting shout of "See you in the morning, boys, at the Houston place gate." The sun was glowing faintly behind its borderland of western ridge spires. Our dogs, seeming to realize that their day's work was done, leaped gladly along to keep our pace. Through field and brake we trotted, and at length, swinging into a black buckshot road, straightened out for the home stretch down Life Boat Chapel lane. It was to me a familiar way, past homely daubed shacks and cabins, ashine with the gleam of lowly lamplight, redolent of wood fires, frying bacon and contentment.

And how the dogs did bark when we swung into the grounds of our host! What is there better in life than an evening spent within the domain of Sweet Hospitality? What is more delightful than when, clothed in the refreshened garb of citizenry, one lies at ease in a deep armchair or sits down to such a dinner as only an "Auntie" can dish up and send in to her "white folks"? And surely out upon the sea of night there rides no fairer craft than a towering four-poster.

It was past seven o'clock when we found ourselves at family breakfast. You have, no doubt, often begun the morning meal with a luscious orange. But listen! Have you ever seen a "yard boy" stagger in under a huge platter, wide as the bottom of a boat, piled high with quail, smothered as only Aunt Hannah can turn the trick, with a whole bucket of bird gravy for the hominy and grits? You may suit yourself about the spiced aromatic spirits of little pigs, or slices of float-away omelette, but personally I prefer to rather economize on space until the waffles start flocking in in droves. Did you ever tenderly smear a pair of round, crisp, eat-me-quick-for-the-love-of-Mike members of the waffle family; watching the molten country butter search out the receptive crevices and overflow each hollow? Then slathered the twain with a ruddy coating of home-kettled, right-from-the-heart, ribbon cane molasses? But at length Pud sounded retreat by announcing the horses. Scabbards and saddle pockets were tied on and we were off in the bright sunshine of a perfect day.

At the Houston place gate we found Joe waiting with the ever ready Ticket and Lady, the latter a Marse Ben-Bragg-Gladstone pup. Within two hours we had raised six bevies. Ticket was the first to make birds, stiffening in a clover patch along a railroad cut. Then little Lady raced away across a hill and made a neat find on the cast. Flash and Jim were old stagers on these grounds. Jim nailed a gang for Andrew near a blackjack stretch and Flash, after handling some of the singles, delved far into the interior and fastened upon a covey. For some time we had royal sport trying to make respectable averages in the dense tangle and the dogs tried hard to overlook the messy work their masters were doing when brown bullets would whir from the dead leaves and top the blackjacks in whizzing farewell.

After lunch we rode the hill crests, letting the dogs cut up the sides and valleys. On an opposite ridge we saw Andrew approach the top with Lady and Jim flagging ahead. Down went the pair on a clean-cut point.

"It's a shame to take the money," shouted Andrew, and, sure enough, he whirled two of the crowd into bird paradise. Midafternoon is the ideal time for bird finding and it was a treat to see the Boston Boy's eyes widen in wonderment when the dogs picked up bunch after bunch.

"By the gills of the sacred codfish," he exclaimed, feverishly ripping open a fresh box of shells, "I never knew there were this many birds in existence." But at length it again neared knocking-off time, so we spurred through the fields hoping for just one more find to make the day complete.

"There they are," called Joe, rising in his stirrups, pointing to Flash and Jim. And, sure enough, they were at it again, and such a whopper the covey proved! We were actually too amazed to shoot on the rise, but watched the fugitives settle in a marshy strip of iron weed bordering a willow "dreen." Suffice to say that we gave them our personal attention and when the war was over the result proved a fitting climax to another red-letter day. Twenty or twenty-five birds doesn't sound so many to a game hog, perhaps, but shooting four in a party, turn about or shooting alone, when a man has spent the hours afield with nature and taken from her cherished stores the satisfaction of twenty clean kills and the vagrant clinging pangs of many misses, he has done pretty much all that an unselfish heart could ever crave.

"Well," questioned Andrew, when our horses' heads were set toward home, "how does the Minute Man from ye Boston Towne like an everyday, Down-in-Dixie bird hunt, with a little Rebel Yell stuff on the side?"

The Gentleman from Boston sighed a sigh of rich content and stretched wearily in his saddle.

"You are now speaking," said he, with that methodical diction characteristic of the ultra-grammatical Bostonian, "of the very best thing in the universe."

"D'm'f'taint," I echoed softly.

And Andrew triple-plated this confirmation in the tongue of our Fatherland.

"Sho' is!"

HUNTING ON THE OREGON TRAIL

FRANCIS PARKMAN

The country before us was now thronged with buffalo, and a sketch of the manner of hunting them will not be out of place. There are two methods commonly practised, "running" and "approaching." The chase on horseback, which goes by the name of "running," is the more violent and dashing mode of the two, that is to say, when the buffalo are in one of their wild moods; for otherwise it is tame enough. A practised and skilful hunter, well mounted, will sometimes kill five or six cows in a single chase, loading his gun again and again as his horse rushes through the tumult. In attacking a small band of buffalo, or in separating a single animal from the herd and assailing it apart from the rest, there is less excitement and less danger. In fact, the animals are at times so stupid and lethargic that there is little sport in killing them. With a bold and well-trained horse the hunter may ride so close to the buffalo that as they gallop side by side he may touch him with his hand; nor is there much danger in this as long as the buffalo's strength and breath continue unabated; but when he becomes tired and can no longer run with ease, when his tongue lolls out and the foam flies from his jaws, then the hunter had better keep a more respectful distance; the distressed brute may turn upon him at any instant; and especially at the moment when he fires his gun. The horse then leaps aside, and the hunter has need of a tenacious seat in the saddle, for if he is thrown to the ground there is no hope for him. When he sees his attack defeated, the buffalo resumes his flight, but if the shot is well directed he soon stops; for a few moments he stands still, then totters and falls heavily upon the prairie.

The chief difficulty in running buffalo, as it seems to me, is that of loading the gun or pistol at full gallop. Many hunters for convenience's sake carry three or four bullets in the mouth; the powder is poured down the muzzle of the piece, the bullet dropped in after it, the stock struck hard upon the pommel of the saddle, and the work is done. The danger of this is obvious. Should the blow on the pommel fail to send the bullet home, or should the bullet, in the act of aiming, start from its place and roll towards the muzzle, the gun would probably burst in discharging. Many a shattered hand and worse casualties besides have been the result of such an accident. To obviate it, some hunters make use of a ramrod, usually hung by a string from the neck, but this materially increases the difficulty of loading. The bows and arrows which the Indians use in running buffalo have many advantages over firearms, and even white men occasionally employ them.

The danger of the chase arises not so much from the onset of the wounded animal as from the nature of the ground which the hunter must ride over. The prairie does not always present a smooth, level, and uniform surface; very often it is broken with hills and hollows, intersected by ravines, and in the remoter parts studded by the stiff wild-sage bushes. The most formidable obstructions, however, are the burrows of wild animals, wolves, badgers, and particularly prairie-dogs, with whose holes the ground for a very great extent is frequently honeycombed. In the blindness of the chase the hunter rushes over it unconscious of danger; his horse, at full career, thrusts his leg deep into one of the burrows;

the bone snaps, the rider is hurled forward to the ground and probably killed. Yet accidents in buffalo running happen less frequently than one would suppose; in the recklessness of the chase, the hunter enjoys all the impunity of a drunken man, and may ride in safety over gullies and declivities, where, should he attempt to pass in his sober senses, he would infallibly break his neck.

The method of "approaching," being practised on foot, has many advantages over that of "running"; in the former, one neither breaks down his horse nor endangers his own life; he must be cool, collected, and watchful; must understand the buffalo, observe the features of the country and the course of the wind, and be well skilled in using the rifle. The buffalo are strange animals; sometimes they are so stupid and infatuated that a man may walk up to them in full sight on the open prairie, and even shoot several of their number before the rest will think it necessary to retreat. At another moment they will be so shy and wary that in order to approach them the utmost skill, experience, and judgment are necessary. Kit Carson, I believe, stands preeminent in running buffalo; in approaching, no man living can bear away the palm from Henry Chatillon.

After Tête Rouge had alarmed the camp, no further disturbance occurred during the night. The Arapahoes did not attempt mischief, or if they did the wakefulness of the party deterred them from effecting their purpose. The next day was one of activity and excitement, for about ten o'clock the man in advance shouted the gladdening cry of buffalo, buffalo! and in the hollow of the prairie just below us, a band of bulls was grazing. The temptation was irresistible, and Shaw and I rode down upon them. We were badly mounted on our travelling horses, but by hard lashing we overtook them, and Shaw, running alongside a bull, shot into him both balls of his double-barreled gun. Looking round as I galloped by, I saw the bull in his mortal fury rushing again and again upon his antagonist, whose horse constantly leaped aside, and avoided the onset. My chase was more protracted, but at length I ran close to the bull and killed him with my pistols. Cutting off the tails of our victims by way of trophy, we rejoined the party in about a quarter of an hour after we had left it. Again and again that morning rang out the same welcome cry of buffalo, buffalo! Every few moments, in the broad meadows along the river, we saw bands of bulls, who, raising their shaggy heads, would gaze in stupid amazement at the approaching horsemen, and then breaking into a clumsy gallop, file off in a long line across the trail in front, towards the rising prairie on the left. At noon, the plain before us was alive with thousands of buffalo,—bulls, cows, and calves,—all moving rapidly as we drew near; and far off beyond the river the swelling prairie was darkened with them to the very horizon. The party was in gayer spirits than ever. We stopped for a nooning near a grove of trees by the river.

"Tongues and hump-ribs tomorrow," said Shaw, looking with contempt at the venison steaks which Deslauriers placed before us. Our meal finished, we lay down to sleep. A shout from Henry Chatillon aroused us, and we saw him standing on the cart-wheel, stretching his tall figure to its full height, while he looked towards the prairie beyond the river. Following the direction of his eyes, we could clearly distinguish a large, dark object, like the black shadow of a cloud, passing rapidly over swell after swell of the distant plain; behind it followed another of similar appearance, though smaller, moving more rapidly, and drawing closer and closer to the first. It was the hunters of the Arapahoe camp chasing a band of buffalo. Shaw and I caught and saddled our best horses, and went plunging through sand and water to the farther bank. We were too late. The hunters had already mingled with the herd, and the work of slaughter was nearly over. When we reached the ground we found it strewn far and near with numberless carcasses, while the remnants of the herd, scattered in all directions, were flying away in terror, and the Indians still rushing in pursuit. Many of the hunters, however, remained upon the spot, and among the rest was our yesterday's acquaintance, the chief of the village. He had alighted by the side of a cow, into which he had shot five or six arrows, and his squaw, who had followed him on horseback to the hunt, was giving him a draught of water from a canteen, purchased or plundered from some volunteer soldier. Recrossing the river, we overtook the party, who were already on their way.

We had gone scarcely a mile when we saw an imposing spectacle. From the river-bank on the right, away over the swelling prairie on the left, and in front as far as the eye could reach, was one vast host of buffalo. The outskirts of the herd were within a quarter of a mile. In many parts they were crowded so densely together that in the distance their rounded backs presented a surface of uniform blackness; but elsewhere they were more scattered, and from amid the multitude rose little columns of dust where some of them were rolling on the ground. Here and there a battle was going forward among the bulls. We could distinctly see them rushing against each other, and hear the clattering of their horns and their hoarse bellowing. Shaw was riding at some distance in advance, with Henry Chatillon; I saw him stop and draw the leather covering from his gun. With such a sight before us, but one thing could be thought of. That morning I had used pistols in the chase. I had now a mind to try the virtue of a gun. Deslauriers had one, and I rode up to the side of the cart; there he sat under the white covering, biting his pipe between his teeth and grinning with excitement.

"Lend me your gun, Deslauriers."

"Oui, Monsieur, oui," said Deslauriers, tugging with might and main to stop the mule, which seemed obstinately bent on going forward. Then everything but his moccasons disappeared as he crawled into the cart and pulled at the gun to extricate it.

"Is it loaded?" I asked.

"Oui, bien chargé; you'll kill, mon bourgeois; yes, you'll kill—c'est un bon fusil."

I handed him my rifle and rode forward to Shaw.

"Are you ready?" he asked.

"Come on," said I.

"Keep down that hollow, "said Henry," and then they won't see you till you get close to them."

The hollow was a kind of wide ravine; it ran obliquely towards the buffalo, and we rode at a canter along the bottom until it became too shallow; then we bent close to our horses' necks, and, at last, finding that it could no longer conceal us, came out of it and rode directly towards the herd. It was within gunshot; before its outskirts, numerous grizzly old bulls were scattered, holding guard over their females. They glared at us in anger and astonishment, walked towards us a few yards, and then turning slowly round, retreated at a trot which afterwards broke into a clumsy gallop. In an instant the main body caught the alarm. The buffalo began to crowd away from the point towards which we were approaching, and a gap was opened in the side of the herd. We entered it, still restraining our excited horses. Every instant the tumult was thickening. The buffalo, pressing together in large bodies, crowded away from us on every hand. In front and on either side we could see dark columns and masses, half hidden by clouds of dust, rushing along in terror and confusion, and hear the tramp and clattering of ten thousand hoofs. That countless multitude of powerful brutes, ignorant of their own strength, were flying in a panic from the approach of two feeble horsemen. To remain quiet longer was impossible.

"Take that band on the left," said Shaw; "I'll take these in front."

He sprang off, and I saw no more of him. A heavy Indian whip was fastened by a band to my wrist; I swung it into the air and lashed my horse's flank with all the strength of my arm. Away she darted, stretching close to the ground. I could see nothing but a cloud of dust before me, but I knew that it concealed a band of many hundreds of buffalo. In a moment I was in the midst of the cloud, half suffocated by the dust and stunned by the trampling of the flying herd; but I was drunk with the chase and cared for nothing but the buffalo. Very soon a long dark mass became visible, looming through the dust; then I could distinguish each bulky carcass, the hoofs flying out beneath, the short tails held rigidly erect. In a moment I was so close that I could have touched them with my gun. Suddenly, to my amazement, the hoofs were jerked upwards, the tails flourished in the air, and amid a cloud of dust the buffalo seemed to sink into the earth before me. One vivid impression of that instant remains upon my mind. I remember looking down upon the backs of several buffalo dimly visible through the dust. We had run unawares upon a ravine. At that moment I was not the most accurate judge of depth and width, but when I passed it on my return, I found it about twelve feet deep and not quite twice as wide at the bottom. It was impossible to stop; I would have done so gladly if I could; so, half sliding, half plunging, down went the little mare. She came down on her knees in the loose sand at the bottom; I was pitched forward against her neck and nearly thrown over her head among the buffalo, who amid dust and confusion came tumbling in all around. The mare was on her feet in an instant and scrambling like a cat up the opposite side. I thought for a moment that she would have fallen back and crushed me, but with a violent effort she clambered out and gained the hard prairie above. Glancing back, I saw the huge head of a bull clinging as it were by the forefeet at the edge of the dusty gulf. At length I was fairly among the buffalo. They were less densely crowded than before, and I could see nothing but bulls, who always run at the rear of a herd to protect their females. As I passed among them they would lower their heads, and turning as they ran, try to gore my horse; but as they were already at full speed there was no force in their onset, and as Pauline ran faster than they, they were always thrown behind her in the effort. I soon began to distinguish cows amid the throng. One just in front of me seemed to my liking, and I pushed close to her side. Dropping the reins, I fired, holding the muzzle of the gun within a foot of her shoulder. Quick as lightning she sprang at Pauline; the little mare dodged the attack, and I lost sight of the wounded animal amid the tumult. Immediately after, I selected another, and urging forward Pauline, shot into her both pistols in succession. For a while I kept her in view, but in attempting to load my gun, lost sight of her also in the confusion. Believing her to be mortally wounded and unable to keep up with the herd, I checked my horse. The crowd rushed onwards. The dust and tumult passed away, and on the prairie, far behind the rest, I saw a solitary buffalo galloping heavily. In a moment I and my victim were running side by side. My firearms were all empty, and I had in my pouch nothing but rifle bullets, too large for the pistols and too small for the gun. I loaded the gun, however, but as often as I levelled it to fire, the bullets would roll out of the muzzle and the gun returned only a report like a squib, as the powder harmlessly exploded. I rode in front of the buffalo and tried to turn her back; but her eyes glared, her mane bristled, and lowering her head, she rushed at me with the utmost fierceness and activity. Again and again I rode before her, and again and again she repeated her furious charge. But little Pauline was in her element. She dodged her enemy at every rush, until at length the buffalo stood still, exhausted with her own efforts, her tongue lolling from her jaws.

Riding to a little distance, I dismounted, thinking to gather a handful of dry grass to serve the purpose of wadding, and load the gun at my leisure. No sooner were my feet on the ground than the buffalo came bounding in such a rage towards me that I jumped back again into the saddle and with all possible despatch. After waiting a few minutes more, I made an attempt to ride up and stab her with my knife; but Pauline was near being gored in the attempt. At length, bethinking me of the fringes at the seams of my buckskin trousers, I jerked off a few of them, and, reloading the gun, forced them down the barrel to keep the bullet in its place; then approaching, I shot the wounded buffalo through the heart. Sinking to her knees, she rolled over lifeless on the prairie. To my astonishment, I found that, instead of a cow, I had been slaughtering a stout yearling bull. No longer wondering at his fierceness, I opened his throat, and cutting out his tongue, tied it at the back of my saddle. My mistake was one which a more experienced eye than mine might easily make in the dust and confusion of such a chase.

Then for the first time I had leisure to look at the scene around me. The prairie in front was darkened with the retreating multitude, and on either hand the buffalo came filing up in endless columns from the low plains upon the river. The Arkansas was three or four miles distant. I turned and moved slowly towards it. A long time passed before, far in the distance, I distinguished the white covering of the cart and the little black specks of horsemen before and behind it. Drawing near, I recognized Shaw's elegant tunic, the red flannel shirt, conspicuous far off. I overtook the party, and asked him what success he had had. He had assailed a fat cow, shot her with two bullets, and mortally wounded her. But neither of us was prepared for the chase that afternoon, and Shaw, like myself, had no spare bullets in his pouch; so he abandoned the disabled animal to Henry Chatillon, who followed, despatched her with his rifle, and loaded his horse with the meat.

We encamped close to the river. The night was dark, and as we lay down we could hear, mingled with the howling of wolves, the hoarse bellowing of the buffalo, like the ocean beating upon a distant coast.

~~~~~~

No one in the camp was more active than Jim Gurney, and no one half so lazy as Ellis. Between these two there was a great antipathy. Ellis never stirred in the morning until he was compelled, but Jim was always on his feet before daybreak; and this morning as usual the sound of his voice awakened the party.

"Get up, you booby! up with you now, you're fit for nothing but eating and sleeping. Stop your grumbling and come out of that buffalo-robe, or I'll pull it off for you."

Jim's words were interspersed with numerous expletives, which gave them great additional effect. Ellis drawled out something in a nasal tone from among the folds of his buffalo-robe; then slowly disengaged himself, rose into a sitting posture, stretched his long arms, yawned hideously, and, finally raising his tall person erect, stood staring about him to all the four quarters of the horizon. Deslauriers' fire was soon blazing, and the horses and mules, loosened from their pickets, were feeding on the neighboring meadow. When we sat down to breakfast the prairie was still in the dusky light of morning; and as the sun rose we were mounted and on our way again.

"A white buffalo!" exclaimed Munroe.

"I'll have that fellow," said Shaw, "if I run my horse to death after him."

He threw the cover of his gun to Deslauriers and galloped out upon the prairie.

"Stop, Mr. Shaw, stop!" called out Henry Chatillon, "you'll run down your horse for nothing; it's only a white ox."

But Shaw was already out of hearing. The ox, which had no doubt strayed away from some of the government wagon trains, was standing beneath some low hills which bounded the plain in the distance. Not far from him a band of veritable buffalo bulls were grazing; and startled at Shaw's approach, they all broke into a run, and went scrambling up the hillsides to gain the high prairie above. One of them in his haste and terror involved himself in a fatal catastrophe. Along the foot of the hills was a narrow strip of deep marshy soil, into which the bull plunged and hopelessly entangled himself. We all rode to the spot. The huge carcass was half sunk in the mud, which flowed to his very chin, and his shaggy mane was outspread upon the surface. As we came near, the bull began to struggle with convulsive strength; he writhed to and fro, and in the energy of his fright and desperation would lift himself for a moment half out of the slough, while the reluctant mire returned a sucking sound as he strained to drag his limbs from its tenacious depths. We stimulated his exertions by getting behind him and twisting his tail; nothing would do. There was clearly no hope for him. After every effort his heaving sides were more deeply embedded, and the mire almost overflowed his nostrils; he lay still at length, and looking round at us with a furious eye, seemed to resign himself to fate. Ellis slowly dismounted, and, levelling his boasted yager, shot the old bull through the heart; then lazily climbed back again to his seat, pluming himself no doubt on having actually killed a buffalo. That day the invincible yager drew blood for the first and last time during the whole journey.

The morning was a bright and gay one, and the air so clear that on the farthest horizon the outline of the pale blue prairie was sharply drawn against the sky. Shaw was in the mood for hunting; he rode in advance of the party, and before long we saw a file of bulls galloping at full speed upon a green swell of the prairie at some distance in front.

Shaw came scouring along behind them, arrayed in his red shirt, which looked very well in the distance; he gained fast on the fugitives, and as the foremost bull was disappearing behind the summit of the swell, we saw him in the act of assailing the hindmost; a smoke sprang from the muzzle of his gun and floated away before the wind like a little white cloud; the bull turned upon him, and just then the rising ground concealed them both from view.

We were moving forward until about noon, when we stopped by the side of the Arkansas. At that moment Shaw appeared riding slowly down the side of a distant hill; his horse was tired and jaded, and when he threw his saddle upon the ground, I observed that the tails of two bulls were dangling behind it. No sooner were the horses turned loose to feed than Henry, asking Munroe to go with him, took his rifle and walked quietly away. Shaw, Tête Rouge, and I sat down by the side of the cart to discuss the dinner which Deslauriers placed before us, and we had scarcely finished when we saw Munroe walking towards us along the river-bank. Henry, he said, had killed four fat cows, and had sent him back for horses to bring in the meat. Shaw took a horse for himself and another for Henry, and he and Munroe left the camp together. After a short absence all three of them came back, their horses loaded with the choicest parts of the meat. We kept two of the cows for ourselves, and gave the others to Munroe and his companions. Deslauriers seated himself on the grass before the pile of meat, and worked industriously for some time to cut it into thin broad sheets for drying, an art in which he had all the skill of an Indian squaw. Long before night, cords of raw hide were stretched around the camp, and the meat was hung upon them to dry in the sunshine and pure air of the prairie. Our California companions were less successful at the work; but they accomplished it after their own fashion, and their side of the camp was soon garnished in the same manner as our own.

We meant to remain at this place long enough to prepare provisions for our journey to the frontier, which, as we supposed, might occupy about a month. Had the distance been twice as great and the party ten times as large, the rifle of Henry Chatillon would have supplied meat enough for the whole within two days; we were obliged to remain, however, until it should be dry enough for transpor-tation; so we pitched our tent and made other arrangements for a permanent camp. The California men, who had no such shelter, contented themselves with arranging their packs on the grass around their fire. In the mean time we had nothing to do but amuse ourselves. Our tent was within a rod of the river, if the broad sand-beds, with a scanty stream of water coursing here and there along their surface, deserve to be dignified with the name of river. The vast flat plains on either side were almost on a level with the sand-beds, and they were bounded in the distance by low, monotonous hills, parallel to the course of the stream. All was one expanse of grass; there was no wood in view, except some trees and stunted bushes upon two islands which rose from the wet sands of the river. Yet far from being dull and tame, the scene was often a wild and animated one; for twice a day, at sunrise and at noon, the buffalo came issuing from the hills, slowly advancing in their grave processions to drink at the river. All our amusements were to be at their expense. An old buffalo bull is a brute of unparalleled ugliness. At first sight of him every feeling of pity vanishes. The cows are much smaller and of a gentler appearance, as becomes their sex. While in this camp we forbore to attack them, leaving to Henry Chatillon, who could better judge their quality, the task of killing such as we wanted for use; but against the bulls we waged an unrelenting war. Thousands of them might be slaughtered without causing any detriment to the species, for their numbers greatly exceed those of the cows; it is the hides of the latter alone which are used for the purposes of commerce and for making the lodges of the Indians; and the destruction among them is therefore greatly disproportionate.

Our horses were tired, and we now usually hunted on foot. While we were lying on the grass after dinner, smoking, talking, or laughing at Tête Rouge, one of us would look up and observe, far out on the plains beyond the river, certain black objects slowly approaching. He would inhale a parting whiff from the pipe, then rising lazily, take his rifle, which leaned against the cart, throw over his shoulder the strap of his pouch and powder-horn, and with his moccasons in his hand, walk across the sand towards the opposite side of the river. This was very easy; for though the sands were about a quarter of a mile wide, the water was nowhere more than two feet deep. The farther bank was about four or five feet high, and quite perpendicular, being cut away by the water in spring. Tall grass grew along its edge. Putting it aside with his hand, and cautiously looking through it, the hunter can discern the huge shaggy back of the bull slowly swaying to and fro, as, with his clumsy, swinging gait, he advances towards the river. The buffalo have regular paths by which they come down to drink. Seeing at a glance along which of these his intended victim is moving, the hunter crouches under the bank within fifteen or twenty yards, it may be, of the point where the path enters the river. Here he sits down quietly on the sand. Listening intently, he hears the heavy, monotonous tread of the approaching bull. The moment after, he sees a motion among the long weeds and grass just at the spot where the path is channelled through the bank. An enormous black head is thrust out, the horns just visible amid the mass of tangled mane. Half sliding, half plunging, down comes the buffalo upon the river-bed below. He steps out in full sight upon the sands. Just before him a runnel of water is gliding, and he bends his head to drink. You may hear the water as it gurgles down his capacious throat. He raises his head, and the drops trickle from his wet beard. He stands with an air of stupid abstraction, unconscious of the lurking danger. Noiselessly the hunter cocks his rifle. As he sits upon the sand, his knee is raised, and his elbow rests upon it, that he may level his heavy weapon with a steadier aim. The stock is at his shoulder; his eye ranges along the barrel. Still he is in no haste to fire. The bull, with slow deliberation, begins his march over the sands to the other side. He advances his foreleg, and exposes to view a small spot, denuded of hair, just behind the point of his shoulder; upon this the hunter brings the sight of his rifle to bear; lightly and delicately his finger presses the hair-trigger. The spiteful crack of the rifle responds to his touch, and instantly in the middle of the bare spot appears a small red dot. The buffalo shivers; death has overtaken him, he cannot tell from whence; still he does not fall, but walks heavily forward, as if nothing had happened. Yet before he has gone far out upon the sand, you see him stop; he totters; his knees bend under him, and his head sinks forward to the ground. Then his whole vast bulk sways to one side; he rolls over on the sand, and dies with a scarcely perceptible struggle.

Waylaying the buffalo in this manner, and shooting them as they come to water, is the easiest method of hunting them. They may also be approached by crawling up ravines or behind hills, or even over the open prairie. This is often surprisingly easy; but at other times it requires the utmost skill of the most experienced hunter. Henry Chatillon was a man of extraordinary strength and hardihood; but I have seen him return to camp quite exhausted with his efforts, his limbs scratched and wounded, and his buckskin dress stuck full of the thorns of the prickly-pear, among which he had been crawling. Sometimes he would lie flat upon his face, and drag himself along in this position for many rods together.

On the second day of our stay at this place, Henry went out for an afternoon hunt. Shaw and I remained in camp, until, observing some bulls approaching the water upon the other side of the river, we crossed over to attack them. They were so near, however, that before we could get under cover of the bank our appearance as we walked over the sands alarmed them. Turning round before coming within gun-shot, they began to move off to the right in a direction parallel to the river. I climbed up the bank and ran after them. They were walking swiftly, and before I could come within gun-shot distance they slowly wheeled about and faced me. Before they had turned far enough to see me I had fallen flat on my face. For a moment they stood and stared at the strange object upon the grass; then turning away, again they walked on as before; and I, rising immediately, ran once more in pursuit. Again they wheeled about, and again I fell prostrate. Repeating this three or four times, I came at length within a hundred yards of the fugitives, and as I saw them turning again, I sat down and levelled my rifle. The one in the centre was the largest I had ever seen. I shot him behind the shoulder. His two companions ran off. He attempted to follow, but soon came to a stand, and at length lay down as quietly as an ox chewing the cud. Cautiously approaching him, I saw by his dull and jelly-like eye that he was dead.

When I began the chase, the prairie was almost tenantless; but a great multitude of buffalo had suddenly thronged upon it, and looking up I saw within fifty rods a heavy, dark column stretching to the right and left as far as I could see. I walked towards them. My approach did not alarm them in the least. The column itself consisted almost entirely of cows and calves, but a great many old bulls were ranging about the prairie on its flank, and as I drew near they faced towards me with such a grim and ferocious look that I thought it best to proceed no farther. Indeed, I was already within close rifle-shot of the column, and I sat down on the ground to watch their movements. Sometimes the whole would stand still, their heads all one way; then they would trot forward, as if by a common impulse, their hoofs and horns clattering together as they moved. I soon began to hear at a distance on the left the sharp reports of a rifle, again and again repeated; and not long after, dull and heavy sounds succeeded, which I recognized as the familiar voice of Shaw's double-barreled gun. When Henry's rifle was at work there was always meat to be brought in. I went back across the river for a horse, and, returning, reached the spot where the hunters were standing. The buffalo were visible on the distant prairie. The living had retreated from the ground, but ten or twelve carcasses were scattered in various directions. Henry, knife in hand, was stooping over a dead cow, cutting away the best and fattest of the meat.

When Shaw left me he had walked down for some distance under the river-bank to find another bull. At length he saw the plains covered with the host of buffalo, and soon after heard the crack of Henry's rifle. Ascending the bank, he crawled through the grass, which for a rod or two from the river was very high and rank. He had not crawled far before to his astonishment he saw Henry standing erect upon the prairie, almost surrounded by the buffalo. Henry was in his element. Quite unconscious that any one was looking at him, he stood at the full height of his tall figure, one hand resting upon his side, and the other arm leaning carelessly on the muzzle of his rifle. His eye was ranging over the singular assemblage around him. Now and then he would select such a cow as suited him, level his rifle, and shoot her dead; then quietly reloading, he would resume his former position. The buffalo seemed no more to regard his presence than if he were one of themselves; the bulls were bellowing and butting at each other, or rolling about in the dust. A group of buffalo would gather about the carcass of a dead cow, snuffing at her wounds; and sometimes they would come behind those that had not yet fallen, and endeavor to push them from the spot. Now and then some old bull would face towards Henry with an air of stupid amazement, but none seemed inclined to attack or fly from him. For some time Shaw lay among the grass, looking in surprise at this extraordinary sight; at length he crawled cautiously forward, and spoke in a low voice to Henry, who told him to rise and come on. Still the buffalo showed no sign of fear; they remained gathered about their dead companions. Henry had already killed as many cows as he wanted for use, and Shaw, kneeling behind one of the carcasses, shot five bulls before the rest thought it necessary to disperse.

The frequent stupidity and infatuation of the buffalo seems the more remarkable from the contrast it offers to their wildness and wariness at other times. Henry knew all their peculiarities; he had studied them as a scholar studies his books, and derived quite as much pleasure from the occupation. The buffalo were in a sense companions to him, and, as he said, he never felt alone when they were about him. He took great pride in his skill in hunting. He was one of the most modest of men; yet in the simplicity and frankness of his character, it was clear that he looked upon his pre-eminence in this respect as a thing too palpable and well established to be disputed. But whatever may have been his estimate of his own skill, it was rather below than above that which others placed upon it. The only time that I ever saw a shade of scorn darken his face was when two volunteer soldiers, who had just killed a buffalo for the first time, undertook to instruct him as to the best method of "approaching." Henry always seemed to think that he had a sort of prescriptive right to the buffalo, and to look upon them as something belonging to himself. Nothing excited his indignation so much as any wanton destruction committed among the cows, and in his view shooting a calf was a cardinal sin.

Henry Chatillon and Tête Rouge were of the same age; that is, about thirty. Henry was twice as large, and about six times as strong as Tête Rouge. Henry's face was roughened by winds and storms; Tête

Rouge's was bloated by sherry-cobblers and brandy-toddy. Henry talked of Indians and buffalo; Tête Rouge of theatres and oyster-cellars. Henry had led a life of hardship and privation; Tête Rouge never had a whim which he would not gratify at the first moment he was able. Henry moreover was the most disinterested man I ever saw; while Tête Rouge, though equally good natured in his way, cared for nobody but himself. Yet we would not have lost him on any account; he served the purpose of a jester in a feudal castle; our camp would have been lifeless without him. For the past week he had fattened in a most amazing manner; and, indeed, this was not at all surprising, since his appetite was inordinate. He was eating from morning till night; half the time he would be at work cooking some private repast for himself, and he paid a visit to the coffee-pot eight or ten times a day. His rueful and disconsolate face became jovial and rubicund, his eyes stood out like a lobster's, and his spirits, which before were sunk to the depths of despondency, were now elated in proportion; all day he was singing, whistling, laughing, and telling stories. Being mortally afraid of Jim Gurney, he kept close in the neighborhood of our tent. As he had seen an abundance of low fast life, and had a considerable fund of humor, his anecdotes were extremely amusing, especially since he never hesitated to place himself in a ludicrous point of view, provided he could raise a laugh by doing so. Tête Rouge, however, was some-times rather troublesome; he had an inveterate habit of pilfering pro-visions at all times of the day. He set ridicule at defiance, and would never have given over his tricks, even if they had drawn upon him the scorn of the whole party. Now and then, indeed, something worse than laughter fell to his share; on these occasions he would exhibit much contrition, but half an hour after we would generally observe him stealing round to the box at the back of the cart, and slyly making off with the provisions which Deslauriers had laid by for supper. He was fond of smoking; but having no tobacco of his own, we used to provide him with as much as he wanted, a small piece at a time. At first we gave him half a pound together; but this experiment proved an entire failure, for he invariably lost not only the tobacco, but the knife intrusted to him for cutting it, and a few minutes after he would come to us with many apologies and beg for more.

We had been two days at this camp, and some of the meat was nearly fit for transportation, when a storm came suddenly upon us. About sunset the whole sky grew as black as ink, and the long grass at the edge of the river bent and rose mournfully with the first gusts of the approaching hurricane. Munroe and his two companions brought their guns and placed them under cover of our tent. Having no shelter for themselves, they built a fire of driftwood that might have defied a cataract, and, wrapped in their buffalo-robes, sat on the ground around it to bide the fury of the storm. Deslauriers esconced himself under the cover of the cart. Shaw and I, together with Henry and Tête Rouge, crowded into the little tent; but first of all the dried meat was piled together, and well protected by buffalo-robes pinned firmly to the ground. About nine o'clock the storm broke amid absolute darkness; it blew a gale, and torrents of rain roared over the boundless expanse of open prairie. Our tent was filled with mist and spray beating through the canvas, and saturating everything within. We could only distinguish each other at short intervals by the dazzling flashes of lightning, which displayed the whole waste around us with its momentary glare. We had our fears for the tent; but for an hour or two it stood fast, until at length the cap gave way before a furious blast; the pole tore through the top, and in an instant we were half suffocated by the cold and dripping folds of the canvas, which fell down upon us. Seizing upon our guns, we placed them erect, in order to lift the saturated cloth above our heads. In this agreeable situation, involved among wet blankets and buffalo-robes, we spent several hours of the night, during which the storm would not abate for a moment, but pelted down with merciless fury. Before long the water gathered beneath us in a pool two or three inches deep; so that for a considerable part of the night we were partially immersed in a cold bath. In spite of all this, Tête Rouge's flow of spirits did not fail him; he laughed, whistled, and sang in defiance of the storm, and that night paid off the long arrears of ridicule which he owed us. While we lay in silence, enduring the infliction with what philosophy we could muster, Tête Rouge, who was intoxicated with animal spirits, cracked jokes at our expense by the hour together. At about three o'clock in the morning, preferring "the tyranny of the open night" to such a wretched shelter, we crawled out from beneath the fallen canvas. The wind had abated, but the rain fell steadily. The fire of the California men still blazed amid the darkness, and we joined them as they sat around it. We made ready some hot coffee by way of refreshment; but when some of the party sought to replenish their cups, it was found that Tête Rouge, having disposed of his own share, had privately abstracted the coffee-pot and drunk the rest of the contents out of the spout.

In the morning, to our great joy, an unclouded sun rose upon the prairie. We presented a rather laughable appearance, for the cold and clammy buck-skin, saturated with water, clung fast to our limbs. The light wind and warm sunshine soon dried it again, and then we were all encased in armor of intolerable stiffness. Roaming all day over the prairie and shooting two or three bulls, were scarcely enough to restore the stiffened leather to its usual pliancy.

Besides Henry Chatillon, Shaw and I were the only hunters in the party. Munroe this morning made an attempt to run a buffalo, but his horse could not come up to the game. Shaw went out with him, and being better mounted, soon found himself in the midst of the herd. Seeing nothing but cows and calves around him, he checked his horse. An old bull came galloping on the open prairie at some distance behind, and turning, Shaw rode across his path, levelling his gun as he passed, and shooting him through the shoulder into the heart.

A great flock of buzzards was usually soaring about a few trees that stood on the island just below our camp. Throughout the whole of yesterday we had noticed an eagle among them; today he was still there; and Tête Rouge, declaring that he would kill the bird of America, borrowed Deslauriers's gun and set out on his unpatriotic mission. As might have been expected, the eagle suffered no harm at his hands. He soon returned, saying that he could not find him, but had shot a buzzard instead. Being required to produce the bird in proof of his assertion, he said he believed that he was not quite dead, but he must be hurt, from the swiftness with which he flew off.

"If you want," said Tête Rouge, "I'll go and get one of his feathers; I knocked off plenty of them when I shot him."

Just opposite our camp, was another island covered with bushes, and behind it was a deep pool of water, while two or three considerable streams coursed over the sand not far off. I was bathing at this place in the afternoon when a white wolf, larger than the largest Newfoundland dog, ran out from behind the point of the island, and galloped leisurely over the sand not half a stone's-throw distant. I could plainly see his red eyes and the bristles about his snout; he was an ugly scoundrel, with a bushy tail, a large head, and a most repulsive countenance. Having neither rifle to shoot nor stone to pelt him with, I was looking after some missile for his benefit, when the report of a gun came from the camp, and the ball threw up the sand just beyond him; at this he gave a slight jump, and stretched away so swiftly that he soon dwindled into a mere speck on the distant sand-beds. The number of carcasses that by this time were lying about the neighboring prairie summoned the wolves from every quarter; the spot where Shaw and Henry had hunted together soon became their favorite resort, for here about a dozen dead buffalo were fermenting under the hot sun. I used often to go over the river and watch them at their meal. By lying under the bank it was easy to get a full view of them. There were three different kinds: the white wolves and the gray wolves, both very large, and besides these the small prairie wolves, not much bigger than spaniels. They would howl and fight in a crowd around a single carcass, yet they were so watchful, and their senses so acute, that I never was able to crawl within a fair shooting distance; whenever I attempted it, they would all scatter at once and glide silently away through the tall grass. The air above this spot was always full of turkey-buzzards or black vultures; whenever the wolves left a carcass they would descend upon it, and cover it so densely that a rifle bullet shot at random among the gormandizing crowd would generally strike down two or three of them. These birds would often sail by scores just above our camp, their broad black wings seeming half transparent as they expanded them against the bright sky. The wolves and the buzzards thickened about us every hour, and two or three eagles also came to the feast. I killed a bull within rifle-shot of the camp; that night the wolves made a fearful howling close at hand, and in the morning the carcass was completely hollowed out by these voracious feeders.

After remaining four days at this camp we prepared to leave it. We had for our own part about five hundred pounds of dried meat, and the California men had prepared some three hundred more; this consisted of the fattest and choicest parts of eight or nine cows, a small quantity only being taken from each, and the rest abandoned to the wolves. The pack animals were laden, the horses saddled, and the mules harnessed to the cart. Even Tête Rouge was ready at last, and slowly moving from the ground, we resumed our journey eastward. When we had advanced about a mile, Shaw missed a valuable hunting-knife, and turned back in search of it, thinking that he had left it at the camp. The day was dark and gloomy. The ashes of the fires were still smoking by the river-side; the grass around them was trampled down by men and horses, and strewn with all the litter of a camp. Our departure had been a gathering signal to the birds and beasts of prey. Scores of wolves were prowling about the smouldering fires, while multitudes were roaming over the neighboring prairie; they all fled as Shaw approached, some running over the sand-beds and some over the grassy plains. The vultures in great clouds were soaring overhead, and the dead bull near the camp was completely blackened by the flock that had alighted upon it; they flapped their broad wings, and stretched upwards their crested heads and long skinny necks, fearing to remain, yet reluctant to leave their disgusting feast. As he searched about the fires he saw the wolves seated on the hills waiting for his departure. Having looked in vain for his knife, he mounted again, and left the wolves and the vultures to banquet undisturbed.

THE MOUNTAIN GOAT AT HOME

WILLIAM T. HORNADAY, SC. D.

John Phillips and I were scrambling along the steep and rough eastern face of Bald Mountain, a few yards below timberline, half-way up 'twixt creek and summit. He was light of weight, well-seasoned and nimble-footed; I was heavy, ill-conditioned, and hungry for more air. Between the sliderock, down timber and brush, the going had been undeniably bad, and in spite of numerous rests I was almost fagged.

Far below us, at the bottom of the V-shaped valley, the horse-bell faintly tinkled, and as Mack and Charlie whacked out the trail, the packtrain crept forward. We were thankful that the camping-place, on Goat Pass, was only a mile beyond.

Presently we heard a voice faintly shouting to us from below.

"Look above you—at the goats!"

Hastily we moved out of a brush-patch, and looked aloft. At the top of the precipice that rose above our slope, a long, irregular line of living forms perched absurdly on the skyline, and looked over the edge, at us. Quickly we brought our glasses to bear, and counted fourteen living and wild Rocky Mountain goats.

"All nannies, young billies, and kids," said Mr. Phillips. "They are trying to guess what kind of wild animals we are." I noticed that he was quite calm; but I felt various things which seemed to sum themselves up in the formula— "the Rocky Mountain goat—at last!"

For fully ten minutes, the entire fourteen white ones steadfastly gazed down upon us, with but few changes of position, and few remarks. Finally, one by one they drew back from the edge of the precipice, and quietly drifted away over the bald crest of the mountain.

For twenty years I had been reading the scanty scraps of mountain-goat literature that at long intervals have appeared in print. I had seen seven specimens alive in captivity, and helped to care for four of them. With a firm belief that the game was worth it, I had traveled twenty-five hundred miles or more in order to meet this strange animal in its own home, and cultivate a close acquaintance with half a dozen wild flocks.

At three o'clock we camped at timberline, on a high and difficult pass between the Elk River and the Bull. That night we christened the ridge Goat Pass. While the guides and the cook unpacked the outfit and pitched the tents, Mr. Phillips hurried down the western side of the divide. Fifteen minutes later he and Kaiser—in my opinion the wisest hunting-dog in British Columbia—had twenty-eight nanny goats and kids at bay on the top of a precipice, and were photographing them at the risk of their lives.

Rifle and glass in hand, I sat down on a little knoll a few yards above the tents, to watch a lame billy goat who was quietly grazing and limping along the side of a lofty ridge that came down east of us from Phillips Peak. A lame wild animal in a country wherein a shot had not been fired for five years, was, to all of us, a real novelty; and with my glasses I watched the goat long and well. It was his left foreleg that was lame, and it was the opinion of the party that the old fellow was suffering from an accident received on the rocks. Possibly a stone had been rolled down upon him, by another goat.

Suddenly sharp cries of surprise came up from the camp, and I sprang up to look about. Three goats were running past the tents at top speed—a big billy, and two smaller goats.

"Hi, there! Goats! Goats!" cried Smith and Norboe.

The cook was stooping over the fire, and looking under his right arm he saw the bunch charging straight toward him, at a gallop. A second later, the big billy was almost upon him.

"Hey! You son-of-a-gun!" yelled Huddleston, and as the big snow-white animal dashed past him he struck it across the neck with a stick of firewood. The goat's tracks were within six feet of the campfire.

The billy ran straight through the camp, then swung sharply to the left, and the last I saw of him was his humpy hindquarters wildly bobbing up and down among the dead jack pines, as he ran for Bald Mountain.

The two smaller goats held their course, and one promptly disappeared. The other leaped across our water-hole, and as it scrambled out of the gully near my position, and paused for a few seconds to look backward, instinctively I covered it with my rifle. But only for an instant. "Come as they may," thought I, "my first goat shall not be a small one!" And as the goat turned and raced on up, my .303 Savage came down.

We laughed long at the utter absurdity of three wild goats actually breaking into the privacy of our camp, on our first afternoon in Goatland. In the Elk Valley, Charlie Smith had promised me that we would camp "right among the goats," and he had royally kept his word.

At evening, when we gathered round the campfire, and counted up, we found that on our first day in Goatland, we had seen a total of fifty-three goats; and no one had fired a shot. As for myself, I felt quite set up over my presence of mind in not firing at the goat which I had "dead to rights" after it had invaded our camp, and which might have been killed as a measure of self-defence.

Our camp was pitched in a most commanding and awe-inspiring spot. We were precisely at timberline, in a grassy hollow on the lowest summit between Bald and Bird Mountains, on the north, and Phillips Peak, on the south. From our tents the ground rose for several hundred feet, like the cables of the Brooklyn Bridge, until it stopped against a rock wall which went on up several hundred feet more. In a notch quite near us was a big bank of eternal ice. In that country, such things are called glaciers; and its melting foot was the starting-point of Goat Creek. Fifty paces taken eastward from our tents brought us to a projecting point from which we looked down a hundred feet to a rope of white water, and on down Goat Creek as it drops five hundred feet to the mile, to the point where it turns a sharp corner to the right, and disappears.

Westward of camp, after climbing up a hundred feet or so, through dead standing timber, the ridge slopes steeply down for a mile and a half to the bottom of a great basin half filled with green timber, that opens toward Bull River. It was on this slope, at a point where a wall of rock cropped out, that Mr. Phillips cornered his flock of goats and photographed them.

At our camp, water and wood were abundant; there was plenty of fine grass for our horses, spruce boughs for our beds, scenery for millions, and what more could we ask?

The day following our arrival on Goat Pass was dull and rainy, with a little snow, and we all remained in camp. At intervals, someone would stroll out to our lookout point above Goat Creek, and eye-search the valley below "to see if an old silver-tip could come a-moochin' up, by accident," as Guide Smith quaintly phrased it.

That gray day taught me something of color values in those mountains. As seen from our lookout point, the long, even stretch of house-roof mountain-slope on the farther side of Goat Creek was a revelation. In the full sunlight of a clear day, its tints were nothing to command particular attention. Strong light seemed to take the colors out of everything. But a cloudy day, with a little rain on the face of nature, was like new varnish on an old oil-painting.

During the forenoon, fleecy white clouds chased each other over the pass and through our camp, and for much of the time the Goat Creek gorge was cloud-filled. At last, however, about noon, they rose and drifted away, and then the mountain opposite revealed a color pattern that was exquisitely beautiful.

For a distance of a thousand yards the ridge-side stretched away down the valley, straight and even; and in that distance it was furrowed from top to bottom by ten or twelve gullies, and ribbed by an equal number of ridges. At the bottom of the gorge was a dense green fringe of tall, obelisk spruces, very much alive. In many places, ghostly processions of dead spruces, limbless and gray, forlornly climbed the ridges, until half-way up the highest stragglers stopped. Intermixed with these tall poles were patches of trailing juniper of a dark olive-green color, growing tightly to the steep slope.

The apex of each timbered ridge was covered with a solid mass of great willow-herb or "fireweed" (*Chamaenerion anguistifolium*), then in its brightest autumn tints of purple and red. The brilliant patches of color which they painted on the mountainside would have rejoiced the heart of an artist. This glorious plant colored nearly every mountainside in that region during our September there.

Below the fireweed, the ridges were dotted with small, cone-shaped spruces, and trailing junipers (*Juniperus prostrata*), of the densest and richest green. The grassy sides of the gullies were all pale yellow—green, softly blended at the edges with the darker colors that framed them in. At the bottom of each washout was a mass of light-gray sliderock, and above all this rare pattern of soft colors loomed a lofty wall of naked carboniferous limestone rock, gray, grim and forbidding.

It seemed to me that I never elsewhere had seen mountains so rich in colors as the ranges between the Elk and the Bull in that particular September.

The rain and the drifting clouds were with us for one day only. Very early on the second morning, while Mr. Phillips and I lay in our sleeping-bags considering the grave question of getting or not getting up, Mack Norboe's voice was heard outside, speaking low but to the point:

"Director, there's an old billy goat, lying right above our camp!"

It was like twelve hundred volts. We tumbled out of our bags, slipped on our shoes, and ran out. Sure enough, a full-grown male goat was lying on the crest of the divide that led up to the summit of Bald Mountain, seventy-five feet above us, and not more than two hundred and fifty yards away. The shooting of him was left to me.

I think I could have bagged that animal as he lay; but what would there have been in that of any interest to a sportsman? I had not asked any goats to come down to our camp, and lie down to be shot!

Not caring greatly whether I got that goat or not, I attempted a stalk along the western side of the ridge, through the dead timber, and well below him. But the old fellow was not half so sleepy as he looked. When finally I came up to a point that was supposed to command his works, I found that he had winded me. He had vanished from his resting-place, and was already far up the side of Bald Mountain, conducting a masterly retreat.

After a hurried breakfast, we made ready for a day with the goats on the northern mountains. Although there are many things in favor of small parties—the best consisting of one guide and one hunter—we all went together—Mr. Phillips, Mack, Charlie and I. Our leader declared a determination to "see the Director shoot his first goat," and I assured the others that the services of all would be needed in carrying home my spoils.

As we turned back toward camp, and took time to look "at the sceneries," the view westward, toward Bull River, disclosed a cloud effect so beautiful that Mr. Phillips insisted upon photographing it, then and there. To give the "touch of life" which he always demanded, I sat in, as usual.

By Mr. Phillips' advice, I put on suspenders and loosened my cartridge-belt, in order to breathe with perfect freedom. We wore no leggings. Our shoes were heavily hobnailed, and while I had thought mine as light as one dared use in that region of ragged rocks, I found that for cliff-climbing they were too heavy, and too stiff in the soles. Of course knee-breeches are the thing, but they should be so well cut that in steep climbing they will not drag on the knees, and waste the climber's horsepower; and there should be a generous opening at the knee.

In those mountains, four things, and only four, are positively indispensable to every party: rifles, axes, fieldglasses and blankets. Each member of our hunting party carried a good glass, and never stirred from camp without it. For myself, I tried an experiment. Two months previously Mrs. Hornaday selected for me, in Paris, a very good opera-glass, made by Lemaire, with a field that was delightfully large and clear. While not quite so powerful a magnifier as the strongest binoculars now on the market, its field was so much clearer that I thought I would prefer it. It was much smaller than any regulation fieldglass, and I carried it either in a pocket of my trousers, or loose inside my hunting-shirt, quite forgetful of its weight.

It proved a great success. We found much interest in testing it with binoculars five times as costly, and the universal verdict was that it would reveal an animal as far as a hunter could go to it, and find it. I mention this because in climbing I found it well worthwhile to be free from a dangling leather case that is always in the way, and often is too large for comfort.

From our camp we went north, along the top of the eastern wall of Bald Mountain. Two miles from home we topped a sharp rise, and there directly ahead, and only a quarter of a mile away on an eastern slope lay a band of eleven goats, basking in the welcome sunshine. The flock was composed of nannies, yearling billies and kids, with not even one old billy among those present. Two old chaperons lay with their heads well up, on the lookout, but all the others lay full length upon the grass, with their backs uphill. Three of the small kids lay close against their mothers.

They were on the northerly point of a fine mountain meadow, with safety rocks on three sides. Just beyond them lay a ragged hog-back of rock, both sides of which were so precipitous that no man save an experienced mountaineer would venture far upon it. It was to this rugged fortress that the goats promptly retreated for safety when we left off watching them, and rose from our concealment. Their sunning-ground looked like a sheep-yard, and we saw that goats had many times lain upon that spot.

Nearby, behind a living windbreak, was a goat-bed, that looked as if goats had lain in it five hundred times. By some curious circumstance, a dozen stunted spruces had woven themselves together, as if for mutual support, until they formed a tight evergreen wall ten feet long and eight feet high. It ranged north and south, forming an excellent hedge-like shield from easterly winds, while the steep mountain partially cut off the winds from the west. On the upper side of that natural windbreak, the turf had been worn into dust, and the droppings were several inches deep. Apparently it was liked because it was a good shelter, in the center of a fine sky-pasture, and within a few jumps of ideal safety rocks.

From the spot where the goats had lain, looking ahead and to our left, we beheld a new mountain. Later on we christened it Bird Mountain, because of the flocks of ptarmigan we found upon its summit. Near its summit we saw five more goats, all females and kids. At our feet lay a deep, rich-looking basin, then a low ridge, another basin with a lakelet in it, and beyond that another ridge, much higher than the first. Ridge No. 2 had dead timber upon it, but it was very scattering, for it was timberline; and its upper end snugged up against the eastern wall of Bird Mountain. Later on we found that the northern side of that ridge ended in a wall of rock that was scalable by man in one place only.

"Yonder are two big old billies!" said someone with a glass in action.

"Yes sir; there they are; all alone, and heading this way, too. Those are your goats this time, Director, sure enough."

"Now boys," said I, "if we can stalk those two goats successfully, and bag them both, neatly and in quick time, we can call it genuine goat-hunting!"

They were distant about a mile and a half, jogging along down a rocky hill, through a perfect maze of gullies, ridges, grassplots and rocks, one of them keeping from forty to fifty feet behind the other.

Even at that distance they looked big, and very, very white. Clearly, they were heading for Bird Mountain. We planned to meet them wherever they struck the precipitous side of the mountain ahead of us, and at once began our stalk.

From the basin which contained the little two-acre tarn, the rocky wall of Bird Mountain rose almost perpendicularly for about eight hundred feet. As we were passing between the lake and the cliff, we heard bits of loose rock clattering down.

"Just look yonder!" said Mr. Phillips, with much fervor.

Close at hand, and well within fair rifle-shot, were four goats climbing the wall; and two more were at the top, looking down as if deeply interested. The climbers had been caught napping, and being afraid to retreat either to right or left, they had elected to seek safety by climbing straight up! It was a glorious opportunity to see goats climb in a difficult place, and forthwith we halted and watched as long as the event lasted, utterly oblivious of our two big billies. Our binoculars brought them down to us wonderfully well, and we saw them as much in detail as if we had been looking a hundred feet with the unaided eye.

The wall was a little rough, but the angle of it seemed not more than 10 degrees from perpendicular. The footholds were merely narrow edges of rock, and knobs the size of a man's fist. Each goat went up in a generally straight course, climbing slowly and carefully all the while. Each one chose its own course, and paid no attention to those that had gone before. The eyes looked ahead to select the route, and the front hoofs skillfully sought for footholds. It seemed as if the powerful front legs performed three-fourths of the work, reaching up until a good foothold was secured, then lifting the heavy body by main strength, while the hindlegs "also ran." It seemed that the chief function of the hind limbs was to keep what the forelegs won. As an exhibition of strength of limb, combined with surefootedness and nerve, it was marvelous, no less.

Often a goat would reach toward one side for a new foothold, find none, then rear up and pivot on its hindfeet, with its neck and stomach pressed against the wall, over to the other side. Occasionally a goat would be obliged to edge off five or ten feet to one side in order to scramble on up. From first to last, no goat slipped and no rocks gave way under their feet, although numerous bits of loose sliderock were disturbed and sent rattling down.

It was a most inspiring sight, and we watched it with breathless interest. In about ten minutes the four goats had by sheer strength and skill climbed about two hundred feet of the most precipitous portion of the cliff, and reached easy going. After that they went on up twice as rapidly as before, and soon passed over the summit, out of our sight. Then we compared notes.

Mr. Phillips and I are of the opinion that nothing could have induced mountain sheep to have made that appalling climb, either in the presence of danger or otherwise. Since that day we have found that there are many mountain hunters who believe that as a straight-away cliff-climber, the goat does things that are impossible for sheep.

As soon as the goat-climbing exhibition had ended, we hurried on across the basin, and up the side of Ridge No. 2. This ridge bore a thin sprinkling of low spruces, a little fallen timber, much purple fireweed and some good grass. As seen at a little distance, it was a purple ridge. The western end of it snugged up against the mountain, and it was there that we met our two big billy goats. They had climbed nearly to the top of our ridge, close up to the mountain, and when we first sighted them they were beginning to feed upon a lace-leaved anemone (*Pulsatilla occidentalis*), at the edge of their newly found pasture. We worked toward them, behind a small clump of half-dead spruces, and finally halted to wait for them to come within range.

After years of waiting, Rocky Mountain goats, at last! How amazingly white and soft they look; and how big they are! The high shoulder hump, the big, round barrel of the body, and the knee-breeches on the legs make the bulk of the animal seem enormous. The whiteness of "the driven snow," of cotton and of paper seem by no means to surpass the incomparable white of those soft, fluffy-coated animals as they appear in a setting of hard, gray limestone, rugged sliderock and dark-green vegetation. They impressed me as being the whitest living objects I ever beheld, and far larger than I had expected to find them. In reality, their color had the effect of magnifying their size; for they looked as big as two-year-old buffaloes.

Of course only Mr. Phillips and I carried rifles; and we agreed that the left man should take the left animal.

"It's a hundred and fifty yards!" said Mack Norboe, in a hoarse whisper.

My goat was grazing behind the trunk of a fallen tree, which shielded his entire body. I waited, and waited; and there he stood, with his head down, and calmly cropped until I became wildly impatient. I think he stood in one spot for five minutes, feeding upon *Pulsatilla*.

"Why don't you shoot?" queried Phillips, in wonder.

"I can't! My goat's hiding behind a tree."

"Well, fire when you're ready, Gridley, and I'll shoot when you do!"

It must have been five minutes, but it seemed like twenty-five, before that goat began to feel a thrill of life along his keel, and move forward. The annoying suspense had actually made me unsteady; besides which, my Savage was a new one, and unchristened. Later on I found that the sights were not right for me, and that my first shooting was very poor.

At last my goat stood forth, in full view—white, immaculate, high of hump, low of head, big and bulky. I fired for the vitals behind the shoulder.

"You've overshot!" exclaimed Norboe, and

"Bang!" said Mr. Phillips' Winchester.

Neither of us brought down our goat at the first fire!

I fired again, holding much lower, and the goat reared up a foot. Mr. Phillips fired again, whereupon his goat fell over like a sack of oats, and went rolling down the hill. My goat turned to run, and as he did so I sent two more shots after him. Then he disappeared behind some rocks. Mack, John and I ran forward, to keep him in sight, and fire more shots if necessary. But no goat was to be seen.

"He can't get away!" said Norboe, reassuringly.

"He's dead!" said I, by way of an outrageous bluff. "You'll find him down on the sliderock!" But inwardly I was torn by doubts.

We hurried down the steep incline, and presently came to the top of a naked wall of rock. Below that was a wide expanse of sliderock.

"Thar he is!" cried Norboe. "Away down yonder, out on the sliderock, dead as a wedge."

From where he stood when I fired, the goat had run back about two hundred feet, where he fell dead, and then began to roll. We traced him by a copious stream of blood on the rocks. He fell down the rock wall, for a hundred feet, in a slanting direction, and then— to my great astonishment—he rolled two hundred feet farther (by measurement) on that ragged, jagged slide-rock before he fetched up against a particularly large chunk of stone, and stopped. We expected to find his horns broken, but they were quite uninjured. The most damage had been inflicted upon his nose, which was badly cut and bruised. The bullet that ended his life (my second shot) went squarely through the valves of his heart; but I regret to add that one thigh-bone had been broken by another shot, as he ran from me.

Mr. Phillips' goat behaved better than mine. It rolled down the grassy slope, and lodged on a treacherous little shelf of earth that overhung the very brink of the precipice. One step into that innocent-looking fringe of green juniper bushes meant death on the sliderock below; and it made me nervous to see Mack and Charlie stand there while they skinned the animal.

As soon as possible we found the only practicable route down the rock wall, and scrambled down. The others say that I slid down the last twenty feet; but that is quite immaterial. I reached the goat a few paces in advance of the others, and thought to divert my followers by reciting a celebrated quotation beginning, "To a hunter, the moment of triumph," etc. As I laid my hand upon the goat's hairy side and said my little piece, I heard a deadly "click."

"Got him!" cried Mr. Phillips; and then three men and a dog laughed loud and derisively. Since seeing the picture I have altered that quotation, to this: "To a hunter, the moment of humiliation is when he first sees his idiotic smile on a surreptitious plate." It is inserted solely to oblige Mr. Phillips, as evidence of the occasion when he got ahead of me.

The others declared that the goat was "a big one, though not the very biggest they ever grow." Forthwith we measured him; and in taking his height we shoved his foreleg up until the elbow came to the position it occupies under the standing, living animal. The measurements were as follows:

rocky mountain goat

Oreamnos montanus

Male, six years old. Killed September 8, 1905,
near the Bull River,-British Columbia.

	Inches
Standing height at shoulder	38
Length, nose to root of tail	59.25
Length of tail vertebrae	3.50
Girth behind foreleg	55
Girth around abdomen	58
Girth of neck behind ears (unskinned)	18

Circumference of forearm, skinned	11.25
Width of chest	14
Length of horn on curve	9.75
Spread of horns at tips	5
Circumference of horn at base	5.60
Circumference of front hoof	10.50
Circumference of rear hoof	7.75
Base of ear to end of nostrils	10.50
Front corner of eye to rear corner	9
Nostril opening	7
Widest spread of ears, tip to tip	15
Total weight of animal by scales, allowing 8 lbs. for blood lost	258 lbs.

The black and naked glands in the skin behind the horn were on that date small, and inconspicuous; but they stood on edge, with the naked face of each closely pressed against the base of the horn in front of it.

On another occasion I shot a thin old goat that stood forty-two inches high at the shoulders, and Mr. Phillips shot another that weighed two hundred and seventy-six pounds. After we had thoroughly dissected my goat, weighed it, examined the contents of its stomach, and saved a good sample of its food for close examination at camp, we tied up the hindquarters, head and pelt, and set out for camp.

And thus ended our first day in the actual hunting of mountain goats, in the course of which we saw a total of forty-two animals. The stalking, killing and dissecting of our two goats was very interesting, but the greatest event of the day was our opportunity to watch those five goats climb an almost perpendicular cliff.

This day, also, was the eleventh of September . . .

Mr. Phillips, Charlie Smith and I descended the steep side of Goat Pass, crossed the basin and slowly climbed the grassy divide that separates it from the source of Avalanche Creek. When half way down the southern side of that divide, we looked far up the side of Phillips Peak and saw two big old billy goats of shootable size. They were well above timberline, lying where a cloud-land meadow was suddenly chopped off at a ragged precipice. The way up to them was long, and very steep.

"That's a long climb, Director," said Mr. Phillips; "but there are no bad rocks."

I said that I could make it, in time—as compared with eternity—if the goats would wait for me.

"Oh, they'll wait! We'll find 'em there, all right," said Charlie, confidently. So we started.

As nearly as I can estimate, we climbed more than a mile, at an angle that for the upper half of the distance was about 30 degrees—a very steep ascent. At first our way up led through green timber, over smooth ground that was carpeted with needles of spruce and pine. That was comparatively easy, no more difficult, in fact, than climbing the stairs of four Washington monuments set one upon another.

At climbing steep mountains, Mr. Phillips, Charlie Smith and the two Norboes are perfect friends. They are thin, tough and long-winded, and being each of them fully forty pounds under my weight, I made no pretence at trying to keep up with them. As it is in an English workshop, the slowest workman set the pace.

In hard climbing, almost every Atlantic-coast man perspires freely, and is very extravagant in the use of air. It frequently happened that when half way up a high mountain, my lungs consumed the air so rapidly that a vacuum was created around me, and I would have to stop and wait for a new supply of oxygen to blow along. My legs behaved much better than my lungs, and to their credit be it said that they never stopped work until my lungs ran out of steam.

As I toiled up that long slope, I thought of a funny little engine that I saw in Borneo, pulling cars over an absurd wooden railway that ran from the bank of the Sadong River to the coalmines. It would run about a mile at a very good clip, then suddenly cease pulling, and stop. Old Walters, the superintendent, said:

"There's only one thing ails that engine. The bloomin' little thing can't make steam fast enough!"

I was like that engine. I couldn't "keep steam"; and whenever my lungs became a perfect vacuum, I had to stop and rest, and collect air. Considering the fact that there was game above us, I thought my comrades were very considerate in permitting me to set the pace. Now had someone glared at me with the look of a hungry cannibal, and hissed between his teeth, "Step lively!" it would have made me feel quite at home.

In due time we left the green timber behind us, and started up the last quarter of the climb. There we found stunted spruces growing like scraggy brush, three feet high, gnarled and twisted by the elements, and enfeebled by the stony soil on which they bravely tried to grow. Only the bravest of trees could even rear their heads on that appalling steep, scorched by the sun, rasped by the wind, drenched by the rains and frozen by the snow. But after a hundred yards or so, even the dwarf spruces gave up the struggle. Beyond them, up to our chosen point, the mountain-roof was smooth and bare, except for a sprinkle of fine, flat sliderock that was very treacherous stuff to climb over.

"Let me take your rifle, Director!" said Charlie, kindly.

"No, thank you. I'll carry it up, or stay down. But you may keep behind me if you will, and catch me if I start to roll!"

On steep slopes, such as that was, my companions had solemnly warned me not to fall backward and start rolling; for a rolling man gathers no moss. A man bowling helplessly down a mountainside at an angle of 30 degrees quickly acquires a momentum which spells death. Often have I looked down a horribly steep stretch, and tried to imagine what I would feel, and think, were I to overbalance backward, and go bounding down. A few hours later we saw a goat carcass take a frightful roll down a slope not nearly so steep as where we climbed up, and several times it leaped six feet into the air.

To keep out of the sight of the goats it was necessary for us to bear well toward our left; and this brought us close to the edge of the precipice, where the mountainside was chopped off. In view of the loose stones underfoot, I felt liked edging more to the right; for the twin chances of a roll down and a fall over began to abrade my nerves. Mr. Phillips and Charlie climbed along so close to the drop that I found myself wondering which of them would be the first to slip and go over.

"Keep well over this way, Director, or the goats may wind you!" said Charlie, anxiously.

"That's all right, Charlie; he's winded now!" said John.

I said we would rest on that; and before I knew the danger, Mr. Phillips had taken a picture of me, resting, and smiling a most idiotic smile.

At last we reached the pinnacle which we had selected when we first sighted our game. As nearly as we could estimate, afterward, by figuring up known elevations, we were at a height of about nine thousand feet, and though not the highest, it was the dizziest point I ever trod. Except when we looked ahead, we seemed to be fairly suspended in mid-air! To look down under one's elbow was to look into miles of dizzy, bottomless space.

The steep slope had led us up to the sharp point of a crag that stuck up like the end of a man's thumb and terminated in a crest as sharp as the comb of a houseroof. Directly in front, and also on the left, was a sheer drop. From the right, the ragged edge of the wall ran on up, to the base of Phillips Peak. Beyond our perch, twelve feet away, there yawned a great basin-abyss, and on beyond that rocky gulf rose a five-hundred-foot wall at the base of the Peak. A little to the right of our position another ragged pinnacle thrust its sharp apex a few feet higher than ours, and eventually caused me much trouble in securing my first shot.

We reached the top of our crag, and peered over its highest rocks just in time to see our two goats quietly walk behind a ragged point of rock farther up the wall, and disappear. They were only a hundred and fifty yards distant; but they had not learned of our existence, and were not in the least alarmed. Naturally, we expected them to saunter back into view, for we felt quite sure they did not mean to climb down that wall to the bottom of the basin. So we lay flat upon the slope, rifles in hand, and waited, momentarily expecting the finish. They were due to cross a grassy slope between two crags, not more than forty feet wide, and if not fired at within about ten seconds of their reappearance, they would be lost behind the rocks! The chance was not nearly so good as it looked.

But minutes passed, and no goats returned. It became evident that the dawdling pair had lain down behind the sheltering crag, for a siesta in the sun. We composed ourselves to await their pleasure, and in our first breath of opportunity, looked off southeasterly, over the meadow whereon the two goats had been feeding. And then we saw a sight of sights.

Rising into view out of a little depression on the farther side of the meadow, lazily sauntering along, there came ten big, snow-white billy goats! They were heading straight toward us, and there was not a nanny, nor a kid, nor even a young billy in the bunch. The air was clear; the sun was shining brightly, the meadow was like dark olive-brown plush, and how grandly those big, pure-white creatures did loom up! When first seen they were about four hundred yards away, but our glasses made the distance seem only one-third of that.

For more than an hour we lay flat on our pinnacle, and watched those goats. No one thought of time. It was a chance of a lifetime. My companions were profoundly surprised by the size of the collection; for previous to that moment, no member of our party ever had seen more than four big male goats in one bunch.

The band before us was at the very top of a sky-meadow of unusual luxuriance, which climbed up out of the valley on our right, and ran on up to the comb of rock that came down from Phillips Peak. In area the meadow was five hundred yards wide, and half a mile long. Afterward, when we walked over it, we found it was free from stones, but full of broad steps, and covered with a dense, greenish-purple matting of ground verdure that was as soft to the foot as the thickest pile carpet. The main body of this verdure is a moss-like plant called mountain avens, closely related to cinquefoil, and known botanically as *Dryas octopetala*. It has a very pretty leaf measuring about 7/16 by 3/16 inches, with finely serrated edges. In September a mass of it contains a mixture of harmonious colors: olive-green, brown, gray and purple. On this the goats were feeding. This plant is very common in those mountains above timberline, especially on southern slopes; but it demands a bit of ground almost exclusively for itself, and thrives best when alone.

Along with this there grew a moss-like saxifrage (*Saxifraga austro-montana*), which to any one not a botanist seems to be straight moss. It grows in cheerful little clumps of bright green, and whenever it is found on a mountain-pasture, one is pleased to meet it.

I record these notes here, because our ten goats had been in no hurry. They were more than deliberate; they were almost stagnant. In an hour, the farthest that any one of them moved was about one hundred yards, and most of them accomplished even less than that. They were already so well fed that they merely minced at the green things around them. Evidently they had fed to satiety in the morning hours, before we reached them.

As they straggled forward, they covered about two acres of ground. Each one seemed steeped and sodden in laziness. When out grazing, our giant tortoises move faster than they did on that lazy afternoon. When the leader of this band of weary Willies reached the geographical center of the sky-meadow, about two hundred yards from us, he decided to take a sunbath on the most luxurious basin possible to him. Slowly he focussed his mind upon a level bench of earth, about four feet wide. It contained an old goat-bed of loose earth, and upon this he lay down, with his back uphill.

At this point, however, he took a sudden resolution. After about a minute of reflection, he decided that the head of his bed was too high and too humpy; so, bracing himself back with his right foreleg, like an ancient Roman senator at a feast, he set his left leg in motion and flung out from under his breast a quantity of earth. The loose soil rose in a black shower, two feet high, and the big hoof flung it several feet down the hill. After about a dozen rakes, he settled down to bask in the warm sunshine, and blink at the scenery of Avalanche Valley.

Five minutes later, a little higher up the slope, another goat did the same thing; and eventually two or three others laid down. One, however, deliberately sat down on his haunches, dog-fashion, with his back uphill. For fully a quarter of an hour he sat there in profile, slowly turning his head from side to side, and gazing at the scenery while the wind blew through his whiskers.

So far as I could determine, no sentinel was posted. There was no leader, and no individual seemed particularly on the alert for enemies. One and all, they felt perfectly secure.

In observing those goats one fact became very noticeable. At a little distance, their legs looked very straight and stick-like, devoid of all semblance of gracefulness and of leaping power. The animals were very white and immaculate—as were all the goats that we saw—and they stood out with the sharpness of clean snow-patches on dark rock. Nature may have known about the much overworked principle of "protective coloration" when she fashioned the mountain goat, but if so, she was guilty of cruelty to goats in clothing this creature with pelage which, in the most comfortable season for hunting, renders it visible for three miles or more. Even the helpless kidling is as white as cotton, and a grand mark for eagles.

That those goats should look so stiff and genuinely ungraceful on their legs, gave me a distinct feeling of disappointment. From that moment I gave up all hope of ever seeing a goat perform any feats requiring either speed or leaping powers; for we saw that of those short, thick legs—nearly as straight as four Indian clubs—nothing is to be expected save power in lifting and sliding, and rocklike stead-fastness. In all the two hundred and thirty-nine goats that we saw, we observed nothing to disprove the conclusive evidence of that day regarding the physical powers of the mountain goat.

While we watched the band of mountain loafers, still another old billy goat, making No. 13, appeared across the rock basin far to our left. From the top of the northern ridge, he set out to walk across the wide rock wall that formed the western face of Phillips Peak. From where we were the wall seemed almost smooth, but to the goat it must have looked otherwise. Choosing a narrow, light-gray line of stratification that extended across the entire width of the wall, the solitary animal set out on its promenade. The distance to be traversed to reach the uppermost point of our sky-pasture was about fifteen hundred feet, and the contour line chosen was about four hundred feet above our position. The incident was like a curtain-raiser to a tragic play.

That goat's walk was a very tame performance. The animal plodded steadily along, never faster, never slower, but still with a purposeful air, like a postman delivering mail. For a mountain goat, not pursued or frightened, it was a rapid walk, probably three miles an hour. Its legs swung to and fro with the regularity and steadiness of four pendulums, and I think they never once paused. The animal held to that one line of stratification, until near the end of its promenade. There a great mass of rock had broken away from the face of the cliff, and the goat was forced to climb down about fifty feet, then up again, to regain its chosen route. A few minutes later its ledge ran out upon the apex of the sky-meadow. There Billy paused for a moment, to look about him; then he picked out a soft spot, precisely where the steep slope of the meadow ended against the rocky peak, and lay down to rest.

Up to that time, Mr. Phillips and I had killed only one goat each, and as we lay there we had time to decide upon the future. He resolved to kill one fine goat as a gift to the Carnegie Museum, and I wished two more for my own purposes. We decided that at a total of three goats each—two less than our lawful right—we would draw the line, and kill no more.

The first shot at the pair of invisible goats was to be mine; and as already suggested, the circumstances were like those surrounding a brief moving target in a shooting-gallery. Before us were two rocky crag-points, and behind the one on the left, the animals lay hidden for full an hour. Between the two crags the V-shaped spot of the meadow, across which I knew my goat would walk or run, looked very small. If he moved a yard too far, the right-hand crag would hide him from me until he would be three hundred yards away. I was compelled to keep my rifle constantly ready, and one eye to the front, in order to see my goat in time to get a shot at him while he crossed that forty feet of ground.

And after all, I came ever so near to making a failure of my vigil. I was so absorbed in watching that unprecedented band of billies that before I knew it, the two goats were in the center of the V-shaped stage, and moving at a good gait across it. Horrors!

Hurriedly I exclaimed to Mr. Phillips, "There they are!" took a hurried aim at the tallest goat, and just as his head was going out of sight, let go. He flinched upward at the shoulders, started forward at a trot, and instantly disappeared from my view.

The instant my rifle cracked, Mr. Phillips said, imperatively,

"Don't move! Don't make a sound, and those goats will stay right where they are."

Instantly we "froze." All the goats sprang up, and stood at attention. All looked fixedly in our direction, but the distant eleven were like ourselves, frozen into statues. In that band not a muscle moved for fully three minutes.

Finally the goats decided that the noise they had heard was nothing at which to be alarmed. One by one their heads began to move, and in five minutes their fright was over. Some went on feeding, but three or four of the band decided that they would saunter down our way and investigate that noise.

But what of my goat?

John slid over to my left, to look as far as possible behind the intercepting crag. Finally he said,

"He's done for! He's lying out there, dead."

As soon as possible I looked at him; and sure enough, he lay stretched upon the grass, back uphill, and apparently very dead. The other goat had gone on and joined the ten.

The investigating committee came walking down toward us with a briskness which soon brought them within rifle-shot; and then Mr. Phillips picked out his Carnegie Museum goat and opened fire, at a range of about three hundred yards. The first shot went high, but at the next the goat came down, hit behind the shoulder. This greatly alarmed all the other goats, but they were so confused that three of them came down toward us at a fast trot. At two hundred yards I picked out one, and fired. At my third shot, it fell, but presently scrambled up, ran for the edge of the precipice and dropped over out of sight. It landed, mortally wounded, on some ragged rocks about fifty feet down, and to end its troubles a shot from the edge quickly finished it.

Mr. Phillips killed his first goat, and before the bunch got away, broke the leg of another. This also got over the edge of the precipice, and had to be finished up from the edge.

But a strange thing remains to be told.

By the time Mr. Phillips and I had each fired about two shots of the last round, in the course of which we ran well over to the right in order to command the field, to our blank amazement my first goat—the dead one!—staggered to his feet, and started off toward the edge of the precipice. It was most uncanny to see a dead animal thus come to life!

"Look, Director," cried Charlie Smith, "your first goat's come to life! Kill him again! Kill him again, quick!"

I did so; and after the second killing he remained dead. I regret to say that in my haste to get those goats measured, skinned and weighed before night, I was so absorbed that I forgot to observe closely where my first shot struck the goat that had to be killed twice. I think however, that it went through his liver and other organs without touching the vital portions of the lungs.

My first goat was the tallest one of the six we killed on that trip, but not the heaviest. He was a real patriarch, and decidedly on the downhill side of life. He was so old that he had but two incisor teeth remaining, and they were so loose they were almost useless. He was thin in flesh, and his pelage was not up to the mark in length. But in height he was tall, for he stood forty-two inches at the shoulders, with the foreleg pushed up where it belongs in a standing animal.

Mr. Phillips' Carnegie Museum goat was the heaviest one shot on that trip, its gross weight being two hundred and seventy-six pounds.

Charlie decided to roll the skinned carcass of my goat down the mountain, if possible within rifle-shot of the highest point of green timber, in the hope that a grizzly might find it, and thereby furnish a shot. He cut off the legs at the knees, and started the body rolling on the sky-pasture, end over end. It went like a wheel, whirling down at a terrific rate, sometimes jumping fifty feet. It went fully a quarter of a mile before it reached a small basin, and stopped. The other carcass, also, was rolled down. It went sidewise, like a bag of grain, and did not roll quite as far as the other.

By the time we had finished our work on the goats—no trifling task—night was fast approaching, and leaving all the heads, skins and meat for the morrow, we started for our new camp, five miles away.

We went down the meadow (thank goodness!), and soon struck the green timber; and then we went on down, down, and still farther down, always at thirty degrees, until it seemed to me we never would stop going down, never reach the bottom and the trail. But everything earthly has an end. At the end of a very long stretch of plunging and sliding, we reached Avalanche Creek, and drank deeply of the icy-cold water for which we had so long been athirst.

After three miles of travel down the creek, over sliderock, through green timber, yellow willows, more green timber and some down timber, we heard the cheerful whack of Huddleston's axe, and saw on tree-trunk and bough the ruddy glow of the new campfire.

The new camp was pitched in one of the most fascinating spots I ever camped within. The three tents stood at the southern edge of a fine, open grove of giant spruces that gave us good shelter on rainy days. Underneath the trees there was no underbrush, and the ground was deeply carpeted with dry needles. Grand mountains rose on either hand, practically from our campfire, and for our front view a fine valley opened southward for six miles, until its lower end was closed by the splendid mass of Roth Mountain and Glacier. Close at hand was a glorious pool of icewater, and firewood "to burn." Yes, there was one other feature, of great moment, abundant grass for our horses, in the open meadow in front of the tents.

To crown all these luxuries, Mr. Phillips announced that, according to mountain customs already established, and precedents fully set, that camp would then and there be named in my honor— "Camp Hornaday." What more could any sportsman possibly desire?

HUNTING THE BLACK BEAR

BY THEODORE ROOSEVELT

Next to the whitetail deer the black bear is the commonest and most widely distributed of American big game. It is still found quite plentifully in northern New England, in the Adirondacks, Catskills, and along the entire length of the Alleghanies, as well as in the swamps and canebrakes of the southern States. It is also common in the great forests of northern Michigan, Wisconsin, and Minnesota, and throughout the Rocky Mountains and the timbered ranges of the Pacific coast. In the East it has always ranked second only to the deer among the beasts of chase. The bear and the buck were the staple objects of pursuit of all the old hunters. They were more plentiful than the bison and elk even in the long vanished days when these two great monarchs of the forest still ranged eastward to Virginia and Pennsylvania. The wolf and the cougar were always too scarce and too shy to yield much profit to the hunters. The black bear is a timid, cowardly animal, and usually a vegetarian, though it sometimes preys on the sheep, hogs, and even cattle of the settler, and is very fond of raiding his corn and melons. Its meat is good and its fur often valuable; and in its chase there is much excitement, and occasionally a slight spice of danger, just enough to render it attractive; so it has always been eagerly followed. Yet it still holds its own, though in greatly diminished numbers, in the more thinly set-tled portions of the country. One of the standing riddles of American zoology is the fact that the black bear, which is easier killed and less prolific than the wolf, should hold its own in the land better than the latter, this being directly the reverse of what occurs in Europe, where the brown bear is generally exterminated before the wolf.

In a few wild spots in the East, in northern Maine for instance, here and there in the neighborhood of the upper Great Lakes, in the east Tennessee and Kentucky mountains and the swamps of Florida and Mississippi, there still lingers an occasional representative of the old wilderness hunters. These men live in log-cabins in the wilderness. They do their hunting on foot, occasionally with the help of a single trailing dog. In Maine they are as apt to kill moose and caribou as bear and deer; but elsewhere the two last, with an occasional cougar or wolf, are the beasts of chase which they follow. Nowadays as these old hunters die there is no one to take their places, though there are still plenty of backwoods settlers in all of the regions named who do a great deal of hunting and trapping. Such an old hunter rarely makes his appearance at the settlements except to dispose of his peltry and hides in exchange for cartridges and provisions, and he leads a life of such lonely isolation as to insure his individual characteristics develop-ing into peculiarities. Most of the wilder districts in the eastern States still preserve memories of some such old hunter who lived his long life alone, waging ceaseless warfare on the vanishing game, whose oddi-ties, as well as his courage, hardihood, and woodcraft, are laughingly remembered by the older settlers, and who is usually best known as having killed the last wolf or bear or cougar ever seen in the locality.

Generally the weapon mainly relied on by these old hunters is the rifle; and occasionally some old hunter will be found even to this day who uses a muzzle loader, such as Kit Carson carried in the middle of the century. There are exceptions to this rule of the rifle however. In the years after the Civil War one of the many noted hunters of southwest Virginia and east Tennessee was Wilber Waters, sometimes called The Hunter of White Top. He often killed black bear with a knife and dogs. He spent all his life in hunting and was very successful, killing the last gang of wolves to be found in his neighborhood; and he slew innumerable bears, with no worse results to himself than an occasional bite or scratch.

In the southern States the planters living in the wilder regions have always been in the habit of following the black bear with horse and hound, many of them keeping regular packs of bear hounds. Such a pack includes not only pure-bred hounds, but also cross-bred animals, and some sharp, agile, hard-biting fierce dogs and terriers. They follow the bear and bring him to bay but do not try to kill him, although there are dogs of the big fighting breeds which can readily master a black bear if loosed at him three or four at a time; but the dogs of these southern bear-hound packs are not fitted for such work, and if they try to close with the bear he is certain to play havoc with them, disemboweling them with blows of his paws or seizing them in his arms and biting through their spines or legs. The riders follow the hounds through the canebrakes, and also try to make cutoffs and station themselves at open points where they think the bear will pass, so that they may get a shot at him. The weapons used are rifles, shotguns, and occasionally revolvers.

Sometimes, however, the hunter uses the knife. General Wade Hampton, who has probably killed more black bears than any other man living in the United States, frequently used the knife, slaying thirty or forty with this weapon. His plan was, when he found that the dogs had the bear at bay, to walk up close and cheer them on. They would instantly seize the bear in a body, and he would then rush in and stab it behind the shoulder, reaching over so as to inflict the wound on the opposite side from that where he stood. He escaped scathless from all these encounters save one, in which he was rather severely torn in the forearm. Many other hunters have used the knife, but perhaps none so frequently as he; for he was always fond of steel, as witness his feats with the "white arm" during the Civil War.

General Hampton always hunted with large packs of hounds, managed sometimes by himself and sometimes by his negro hunters. He occasionally took out forty dogs at a time. He found that all his dogs together could not kill a big fat bear, but they occasionally killed three-year-olds, or lean and poor bears. During the course of his life he has himself killed, or been in at the death of, five hundred bears, at least two thirds of them falling by his own hand. In the year just before the war he had on one occasion, in Mississippi, killed sixty-eight bears in five months. Once he killed four bears in a day; at another time three, and frequently two. The two largest bears he himself killed weighed, respectively, 408 and 410 pounds. They were both shot in Mississippi. But he saw at least one bear killed which was much larger than either of these. These figures were taken down at the time, when the animals were actually weighed on the scales. Most of his hunting for bear was done in northern Mississippi, where one of his plantations was situated, near Greenville. During the half century that he hunted, on and off, in this neighborhood, he knew of two instances where hunters were fatally wounded in the chase of the black bear. Both of the men were inexperienced, one being a raftsman who came down the river, and the other a man from Vicksburg. He was not able to learn the particulars in the last case, but the raftsman came too close to a bear that was at bay, and it broke through the dogs, rushed at and overthrew him, then lying on him, it bit him deeply in the thigh, through the femoral artery, so that he speedily bled to death.

But a black bear is not usually a formidable opponent, and though he will sometimes charge home he is much more apt to bluster and bully than actually to come to close quarters. I myself have but once seen a man who had been hurt by one of these bears. This was an Indian. He had come on the beast close up in a thick wood, and had mortally wounded it with his gun; it had then closed with him, knocking the gun out of his hand, so that he was forced to use his knife. It charged him on all fours, but in the grapple, when it had failed to throw him down, it raised itself on its hind legs, clasping him across the shoulders with its fore-paws. Apparently it had no intention of hugging, but merely sought to draw him within reach of his jaws. He fought desperately against this, using the knife freely, and striving to keep its head back; and the flow of blood weakened the animal, so that it finally fell exhausted, before being able dangerously to injure him. But it had bitten his left arm very severely, and its claws had made long gashes on his shoulders.

Black bears, like grislies, vary greatly in their modes of attack. Sometimes they rush in and bite; and again they strike with their fore-paws. Two of my cowboys were originally from Maine, where I knew them well. There they were fond of trapping bears and caught a good many. The huge steel gins, attached by chains to heavy clogs, prevented the trapped beasts from going far; and when found they were always tied tight round some tree or bush, and usually nearly exhausted. The men killed them either with a little 32-calibre pistol or a hatchet. But once did they meet with any difficulty. On this occasion one of them incautiously approached a captured bear to knock it on the head with his hatchet, but the animal managed to partially untwist itself, and with its free fore-arm made a rapid sweep at him; he jumped back just in time, the bear's claws tearing his clothes—after which he shot it. Bears are shy and have very keen noses; they are therefore hard to kill by fair hunting, living, as they generally do, in dense forests or thick brush. They are easy enough to trap, however. Thus, these two men, though they trapped so many, never but once killed them in any other way. On this occasion one of them, in the winter, found in a great hollow log a den where a she and two well-grown cubs had taken up their abode, and shot all three with his rifle as they burst out.

Where they are much hunted, bear become purely nocturnal; but in the wilder forests I have seen them abroad at all hours, though they do not much relish the intense heat of noon. They are rather comical animals to watch feeding and going about the ordinary business of their lives. Once I spent half an hour lying at the edge of a wood and looking at a black bear some three hundred yards off across an open glade. It was in good stalking country, but the wind was unfavorable and I waited for it to shift—waited too long as it proved, for something frightened the beast and he made off before I could get a shot at him. When I first saw him he was shuffling along and rooting in the ground, so that he looked like a great pig. Then he began to turn over the stones and logs to hunt for insects, small reptiles, and the like. A moderate-sized stone he would turn over with a single clap of his paw, and then plunge his nose down into the hollow to gobble up the small creatures beneath while still dazed by the light. The big logs and rocks he would tug and worry at with both paws; once, over-exerting his clumsy strength, he lost his grip and rolled clean on his back. Under some of the logs he evidently found mice and chipmunks; then, as soon as the log was overturned, he would be seen jumping about with grotesque agility, and making quick dabs here and there, as the little, scurrying rodent turned and twisted, until at last he put his paw on it and scooped it up into his mouth. Sometimes, probably when he smelt the mice underneath, he would cautiously turn the log over with one paw, holding the other lifted and ready to strike. Now and then he would halt and sniff the air in every direction, and it was after one of these halts that he suddenly shuffled off into the woods.

Black bears generally feed on berries, nuts, insects, carrion, and the like; but at times they take to killing very large animals. In fact, they are curiously irregular in their food. They will kill deer if they can get at them; but generally the deer are too quick. Sheep and hogs are their favorite prey, especially the latter, for bears seem to have a special relish for pork. Twice I have known a black bear kill cattle. Once the victim was a bull which had got mired, and which the bear deliberately proceeded to eat alive, heedless of the bellows of the unfortunate beast. On the other occasion, a cow was surprised and slain among some bushes at the edge of a remote pasture. In the spring, soon after the long winter sleep, they are very hungry, and are especially apt to attack large beasts at this time; although during the very first days of their appearance, when they are just breaking their fast, they eat rather sparingly, and by preference the tender shoots of green grass and other herbs, or frogs and crayfish; it is not for a week or two that they seem to be overcome by lean, ravenous hunger. They will even attack and master that formidable fighter the moose, springing at it from an ambush as it passes—for a bull moose would surely be an overmatch for one of them if fronted fairly in the open. An old hunter, whom I could trust, told me that he had seen in the snow in early spring the place where a bear had sprung at two moose, which were trotting together; he missed his spring, and the moose got off, their strides after they settled down into their pace being tremendous, and showing how thoroughly they were frightened. Another time he saw a bear chase a moose into a lake, where it waded out a little distance, and then turned to bay, bidding defiance to his pursuer, the latter not daring to approach in the water. I have been told—but cannot vouch for it—that instances have been known where the bear, maddened by hunger, has gone in on a moose thus standing at bay, only to be beaten down under the water by the terrible fore-hoofs of the quarry, and to yield its life in the contest. A lumberman told me that he once saw a moose, evidently much startled, trot through a swamp, and immediately afterwards a bear came up following the tracks. He almost ran into the man, and was evidently not in a good temper, for he growled and blustered, and two or three times made feints of charging, before he finally concluded to go off.

Bears will occasionally visit hunters' or lumberman's camps, in the absence of the owners, and play sad havoc with all that therein is, devouring everything eatable, especially if sweet, and trampling into a dirty mess whatever they do not eat. The black bear does not average much more than a third the size of the grisly; but, like all its kind, it varies greatly in weight. The largest I myself ever saw weighed was in Maine, and tipped the scale at 346 pounds; but I have a perfectly authentic record of one in Maine that weighed 397, and my friend, Dr. Hart Merriam, tells me that he has seen several in the Adirondacks that when killed weighed about 350.

I have myself shot but one or two black bears, and these were obtained under circumstances of no special interest, as I merely stumbled on them while after other game, and killed them before they had a chance either to run or show fight.

THE QUEST OF
THE PTARMIGAN

REX BEACH

Sell Keno? No—guess not. Need Money? Oh yes—but. No—you can't buy him. That's a big price, I know, and I could buy lots of dog teams for that, but I may as well tell you I would as soon sell my brother—my best friend, or, if I had one, my wife. May be sentiment, but he saved my life, and no other man while he lives shall ever curl the lash of a dog-whip across his shaggy back. He's not a dog to me; he's my friend.

Want to hear about it?—Well—I don't mind. It's cold outside and nothing to do. Better light up. It's mostly a story of a ptarmigan hunt. Kind of a peaceful pastoral prelude, with merry guns cracking, ending up with a dash for life accompanied by a full fledged howling of the storm chorus under the baton of the spirit of the North.

Did you ever have the meat hunger so strong in your vitals that you would wake at night dreaming of the fried chicken that mother made, or could picture the grill-marks on a broiled steak? Just in from the states, eh?

Well, after a continuous diet of bacon, ham and the poorly-embalmed beef that made Chicago famous, the longing for something fresh becomes unbearable, so when McMillan, another old timer, dropped in at the bunk house one night and said that Nome River was "alive with ptarmigan" my partner Jack and I decided to take the dog team and drive over for a day's sport—and a week's grub.

The heavy snows had driven the birds down from the mountains to the coast where the willows were still uncovered. That was the year I had the great team, considered the best on the coast; fifteen as fine dogs as ever stole a ham; kept me broke, too, with dog-feed at 35 cents. Yes, that's the team we rescued the Cooper party with, after the big storm. I brought two of the frozen men to a doctor ninety-six miles in twelve hours, with Keno, here, in the lead. Good drive, eh?

Well, the next morning found us up, not bright and early, as daylight doesn't come till about eight o'clock and isn't any too bright when it does get around, but early nevertheless, and after a breakfast of oatmeal, bacon, evaporated potatoes and "sour dough" flap jacks warranted to stick to your ribs for a week, I slipped the harness over ten of the best dogs, and as the stars began to dim and fade we heard the "swish-swish" of McMillan's twelve-foot skis as he came down the creek. He looked ghostlike and unreal in his long white parka, or hooded shirt, with beard, mustache and eyebrows white from his frozen breath.

"How cold is it by your thermometer?" said he, "The 'quick' in ours is frozen up."

Our spirit thermometer registered 44 degrees below, but as there wasn't a breath of air stirring we anticipated a fairly comfortable day. My "malamoots" had shaken off their sleepiness and seated shivering on the snow with heads to the stars saddened the air with dismal complaints.

Jack took his seat in the bottom of the long basket-sled, behind McMillan. There was a crack of the whip and a "Mush boys" and as the dogs leaped into their collars we were whisked around the cabin and out onto the main trail at railroad speed. Then a word to old Keno here and the pack settled down to the even run which eats up distance and which well-trained dogs maintain for hours.

When we reached the bunch of willows at the mouth of Osborne Creek we slipped into the snowshoes and started back toward the foothills, keeping about a hundred yards apart.

I had been straining my eyes to detect some object on the monotonous expanse of white, when suddenly a spot of snow which I had scanned, broke up under my eyes into four animated, squawking snow-balls, which went whizzing in as many different directions. I wasn't sure on my snow shoes and missed with both barrels.

While the birds remained above the skyline they were readily visible, offering a splendid target, but as they settled lower they were merged into the whiteness of the snow and instantly disappeared.

I heard McMillan's 10-bore explode and concluded he was doing business in his usual way. Then a double from Jack, followed by a peculiarly easy and melodious flow of profanity, showing at least three years' continuous residence "north of 53," explained perfectly the result of his two shots.

Near me I noticed a black dot like a small shoe-button against the field of white, and straining my eyes until the tears came and froze on my cheeks, I detected the outlines of a bird. With shoes well under me I advanced on the enemy's right wing, as it were. This time when my bird rose I cut short his derisive squawk, and with my right barrel knocked the tail out of another which had followed, and saw him wabble off for a hundred yards before giving up the fight.

Again I heard the report of Jack's Parker, and then upon the still air there floated to me a bunch of the most earnest and sincerely heartfelt profanity that an active brain and facile tongue could master, interspersed with recurring prophesies as to the eventual destiny of the individual who invented smokeless powder, the corporation which made it, the store that sold it, and the infernal idiot who would attempt to use it in cold weather. I judged that he had attempted to use frozen nitro-powder and found that it would hardly clear the gun barrel of shot.

When I returned to the sled, the dogs were sleeping peacefully, curled up in the snow like round fur balls. While I straightened them out of the tangle of harness they had formed before lying down, Jack and McMillan cleaned the birds, distributing feathers and refuse impartially among the members of the team. The craving for fresh meat among the inner circles of the dogs is probably more acute than among us and certainly less often gratified.

Having put them in a good humor we were off again up the river in the direction our birds had gone. Jack had turned to ask me something when he interrupted himself to tell me that my nose was frozen. This particular feature is unduly prominent with me and its isolation from the base of supplies renders it "shy" on circulation, so that it grows chill and clammy in Indian summer and has been frozen stiff by Thanksgiving. These frost bites result in an exceedingly red-looking and painful member which later peels off like a boiled potato. After a few moments of vigorous rubbing and pinching I succeeded in restoring animation and thereafter by wrinkling my nose like a cow I could tell whether the circulation had "made good" or was laying off. If the part felt stiff and difficult to move, off would come the mittens and the osteopathy recommence, continuing until the organ became sensible to muscular control.

I had been sitting on the sled rail, engaged in working my nose up to a fever heat, when suddenly, with a jerk that nearly unseated me, the team leaped into a sharp run. Glancing ahead the cause was apparent in the shape of a big Arctic hare that had hopped from the deep snow in the willows to the bare ice of the river and was leisurely working the kinks out of his legs a short distance ahead of us.

The dogs quieted almost instantly, and with noses to the trail began to run madly, making our sled sing over the smooth ice, which allowed them a sure footing and offered no resistance to the sled. In fact, here lay the danger, for with the accelerated speed, our sled, striking the little inequalities of the ice surface, was veering wildly, sometimes sliding nearly broadside on. Striking an obstacle, with a string of sparks from the steel shoe, it would tilt on one runner, nearly hurling us headlong onto the ice, then back again to the other side.

To control a team with the smell of game in their nostrils is impossible, yet a spill on the ice at this rate of speed meant painful results, if not serious ones, while a runaway team would mean loss of outfit and a long trip home on foot.

The duties of the "chauffeur" of the team in addition to "dog punching" consists of preventing an upset, if possible, so bidding the boys keep their seats, I balanced my 200 pounds of avoirdupois on the upper rail of the sled, changing from side to side as it began its erratic flights. This method of shifting ballast was working admirably and we were enjoying our dizzy ride, when our pacemaker, thinking the excitement too tame, increased his speed, and turning abruptly, made for the willows on the river bank.

This particular curve was not graded for our rate of speed, and when the dogs turned the sled swung, skimming around broadside and striking an ice hummock upsetting with such violence as to hurl me flying through the air like a frog. I believe a parabola is the most beautiful curve in geometry, yet although I feel that the one I described was geometrically perfect, its beauty did not appeal to me. Experience on a bicycle track, from the days of the high wheel onward, had taught me a valuable thing about falling, and I rejoiced in the knowledge that unlike a board track there were no splinters here.

I landed amid a rain of dead birds with the breath knocked out of me and a mental photograph of Jack and McMillan in positions absolutely defying the laws of nature. Mac was evidently attempting to rise at the critical moment, and with his long legs curled beneath him, had added to his momentum by jumping at random—so I caught a fleeting glimpse of a giant, red-headed Scotchman apparently seated at ease on the ice, but progressing with surprising rapidity in the direction we had been going. I had never before seen a practical demonstration of the Scotch game of "curling." I believe I would enjoy watching a game.

Jack's early training on the deck of a cattle pony asserted itself, and clinging tightly to the sled he was dragged up the bank through the snow, and into the bushes where the dogs, becoming entangled, came to a stop and awaited us with wagging tails, lolling tongues and an expression plainly saying: "We gave him the run of his life, didn't we?" We found Jack with pipe still clenched between his teeth, gingerly testing his knee caps.

"They were my only points of bearing for fifty yards," said he, "and if they weren't good, thick Missouri knee caps, they'd be looking like a glass of toothpicks, now."

An excited team will tie knots in its harness that would defy a sailor to attempt to straighten out the tangle.

Busied in this way I suddenly became conscious of an ominous movement of the air which till now had been deathly still. Glancing north up the valley I saw that which caused me to snatch the struggling dogs out on the ice with a curse, and utter a cry of warning to my companions. The mountains, towering on either hand, had changed, and instead of standing clear-cut and white in the marble stillness, a dim haze had veiled the landscape while from the peaks flew gossamer streams of whirling snow, like thin smoke of many fires. As yet the air of the valley was scarcely stirring, but as we gazed, the twin walls of mountains gleaming miles northward up the valley were silently blotted out by the gray clouds of snow that swept down upon us. We were in the icy grip of the "Terror of the Northland," the sudden breath of the Arctic which sweeps south without warning over this desolate wilderness.

"We'll have to run before it," said Jack, as we hurriedly donned the fur "parkis" which till now had remained unused. "No living thing could face a wind in this cold."

As we threw the birds in the sled, a puff of snow whirled past, enveloping us in a stinging cloud of frost crystals, while the dogs whined uneasily and strained against the harness.

The storm did not break suddenly, nor did it sweep down upon us with the roar and violence of a hurricane, but rather with a darkening of the heavens there came a restless stirring of the air which rapidly quickened and brought with it a moaning flurry of snow. This writhed along the ground as though loathe to part from its drifts.

McMillan's hooded figure floated ahead of us, visible only above the waist, his long legs invisible in the swirling snow, which clinging close to the earth, hid the dogs from view and seemed to buoy us up on a drifting sea of white. Soon the familiar landscape faded out and we were hurried on through a thick, gray, biting atmosphere, trusting to our general sense of direction.

Given a good sleeping-bag, the proper course to pursue in an extremity of this kind is to free the dogs from the harness and seeking the shelter of the sled, crawl inside the bag and wait for the storm to abate. This is no beauty sleep which one enjoys inside a deerskin sack during the two or three days that a blizzard rages, but with sufficient food to sustain bodily heat, it is a safe resource.

Totally unprepared as we were, the anxiety I saw in Jack's countenance was mirrored in mine, but I thanked my stars for not having a little wife waiting for me back at the claim, as he had.

McMillan paused until we blew up to his side, and speaking through ice-burdened whiskers said, "Either my direction is wrong or the wind is changing. If we keep this course we'll be out on the ice of the Bering sea by night-fall."

"We don't need to complicate this pleasant situation by getting onto the ice-pack with an offshore gale," shouted Jack. "We'd better take the consensus of opinion and strike for the point we think is home."

The plain lying between the foothills and the ocean is devoid of vegetation and makes it extremely easy to wander out upon the ice-floe. Confused by the approaching darkness and the blinding snow, I feared for the result in such a case.

It seemed to our strained imaginations that we had travelled for hours before the early darkness, hastened by the gloom of the storm, settled upon us, and the dogs, wearied by constant plunging through soft snow and heavy with ice-matted coats, stopped, panting and exhausted.

There is no rest for man or beast on the frozen trail, and after cleaning the ice from their faces, with a cheering word to each, we forced them on.

Moving among them, and with hoarse cries of encouragement we plodded onward.

Suddenly with a shout Jack halted us. "We're out on the pack" said he, and stopping he dimly showed us the ragged point of an up-ended ice cake from which the snow had been blown.

With my sheath knife I chipped a piece off and the briny taste told me that we were indeed upon the ice of Bering Sea and perhaps headed for open water a few miles off shore. Fortunately we had not encountered a crevice, for had we done so nothing would have prevented our plunging into it, blinded and driven by the gale and with no question as to the result, for even though regaining the solid ice, the excessive cold would have instantly congealed our heavy clothes into icy armour impossible to bear.

Turning, we fought our way back again into the storm, but the dogs refused to face the cutting sleet. The heavy butt of the dog whip only produced whines of pain, so heading as closely to the wind as possible we changed our course back toward the shore.

I was faint from hunger and very tired. We had traveled for an endless time in this direction when McMillan staggered back to the sled and throwing himself upon it said, "I'm afraid I can't make it much farther. One of my skis is broken and I'm too far gone to travel without it."

Jack listlessly rubbed his cheeks with snow as he sank behind the sled.

"Fellows, my face has started to freeze," said he. "We might as well try to walk around till morning. We may go it till daylight if we keep moving and don't let each other go to sleep."

I was glad to yield to an overpowering desire to stop. Rest was what I wanted and a little doze. It seemed many days since I had slept, and a few moments' sleep now would fix me finely.

Too drowsy and exhausted to answer, I went forward to cut the harness from the dogs, thinking that they at least would sleep the storm out and return safely to the claim.

Immediately upon stopping every animal save one, had curled up and was sleeping in its tracks. "Keno," the leader, sat up and with quivering nostrils was casting the wind for a scent. Three winters on the trail with this shaggy veteran had taught me the significance of his every move and had bred absolute confidence in his instinct.

"He smells a camp!" I shouted, and fell to madly pulling, beating and kicking the weary brutes onto their feet. We yelled and coaxed and entreated, careful not to confuse the leader who, given his head, started rapidly into the very teeth of the storm, occasionally raising his nose to the wind.

Soon one of the big gray wheel-dogs whined eagerly and strained into the harness, and with a chorus of sharp cries the team broke into a run while we clung stubbornly to the sled and plunging heavily were dragged up over a bank where the blizzard howled down from the hills above, and tearing the hoods from our faces, froze our wet streaming hair. Then the dogs were suddenly swallowed up in a dark hole which pierced the depths of a large drift, and with a crash the sled struck the log forming one side of the entrance, throwing us partially into the low black tunnel of an "egloo."

Almost instantly a blaze of light appeared at the end of the passage as a door swung open disclosing the rough interior of a roadhouse, while a man's tall figure was silhouetted against the square of welcome brightness. A ravishing steam of hot cooking assailed our nostrils, and as he waded towards us through the struggling mass of smoking wolf-dogs he cried, "My God, strangers! Who hits the trail on a night like this?"

BLACKTAILS IN THE BAD LANDS

BRONSON RUMSEY

One bright, cold November day I started from a ranch on the Little Missouri, in western Dakota, with the set purpose of getting venison for the ever hungry cow-boys. They depended solely upon me for their supply of fresh meat; and as for some time I had shot nothing, I had been the subject of disparaging comment for several days, and the foreman, in particular, suggested that I should stay at home and kill a steer, and not chase all the black-tails into the next county.

So I stole off this time with an almost guilty conscience, and plunged at once into the dense brush of the river-bottom. In the thicket I startled a Virginia deer, but knew it to be one only by the waving salute of its white flag. I also passed a tree in one of the forks of which I had, at another time, found an old muzzle-loading rifle, rusted, worn, and decaying, a whole history in itself, and beyond, not two hundred yards away, an Indian's skull with a neat round hole through the crown.

The Keogh stage road crossed the river near by, and I found out that the place was the scene of the last Indian deviltry in this section. It was the old story. A man, while looking for the stage-horses, was shot; a second, hearing the report, went out to see what it meant, and was in turn killed; while a third, with perhaps a little more experience, jumped on the only horse left at the station and fled for his life, with half a dozen Indians in full cry in pursuit.

I walked on along the old trail taken by the lucky fugitive, and up out of the river-valley to a level plateau above. From the top could be seen in the distance several big buttes, and a dark pine-tree, which was to be my objective point for the day's hunt. To the right, as I stepped briskly forward, was a large washout, cut deep into the clay soil, broken and irregular, with sage-brush scattered here and there along its sides and bottom. At the head of the washout I spied some yellow long-horned Texas cattle, and gave them a wide berth. I had had some pleasing experiences of their habits, and did not care just then to be stamped flat.

To the left, a few hundred yards away, was a long valley leading to the river and far out into the prairie, wooded in patches, with small pockets at intervals along the sides, filled with low brush. Here at other times I had jumped whitetails from their daytime naps, and once had had a running shot at a large prairie-wolf. Bearing all this in mind, I veered over toward the valley, and had not gone far when I saw in the distance a black-tail buck come skipping out of it, and moving with high, long bounds, as is the way of its kind when frightened or going at speed.

These bounds, by the way, are very curious: the animal lands on all four feet at once, in such a small area that a sombrero would cover the four footprints. On a few occasions, when very badly frightened, I have seen them run level, like a race-horse; but that gait is so unusual as hardly to be considered characteristic of this deer. The deer in question, after a few long jumps, settled down into a trot, then into a walk, and finally stopped and looked about. He did not see me, however, and when he again moved off there was a man jogging quietly along in his wake.

Taking advantage of every little hollow to keep from his sight and make a spurt, I soon reduced the distance between us, and arrived at the further edge of the plateau just in time to see him disappear in some broken country. Continuing cautiously on to where I had last seen him, it became apparent that he had determined upon some definite course, for his tracks led as straight as the nature of the ground would permit to what I knew was the head of a large coulée which ran into the valley from which he had come into view.

As the soil was very hard and dry, and his tracks difficult to follow, I soon determined to leave them and cut straight for the coulée below the point toward which he had been headed, thinking it likely that he would continue his course down the coulée, at least for a short distance. I ought to be able to write that "events turned out exactly as calculated," but they did not. I ran with a fair burst of speed to the edge of the coulée, and when, after quietly watching for twenty minutes, no deer appeared, my mind went back to the foreman's remark about killing a steer.

However, it remained for me to go up to the point where it was probable the buck entered the coulée. I accordingly did so, hunting every inch of the way, and looking for sign and whatever else might turn up. I saw nothing, however, but two grouse that startled me, as they always do, but especially when my nerves are strung up as they were just then. What course the buck had taken, was now the question. Doubling back to my old conclusion that he had gone straight, I went out of the coulée, and followed on the line he had gone. At first it led over another small plateau, then it dipped down again into some more bad lands, cut up and broken with picturesque red scoria hills covered with straggling twisted cedar-trees.

About this time my ardor for this particular buck had begun to subside, and he was now anybody's game. Being somewhat tired as well, I climbed to the top of a round clay butte, sat down, and lighted a pipe. I had been smoking for about ten minutes, enjoying the mysterious scenery and thinking what course it would be best to take, when again my buck loomed up for a few seconds in the distance, and once more walked quickly out of sight. This was a great surprise and pleasure, and the pace at which I set out in pursuit would have rejoiced the heart of a messenger boy. I ran as fast as I could, stopping to peer over every rise in the land, and was soon rewarded by a most interesting sight. The buck had come upon another, fully as large if not larger than himself, and they were exchanging greetings across a small washout, each extending his nose and smelling the other. They would sniff a minute and then turn their heads about, flap their long gray ears, and wiggle their short black tails, acting as if they were old friends.

It seems a great pity to shoot such noble creatures; but unfortunately this thought rarely comes at the right time for the deer. Given, a man having killed nothing for several days, unmercifully guyed by all the cow-boys, and add to that a long and lively chase after constantly vanishing venison,—when, then, the man gets within shooting distance, it is hardly at such a time that his kindly instincts will suggest the propriety of letting the poor beasts escape.

As for myself, with every muscle and nerve at tension from an exciting chase, and mind fairly satisfied of game well earned, it would have taken more self-denial than I pretend to possess not to shoot, especially since we had been living on pork for some time. When fresh meat is plentiful in camp, it is to a real sportsman no sacrifice to let the does and fawns escape, or to shoot them merely with the deadly kodak; but on this day the shack really had to have meat—those lordly heads, too.

There is always a strong desire, when one comes upon game, to shoot at once; but it is a good plan, if possible, to rest and get one's breathing apparatus into proper shape. It is most exasperating, not to say cruel, to wound a deer and have him get away; and there is a good chance of this happening if, before your hand steadies and your head clears, you begin to open fire.

From the direction of the wind it was quite evident that the deer could not scent me, so for some moments I lay watching the animals with lively interest, and wondering what they would do next.

They were apparently satisfied with an occasional sniff at one another, but seemed at the same time to give their attention to something beyond my view. From my position on top of a small mound, or butte, where I had crawled with great caution, nothing could be seen either up or down a large washout that was between me and the deer; and I had poked my gun through a bunch of grass, and was quite prepared to shoot, when the ears, then the head and body, of a large doe, closely followed by a young buck and a yearling, came into full view.

To say that I was surprised but faintly expresses it, and for the time being all idea of shooting left me, as I watched with keenest interest the advent of the new-comers. The old doe, as if aware of her importance as the respected matron of a family, walked sedately past the two bucks without bestowing the least attention upon them, selected a grassy spot in the sun, pivoted around twice to level her bed, and quietly settled to earth, facing me. The young buck and yearling stood as if not quite decided whether to follow her example, but finally began to nibble grass and walk about. Here, indeed, was a pretty picture,— an embarrassment of riches. I thought it quite possible to get one big buck, with the chance of a good running shot at the other; and as there was no hurry, and my gun was at a dead rest for the first shot at least, I decided to shoot at the largest buck behind the ear, and then trust to occasion for whatever should follow.

I felt that excitement was again about to get the upper hand, and I aimed carefully several times before pulling trigger. At last, after a sharp report, the smoke blew directly in my face, and for a second I could see nothing distinctly; but when it cleared away, and I, having pumped a cartridge into place, was again prepared to shoot, what was my astonishment to find that the buck fired at had utterly disappeared, and that the second, far from being frightened, was still standing with his nose poked down into the washout that had been between them.

Without further speculation, I sighted for the neck of buck number two, and at the report he also disappeared; but this time I made out that he fell over forward into the washout. Everything was now afoot and moving about, so taking a quick shot at the doe, behind the shoulder, and three more at the remaining two, the last on the jump, I realized, by seeing them fall, a big day's work, and for the moment felt very proud. It was not until afterward that the feeling came up that my glory would have been quite enough without killing the last three; but then it must be remembered that we needed every pound of meat at the shack.

The two big bucks had fallen into the washout, which was about six feet deep, one directly on top of the other, and it was beyond my strength, without a horse and rope, to pull them out. As it was, I had to clean them in very uncomfortable quarters and not in the most approved manner. During November, in the northern latitudes, the sun is early to bed, and it was four o'clock and getting gray when the last deer had been cared for. At dark I washed all trace of blood from my hands and arms in the river near the shack, and strolled into the kitchen with as woebegone a countenance as I could muster. I intended to get even with the foreman.

A sardonic smile stole over his face, and a disgusted look over those of the others, as they noticed my unstained hands. I remarked to the foreman that I had shot some game. He promptly replied, "You didn't; if you had, you'd have been so proud you'd be as red as a scoria butte with deer blood, to show off. No such luck; and as long as you and that thirty-eight-caliber pop-gun go rustling around this country, I reckon we'll eat pork and be —— glad to get it."

To this I answered that if he would promise to pack in what game I had killed, and would do it, I would give him the hunting-knife that he had been trying to steal for the last week. He instantly called it a bargain, and asked how far it was to the game. I answered that it was about five miles, and that I would take him there in the morning.

So next morning we started on horseback, and I went far enough with him to point out exactly where the deer were, and leaving him, I rode over to call on a friend who had a small horse-ranch in the neighborhood. I stayed at this horse-ranch overnight, and did not get back to our ranch until the following evening about supper-time.

It leaked out that the cow-boys had fairly screamed with delight when the truth was known, and would rather have been discharged than help the foreman pack in the five deer. He did pack them, however, in good faith; and both he and the cow-punchers, now that they had fresh meat, spared me their jokes, and for several days did not try to lend me their pitching ponies.

Thus ended a most eventful hunt; and although it was unquestionably a very exceptional piece of good luck to have killed five deer neatly, still it is none the less a fact that with a thirty-eight-caliber rifle I have always done the best work. With a fifty-caliber I have shot deer in their vital parts and then had them run great distances, whereas with the smaller bullet, when properly hit, they would almost invariably double up on the spot. I can give no explanation that will help to determine why the smaller-bored rifle has always, with me, been the most efficient.

SOURCES

"Hunting the Grisly," by Theodore Roosevelt, *The Wilderness Hunter*, 1893.

"The White Goat and His Country," by Owen Wister, *American Big Game Hunting*, 1893.

"De Shootin'est Gent'man," by Nash Buckingham, *Recreation*, 1916.

"That Twenty-Five-Pound Gobbler," by Archibald Rutledge, *Outing*, 1919.

"In Buffalo Days," by George Bird Grinnell, *American Big Game Hunting*, 1893.

"Tige's Lion," by Zane Grey, *Field & Stream*, 1908.

"Red Letter Days in British Columbia," by Lieutenant Townsend Whelen, *Outdoor Life*, 1906.

"The Alaskan Grizzly," by Harold McCracken, *Field & Stream*, 1920.

"The Plural of Moose Is Mise," by Irwin S. Cobb, *Field & Stream*, 1921.

"Brant Shooting on Great South Bay," by Edwin Main Post, *Field & Stream*, 1910.

"Bear Hunting in the Smokies," by Horace Kephart, *Field & Stream*, 1909.

"An Elk Hunt at Two-Ocean Pass," by Theodore Roosevelt, *The Wilderness Hunter*, 1893.

"Bob White, Down 't Aberdeen," by Nash Buckingham, *Field & Stream*, 1913.

"Hunting on the Oregon Trail," by Francis Parkman, *The Oregon Trail*, 1847.

"The Mountain Goat at Home," by William T. Hornaday, Sc. D., *Camp-Fires in the Canadian Rockies*, 1906.

"Hunting the Black Bear," by Theodore Roosevelt, *The Wilderness Hunter*, 1893.

"The Quest of the Ptarmigan," by Rex Beach, *Outdoor Life*, 1903.

"Blacktails in the Bad Lands," by Bronson Rumsey, *American Big Game Hunting*, 1893.

CPSIA information can be obtained
at www.ICGtesting.com
Printed in the USA
BVHW081056061121
620760BV00003B/3

9 781493 040421